Popular Culture
and
American Life

Selected Topics
in the Study of
American Popular Culture

Popular Culture and American Life

SELECTED TOPICS IN THE STUDY OF AMERICAN POPULAR CULTURE

Martin W. Laforse (Parts 3, 4, & 5)
Ithaca College

James A. Drake (Parts 1 & 2)
University of Tampa

Nelson-Hall nh Chicago

Library of Congress Cataloging in Publication Data

Laforse, Martin W   1927-
    Popular culture and American life.

    Bibliography: p.
    Includes index.
        1.   United States—Popular culture—Addresses,
essays, lectures.   2.   United States—Civilization—
20th century—Addresses, essays, lectures.   1.   Drake,
James A., joint author.   II.   Title.
E169.1.L32   973.9   80-27809
ISBN 0-88229-577-2 (cloth)
ISBN 0-88229-778-3 (paper)

Manufactured in the United States of America

10   9   8   7   6   5   4   3   2

 The paper used in this book meets the minimum requirements of American National Standard for Information Sciences—Permanence of Paper for Printed Library Materials, ANSI Z39.48-1984.

Contents

Introduction

As his seventy-fifth birthday approached, George Bernard Shaw discussed with London newsmen the effects radio might have on serious writing. Would not the great Irish dramatist concede, one newsman asked, that the demand for radio plays could eventually produce a generation of great playwrights? And would not it follow, therefore, that for more reasons than one, radio was a great invention? Always at home with the press and invariably fond of displaying his acid wit, Shaw paused for a moment, and then remarked that, indeed, radio was a great invention. But, he promptly added, the switch turning it off might be an even greater invention.

Whether the comment is apocryphal or not, the incident captures the longstanding tension between the "popular" and the "serious" in the twentieth century. Debates about which kind of art form, the popular or the serious, best contributes to the enrichment of modern society have been intense and, more often than not, fruitless. Unless illuminated by an understanding of a society's structure, values, and general history at a given time, debates of this sort tend to degenerate into emotional wrangling. A synthesis is not only possible but intellectually challenging as well.

Synthesizing a range of seemingly divergent viewpoints will be our task in this introduction. Our purpose will be to inquire into the scope of American popular culture by analyzing its roots, and by contrasting it with what contemporary social scientists often call *high culture* and *folk culture*. For the moment, let us consider as a working definition for the term *popular culture* the range of media products, art forms and artifacts disseminated broadly in American society throughout the twentieth century. Newspapers, magazines, phonograph recordings, radio and television programs, popular photography, fashion, popular art, product design, political campaigns, cartoons, musical comedies and reviews, comic books, films, professional sports, the lyrics of popular songs—all these and more constitute popular culture. The variety of topics and themes includes the nature of success; the meaning of sexual relationships; the impact of social class; the varying modes of courtship, marriage, and childrearing; the multiplicity of advertising and consumer strategies; the changing concepts of masculinity and femininity; the imperatives of patriotism; the evolving social status of immigrants; the searing but often comically portrayed problems of adolescence; the will to win and the hatred of failure; changing styles of work; heroes and heroism; ethnic behavior and its identification for middle-class audiences; and the definition of national problems in the future.

Understood in this broad sense, popular culture may be said to have originated with the appearance of mass society in the period after the Civil War in the United States. Its form was shaped by rapid industrialization, growing urbanization, the newly-freed black masses, the influx of immigrants from eastern and southern Europe, the onset of universal compulsory education, and the creation of new means of mass communication. With the coming of mass culture and the consequent extension of political democracy and educational opportunity, popular culture came to complement the more formal social institutions through which values are instilled. Recordings, radio, television, and motion pictures have come to play an important latent role in the socialization process and thus to complement the roles played by family and home, church, and school.

A fruitful way to view popular culture is to compare it with the folk and high cultures. High culture is generally associated rather closely with class status in society, and typically only the "sophisticates" partake of it. Put simply, high culture is typified by activities centered in art museums, concert halls, and avant-garde film theaters, and by reading literary master-pieces in various genres. The high-culture artists, whatever their mediums happen to be, are the architects of personal universes. Whether an artist is a composer, painter, sculptor, poet, novelist, or dramatist, the art is necessarily an intense personal expression of what Byron called "the soul within"; ideally, it is produced for a public, but usually not for mass public consumption. Sales, royalties, and money in general are viewed, at least in theory, by high-culture artists as being the useful consequence of the public's occasional reaction to quality in art. The public does not always react, although time has a way of rectifying matters. A salient example may be found in the career of Charles Ives, now celebrated as a brilliant and original American composer, whose vision was well ahead of his time. Weaving a variety of elements into the complex fabric of his art, Ives drew from Civil War ballads, hymns, folk songs, ragtime, and popular music in general in his compositions. The superimposed themes which are now considered his genius are the same themes with which audiences found little fascination in his own day, apparently causing him to abandon musical composing during World War I.

Where high culture art forms reflect idealized universal themes, folk art is by contrast the evocation of the life experiences of the artist, as for example in the ballads of Woody Guthrie and the paintings of Grandma Moses. Theoretically at least, a folk artist is one with his or her audience. By being a part of the audience and thus a part of the environment of his art, a folk artist breaks down the artist-audience distinction. With the passing of time, folk art often finds its way into art museums and concert halls where, ironically, it becomes the object of attention for high-culture audiences.

In contrast to both folk and high culture artists, popular artists aim to reach an audience with works that are calculated to sell. Advertisers, popular photographers, magazine illustrators, popular song writers, and movie directors typify the popular artist. To sell widely, such artists attempt to cultivate the feelings and preferences of mass audiences with results which can be catalogued through sales charts, corporate tax records, and best-seller lists. Out of the stream of popular art there have been, there are, and will continue to be art objects which transcend the ephemeral and eventually find a place in a new category. Shifting tastes often account for the retrieval of certain works from near or total obscurity, and as succeeding generations sift through the past their perception of what they find often differs from their predecessors' perceptions.

Perhaps no popular art form better exemplifies this sort of perceptual change than the movies and their evolution into film. The masters of silent screen comedy—Chaplin, Lloyd, Keaton, Langdon—created a truly·popular theater by using their materials and routines to please a mass audience. With the exception of Chaplin, few seem to have held self-conscious social views or to have been the architects of the kinds of social commentary film critics often attribute to them. Most simply did their stuff using time-honored routines to try to be as funny as possible to the greatest number of people.

The coming of the film archive, the programs in the Museum of Modern Art in New York City and similar ones across the country, and the use of old movies in early television programming paved the way for a select, serious, intellectual audience to substitute the honorific term *film* for what their parents and grandparents called movies. The same sequences of frames and images that delighted largely working class audiences some forty years earlier became, in time, intellectually attractive to the *cognoscenti* who frequented university theaters, art museums and avant-garde theatres where they were shown. Today, the abundance of courses in film history taught at many prestigious universities, as well as the proliferation of articles and books written about film by critics, all attest to the elevation of movies to a high-culture art form.

If movies provide an excellent example of the elevation of a popular culture art form into a high-culture one, jazz music illustrates the uncertainty of the distinction among folk, high, and popular culture. Originally a folk art form endemic to late nineteenth century blacks in the South, jazz became the object of "serious" analysis by the late 1930s. By the 1950s jazz became newsworthy enough for the *New York Times* to run lengthy obituaries of New Orleans jazzmen who had been ignored by the establishment news media in their productive years. Through the greater part of the twentieth century, jazz gained public acceptance on two levels. On the one hand it bred a coterie of aficionados, insiders to whom the jazz world and its players were part of a separate society. Their heroes were the laureled artists of the medium, the Louis Armstrongs, Bessie Smiths, Dizzy Gillespies, and Charlie Parkers whose work was understood by only a rather small group of insiders. On the other hand, jazz was accorded its place in the symphonic world from the February day in 1924 when Paul Whiteman's Concert Orchestra first performed George Gershwin's *Rhapsody in Blue*. At the same time, through Whiteman's and other dance band recordings in the mid-1920s, jazz was packaged in the form of popular songs and arranged dance music. Like symphonic jazz, the so-called jazz played by many of the dance bands of the 1920s was a derivative and diluted form of the authentic black folk musical form. The relation of jazz to popular culture is, then, rather ambiguous, and it shows that the same art form can be part of folk, high, *and* popular culture at different stages.

Popular culture is now so intimately connected with the entertainment media that social analysts tend to focus on them in discussions of the alleged debasement of aesthetic values caused by popular culture. The sociologists C. Wright Mills and Herbert Gans exemplify two different types of interpretation. Mills condemned the media for slighting their educational functions and considered them "malignant forces" which obscured from viewers the causes of their tensions and anxieties. By presenting what he called "malarkey" Mills saw the media as hindering audiences from confronting reality and forcing upon them instead "second-hand worlds."

Gans countered these arguments by discounting the supposed ill-effects of media on viewers. He constructed a model of taste cultures based on the class structure and claimed that television, for example, tended to reinforce desires already present in viewers. Far from debasing high culture, which continues to flourish, media tend to enlarge perspectives by presenting taste and value models unfamiliar to many sections of the audience. Indeed, Gans asserted that each taste culture had an operating aesthetic and that high culture had borrowed generously from popular culture. Gans claimed that at certain key points the various taste cultures and their producers had more in common than most critics had assumed. In contrast with Mills, Gans was hopeful about the future possibilities of the media and called for multicultural programming.

In the midst of the debate over the relationship between media and society, there stands the fact that popular culture and the media, especially the entertainment media, are for all practical purposes inseparable. Because so much about twentieth century popular culture must be inferred from the products of the entertainment media, a brief inquiry into the origins and development of those media will be essential here. In part 1 we will inquire into the complex effects the media have had on society by taking into account the technology which made possible their rise. Then, in part 2, we will inquire into American vaudeville. Both as a business and as a medium of entertainment vaudeville in its rise and fall mirrors many turn-of-the-century social attitudes in American life. The same holds true for popular music, from the beginning of the century onward, and for jazz as both a uniquely American musical form and as a tragic setting for some of its best interpreters. These become our focus in parts 3 and 4 of this book. Thereafter, in part 5, the focus of our analysis is expanded to include American sports, notably the reflexive relationship between the growth of baseball and urban change in twentieth century America. Each of the topics we treat has a viability of its own in analyzing American society and its evolution over the past hundred years.

Part One

The Entertainment Media

Sweeping across the country with the speed of transient fashion in slang or Panama hats, political war cries, or popular novels, comes now the mechanical device to sing for us a song or play for us a piano, in substitute for human skill, intelligence, and soul.

John Philip Sousa, 1906

1.

Recordings and Motion Pictures

The excitement surrounding the invention of sound recording can be gathered from the eyewitness accounts of the first persons who saw demonstrations of Edison's phonograph.

> If it were not that the days of belief in witchcraft are long since past, witch-hunters such as those who figured so conspicuously in the early history of our country would now find a rich harvest of victims in the Tribune Building. Here are located two marvels of a marvellous age. The telephone, which created such a sensation a short time ago by demonstrating the possibility of transmitting vocal sounds by telegraph, is now eclipsed by a new wonder called the phonograph. This little instrument records the utterance of the human voice and like a faithless confidante repeats every secret confided to it whenever requested to do so. It will talk, sing, whistle, cough, sneeze, or perform any other acoustic feat. With charming impartiality it will express itself in the divine strains of a lyric goddess, or use the startling vernacular of a street Arab.[1]

Even greater excitement must have been felt when John Kruesi, one of Edison's most trusted associates and most

3

gifted mechanics, presented the inventor with the first working model of the phonograph Edison had designed. The machine was a simple affair and had no electric parts at all, working entirely upon mechanical energy. Its main component was a metal diaphragm to which a needle or "stylus" was affixed; when this diaphragm was set in motion by sound waves generated by the voice or an instrument, the stylus was also set in motion and, Edison reasoned, could be made to emboss these sound-wave patterns in a suitably strong material, such as tinfoil. This was the language he used to describe his invention both in his American and British patent applications. As the handful of Edison employees who witnessed the first recording and reproduction of the human voice were to recount later, Edison's reasoning was correct: he turned a small crank on the machine, setting the cylindrical tinfoil sheet in motion, and then spoke the words to the childhood nursery rhyme "Mary Had a Little Lamb." Moments later he heard the rhyme spoken back to him in his own voice. Later he was to say of the event, "I was never so taken aback in my life!"[2]

Though Edison was granted the basic patents on phonograph recording, others were responsible for the refinement of his concept. The inventor of the telephone, Alexander Graham Bell, and his associates Charles Sumner Tainter and Chichester Bell produced what can be called the first practical phonograph. In place of the fragile tinfoil sheets Edison employed as records, the Bells and Tainter substituted wax cylinders having a cardboard core. Since tinfoil sheets were prone to tear easily, this resulted in more permanent recordings, and it also yielded much clearer recordings of the voice. The man who contributed the most to phonograph recording as we know it today was Emil Berliner, a German mechanic who invented the flat-disc record and who held the basic patents on the method of recording in use until the advent of stereo in the 1950s. The various Edison corporate interests, and also those of the Bells and Tainter, figured prominently in the United States recording industry until well into the 1920s. Both came to be dominated, however, by a third interest—the Victor Talking Machine Company, formed in 1901 by Eldridge R. Johnson, who had first become associated with the Berliner Company as a licensed manufacturer. Like Berliner's, Johnson's interests lay solely with the flat-disc record and not the cylindrical-type recordings associated with the Edison and Columbia concerns, both of which eventually marketed the two types of records.

The recordings produced and marketed by each of these companies differed in significant ways, both technically and artistically. The Edison recordings made from 1912 through about 1920 were technically superior to any other records on the market. Part of the reason for this lies in the nature of the process used to make them, commonly called the "acoustical" or "mechanical" method of recording. No amplifiers, micro-phones, or any other electrical equipment were employed in this process; rather, the mechanical energy generated by the source of a particular sound was used to actuate the dia-phragm-and-stylus apparatus.

There were definite laws which governed this process, the most important of which was that the volume of the final re-cording depended directly upon the volume of the voices or instruments recorded, since there was no way to amplify these electrically. The performers merely grouped themselves as closely as possible in front of a large megaphone to which the diaphragm and stylus were attached and tried to play or vocalize loudly enough to produce an evenly balanced recording.

The results were often severely affected, however, by a host of variables, some of which are present even in the finest acoustical records. First, the recording apparatus was not sensitive at all to certain kinds of sounds. Only vowels and hard consonants recorded well, and some sounds, such as the sibilant *s,* did not record at all. Large orchestras could not be recorded because it was impossible for more than twenty players to be grouped around the megaphone, or "horn," in such a way that a balanced record could be made. Other complications were added by the diaphragm's sensitivity range. String instruments, for example, did not generally record well, and brass instruments were often used in their place in orchestral recordings. Musical *fortissimi,* or loud tones, often caused the stylus to vibrate too intensely, ruining the record altogether; and *pianissimi,* or very soft tones, often became lost in the scratching sound of the surface noise associated with all acoustic records.

The Edison records, however, held these variables in considerable check. They contain audible sibilants, and some of the orchestral recordings the company issued are known to have employed thirty-five musicians, all of whom can be clearly heard in the commercially issued recordings. The final credit for the technical superiority of the Edison records goes entirely to the inventor himself, who continually perfected his acoustical process to the point that the solo human voice and many instruments were almost perfectly recorded.

The 1920s saw a technical development in the recording process which was almost as significant as Edison's first achievements. In 1925 the Western Electric Company offered rights to an electric recording process developed by J. P. Maxfield and H. C. Harrison. Utilizing microphones and vacuum-tube amplifiers, the new electrically made records were better balanced and usually more brilliant than even the best of the acoustic ones. Where a mere fifteen to twenty players could be grouped before the acoustical "horn," whole symphony orchestras could be recorded electrically; where four to six solo voices could be recorded only with difficulty in the acoustic process, choral groups numbering in the hundreds could be registered by the microphone of the new process. The severe restrictions of the mechanical record were no longer felt in the industry after 1925. Electric recordings continued to be perfected throughout the 1930s and 1940s, culminating in the introduction of the LP or long-playing record by Columbia Records in 1948. Representing the work of researchers Peter Goldmark and William S. Bachman, LP records made possible most of the improvements in sound recording and reproduction seen in recent years. Unlike the standard recordings of its day, which were made of a shellac-based composition that generated an excessive amount of noise, the Columbia LP was made of vinylite, a soft plastic composition which reduced surface noise considerably. And unlike the standard 78 rpm record, which played for a maximum of four minutes, the LP provided uninterrupted listening for twenty-three minutes, having more closely spaced grooves and being made to play at 33⅓ rpm.

RCA, the Radio Corporation of America, with whom Victor had merged in 1929, was still Columbia's chief competitor and countered its rival's new product with a new system of its own. The RCA-Victor system featured a small vinylite record designed to be played at 45 rpm on a special turntable equipped with an unusually fast record-changing mechanism. The introduction of the new "45" brought about considerable speculation concerning which new speed would eventually dominate the industry, and what copywriters called "The War of the Speeds" ensued. In the midst of it, ironically, the 78 rpm gradually lost its importance and eventually disappeared altogether.

Just as the name Edison is linked with the origins of sound recording, so it is also linked with the beginnings of the motion picture, one of the most powerful media of this century. On October 6, 1889, members of the press were invited to the Edison laboratories at West Orange, New Jersey, to witness what was heralded as a demonstration every bit as significant as the phonograph's debut. The press representatives were ushered into a darkened room at one end of which was suspended a white screen, four feet square, and upon which, within a few seconds, the likeness of a man appeared. What was unique about this demonstration was that the man moved about on the screen and suddenly began to talk to the audience. This was the first demonstration of a "talking picture," and it occurred nearly forty years before *The Jazz Singer,* the first large-scale commercial demonstration of a sound picture.

In this early demonstration, both the motion picture projector and the camera used in the photography were made in the Edison laboratories. The projector was designed from French specifications, with several modifications added by the Edison staff. The motion picture camera was entirely an Edison design, and nothing like it had ever been employed in the history of motion picture photography. Previous attempts at creating the illusion of motion had mostly been made by assembling in a sequence large numbers of still photographs which were then made to "move" by mechanical means. The Edison camera actually filmed motion in progress and captured the images on a long strip of flexible, transparent photographic film, which could be wound onto reels for projection.

The film used in this first demonstration was made to Edison's specifications by George Eastman, the founder of the Eastman Kodak Company of Rochester, New York. The film stock which Eastman made for Edison differed substantially from the film supplied for the Kodak box cameras, the inexpensive snapshot camera series which made the young company a financial success. Eastman's box-camera film had a paper base, although the inventor had been experimenting with a flexible, transparent film at the time Edison had contacted him. The importance of the transparent film lay in the fact that the light of the projector could pass through it, and the final specifications for the film Edison designed were drawn up primarily by William K. L. Dickson, like Eastman a pioneer in photography and also a close associate of Edison. Ultimately, both Edison and Eastman profited from this early venture; Eastman applied for a patent on the new film some two months after the motion picture demonstration, and approximately two years afterward Edison applied for a patent on the motion picture camera he and his associates had developed.

Edison employed his own film production company, to which goes the credit for the first motion picture containing a complete story—*The Great Train Robbery*. The Edison company worked in and around West Orange, New Jersey, although as the infant industry began to blossom, the great production centers, like the receding American frontier, gradually moved westward. For a time, the pioneer companies were located in New York State; the Vitagraph Company, for example, had its headquarters in Flatbush, Brooklyn. Upstate New York provided a locale conducive to outdoor comedies, dramas, and serials, and such cities as Ithaca, New York played host to a number of early film companies and their crews. As the East Coast production companies grew successful, branches were opened in Chicago; many large companies produced part of their films there and the remainder in New York. By 1914, however, the industry had a new center: Hollywood, California. The constant Hollywood sunshine proved to be a great attraction for the film companies, which often had to delay production for weeks because of unpredictable weather. Hollywood had another singular appeal in its favor as well. It was close to the Mexican border, which offered refuge to crewmen who used equipment that infringed on Edison's basic patents and those of other inventors whose patents were pooled in what became known as the Motion Picture Patents Corporation. In the event that the Patents Corporation tried to use its legal power against the early Hollywood studios—many of whom used cameras which infringed on these patents—cameras and crew could be transported quickly to Mexico, where they could remain until they were assured a safe return.

It was in Hollywood that the motion picture passed from
the status of an experiment into an art form. There the great
directors of the art's early period—David Wark Griffith,
Thomas H. Ince, Mack Sennett—and its famous cameramen
—G. W. Bitzer, Charles Rosher, and others—combined with
the first motion picture "stars" to produce films which not
only told a story but did so with subtlety, intelligence and
imagination. The artistic achievements which the silent film
had reached by the end of the 1920s is almost impossible to
convey in words, the single element which they lacked.

Motion pictures were able to "talk," however, long before
Al Jolson uttered his now-famous "You ain't heard nothin'
yet!" in *The Jazz Singer*. The first motion picture demonstration, as it was mentioned earlier, had featured sound and motion in conjunction. But this was not "sound film" as it is
known today, in which the sound track is actually part of the
length of film. Rather, in the 1889 demonstration, an Edison
cylinder phonograph was synchronized with the projected
film, to give the impression that the figure on the screen was
speaking to the audience.

As primitive as this synchronization process might seem in
retrospect, the same process, essentially, was used in *The Jazz
Singer* some forty years later. The name given to the syn-
chroniprocess used in this 1927 film was Vitaphone, and it
featured the sound portion recorded and pressed on a disc
record which had to be synchronized with the projector. Although the Vitaphone process was much more reliable than
the Edison attempts had been, it differed from Edison's
process only in that the electrically recorded disc took the
place of the acoustically made cylinder recording of the 1889
demonstration. The process known as "sound on film," the
process in use today, was the product of the combined work
of a number of film experimenters, the most important of
which was Theodore W. Case of Auburn, New York. The
Case Company marketed a series of what could be called

"short subjects" which featured a sound track that was a part of the film itself. Lee DeForest, the inventor of the three-element vacuum tube, also produced a series of sound-on-film shorts, many featuring nationally known entertainers. By the early 1930s the sound-on-film technique had completely displaced such synchronized sound processes as the Vitaphone.

To many people the term "silent movie" denotes a crudely photographed effort in which the principal characters move about with superhuman speed, hurling custard pies at each other in the process. To many, the silent screen is associated primarily with comedy rather than drama, and to some, the dramatic attempts of silent producers and directors seem unintentionally comic, at least by today's standards. But, an understanding of motion picture techniques is necessary in forming retrospective judgments, particularly about silent films.

It is now rather well known that the rapid movement which characterizes many silent films is not a flaw in the films, but rather in their projection. Most silent films were photographed at a speed of twelve to sixteen frames per second, and when they are shown at the rate of twenty-four frames per second— the speed of modern projectors—the action takes on a comical pace. Silent films were photographed by turning the camera's drive mechanism by hand, for which a crank was provided. They were also intended to be projected by hand-cranking, so that any deviations in the speed of the photographed action could be corrected by the projectionist.

Supplying the power for the camera by hand gave the motion picture photographer a great measure of control over the pacing of a scene. If a comedy sequence called for the central character to slip and slide furiously on a newly waxed floor, the camera could be cranked at a relatively slow speed to intensify the motion of the character's feet. Electrically driven cameras, which were introduced at the time sound films appeared, were rarely used in silent photography, first because there was no sound track and hence no need to maintain a precise film speed, and second because electric motor drives required power sources, which were understandably difficult to find in certain shooting locations.

Silent films, like acoustical recordings, are perhaps best appreciated when they are shown in the context of their times. Silent films often appear uninventive when compared to later films, primarily because the camera techniques which made them progressive in their own times are now so much a part of standard cinema technique that audiences are well accustomed to them. When the films of such early directors as Griffith are shown to modern audiences, many of the innovations he introduced go largely unnoticed because viewers are frequently unaware of the creativity they represented at the time they were made.

Among the popular beliefs associated with silent films, the notion that production companies packed their equipment, their stars, and a food supply, and then went to a location where a story line was made up as the shooting was going on is a pervasive one that fosters many misconceptions about silent motion picture art. It is undeniably true that many scenes in silent pictures were shot spontaneously; early silent production companies were much smaller than their counterparts in the sound era, and they were not hampered by the bureaucratization which characterized the immense corporations of later Hollywood. In this way the silent medium was a relatively free one, which not only allowed for spontaneous innovations, but seemed to encourage them as well.

But the story line, or scenario, was rarely created as the cameras were being loaded. Directors had precise scenarios, although they were not always written down, and many of the delays in shooting resulted from deciding which camera angles, lighting directions, and scene arrangements would best translate the story onto the screen. The actors themselves frequently did not know the total scenario of a film, both because the scenes were usually shot out of sequence and because a good director could exact the proper performance from the actors without their having to know the complete story line. When, as in Charles Chaplin's case, the central character, the scenario writer, the director, and the composer of the musical score were all the same person, maximal control over the translation of the story from the realm of ideas to the medium of the screen was possible. To anyone who steadfastly maintains that silent comedies are primitive when compared to those of the sound era, two of the last silent films made—*City Lights* and *Modern Times*—both of which were written, acted, directed, and composed musically by Charles Chaplin, provide direct evidence of the degree of perfection which he brought to the new medium.

If the action and pacing of silent films seem rapid and jerky, the first sound films are notably static and slow by comparison. For technical reasons the camera movement in the first talking pictures was limited, just as it had been in the earliest silent films, where the camera was placed at a distance long enough to capture the entire framing of the scene. In these first silent pictures, the camera was intended to approximate the eyes of a stage or theater audience, and most of the scenes were shot against the backdrop of theater scenery. What some of the silent experimenters apparently did not realize is that the eyes of theater viewers could be selective, where the camera could not; an audience could focus on one small part of the stage and mentally block out the rest but the camera lens, being a mechanical instrument, could record whatever was within the borders of its viewfinder.

Once directors and cameramen began using the camera to approximate and enhance the selectivity of the eye, films ceased being photographic representations of stage scenes. But the same thing, to a lesser and somewhat different degree, plagued the first sound pictures of the late 1920s and early 1930s. Here the inhibiting factor was not the selectivity of the camera, but rather the dynamic range of the microphones used to record the sound tracks. Traveling microphones were not employed in the earliest sound films, and because of the limited mobility and sensitivity of the microphones that were used, they were often hidden in such scenic props as telephones. To insure the proper recording of their voices, actors were often carefully grouped near the microphone or prop and were urged to confine their movement to a certain radius.

The sound generated by the camera motors created other problems, since the noise of the drive motors' gears would frequently be picked up by the microphones. For a time cameras were encased in sound-proof booths, which eliminated the noise factor but at the same time restricted their movement. Noise problems were solved within a short time, however, and by 1932 Hollywood was well on its way to producing the lavish spectacles and musicals typifying the pre-World War II period in American commercial filmmaking. In the interim, radio eclipsed the phonograph as the dominant home entertainment medium, and within two decades radio itself would be eclipsed by the popularity of commercial television.

2.
Radio and Television

Just as it is difficult to assign specific dates to the origins of the phonograph and of the sound film, it is difficult to do so for radio and television. Guglielmo Marconi is popularly associated with the invention of radio, although his work lay in the area of wireless telegraphy, the transmission of telegraphic messages without the use of wires. The history of the development of radio begins before Marconi, however, with the hypotheses of James Clerk Maxwell, who theorized that electrical currents give off a special type of energy. In 1863 Maxwell offered mathematical evidence for the existence of this type of energy, although he was unable to detect it empirically.

Edison, whose inventive career touched upon all of the twentieth century media mentioned so far, built the first device capable of detecting this energy form, which he called "the ethereal force." In his various experiments he discovered that the new force could be used to transmit a signal which could be received without the use of wire connections. This occurred in 1875, and the results of Edison's experiments were published in the December 25, 1875, edition of *Scientific Ameri-*

can. Following Edison's initial work, Heinrich Hertz, for whom radio waves are named, demonstrated that the "ethereal forces" or electromagnetic waves could be altered and tuned to specific frequencies, which would enable them to be transmitted and received. The experiment conclusively demonstrating the feasibility of long-range voice communication without the use of telephone wires took place in 1906; it was overseen by Reginald A. Fessenden, who at an earlier time in his career had been associated with Edison. The Fessenden demonstration took place between Plymouth and Brant Rock, Massachusetts, a distance of eleven miles over which conversations were transmitted without the use of wires.

Six years earlier, the range of radio communication had been one mile, with reception at both ends being very poor in quality. Only one year after the Plymouth-Brant Rock demonstration, Fessenden was able to increase the distance to two hundred miles with excellent results. The importance of all these experiments lay in the fact that Fessenden actually succeeded in transmitting voices, where Marconi had only been able to transmit long-distance telegraph signals. Unfortunately, Reginald Fessenden was deprived of much of the credit due him when the Western Electric Company claimed credit for the wireless telephone in 1919. Fessenden had shown his full experiments to the Bell Telephone Company in 1908 for purposes of negotiating with them to put his devices into use. At the last moment the Bell interests were unable to sign the contracts, though by some means, the Western Electric Company—which was owned entirely by Bell Telephone—was able to duplicate Fessenden's experiments and equipment and eleven years later claimed full credit for wireless telephony.[1]

In 1907 Lee DeForest began to experiment with voice transmission, and late in 1907 he succeeded in broadcasting the voice of concert singer Eugenia Farrar from his Lowell Park Avenue station in New York City to a listening post in

Brooklyn and another in Staten Island. While these distances were rather small in comparison to the Fessenden achievements of the same year, the quality of the reception which DeForest was able to secure was exceptional. DeForest began regular radio broadcasts from his station in the Bronx in 1916. His programming efforts were joined by those of Frank Conrad, a chief engineer at the Westinghouse Electric Company, who broadcast music from a transmitter located in his garage on Wednesday and Saturday evenings. It was Conrad who directed the first broadcasts of station KDKA, located in Pittsburgh, and which had the distinction of being the first licensed commercial radio station. KDKA's first program was aired on November 2, 1920, and it consisted of a report of the Harding-Cox election returns.

A change in the Westinghouse Company's view of wireless telephone transmission brought station KDKA into being. At first, the Westinghouse interests saw the wireless telephone as just that—a device which would greatly improve the utility of the long-distance telephone system. But when a Pittsburgh department store began to market receivers which could pick up the KDKA signal, the Westinghouse personnel began to see the possibilities afforded by wide-range listening. Within months the KDKA facilities were improved, and the transmitting equipment was eventually moved from the company's laboratories to the roof of a downtown manufacturing building. Regular programming continued from there during 1920 and 1921, and for a time a large tent served as the broadcasting studio.

From these infant beginnings radio grew into the dominant entertainment medium in the nation during the early 1930s. A great part of its success was undoubtedly owed to depression economics, which brought the sale of phonograph records to an industry-wide low point in 1932. Radio, unlike the phonograph, seemed tailor-made for depression times; once the receiver or set was paid for, the entertainment it provided came into the home free of charge. Furthermore, radio broadcasts had a spontaneity to them and an absence of the surface noise long associated with phonograph records. In a sense, radio ultimately brought the phonograph record back to the public, as record manufacturers of the early 1930s began to market inexpensive turntables which could be attached to the amplifiers of the radio sets found in most homes. But for a time radio, the new medium, nearly brought about the demise of the phonograph recording. The same fate awaited radio when commercial television became the new medium in the late 1940s.

The story of television's development, similar in a way to radio's, is far too complex to be related adequately here, although a number of the same technical elements which underlay radio broadcasting were incorporated into early television. Experimental telecasts were being conducted as early as the mid-1920s, and a number of television receivers were marketed at this time, primarily on the East Coast. These early sets had viewing screens which were four to six inches in diagonal measurement and whose images were reflected onto a large mirror located at the top of the set's cabinet, directly above the picture tube. When improved television sets were marketed on a large scale in the late 1940s, the measurement of the viewing screens had increased to an average of ten inches, with some receivers having the smaller eight-inch screen and a few having what then seemed to be an unusually large twelve-inch screen. By the late 1950s however, viewing screens measuring twenty-four inches were being sold.

The variety of screen sizes in television sets saw a recurrence of a phenomenon which much earlier had been experienced with phonographs and radio sets. By 1915 phonographs were available in a wide variety of cabinet styles, many of which were designed after classic furniture styles. Some of these had retail prices exceeding $1,000, which in 1915 could hardly be termed a casual purchase. Also, some brand names cost more than others in the phonograph industry. An immediate consequence of this discrepancy was the social importance attached to owning certain kinds of phonographs, in which expensive models with elaborate cabinetry took precedence over less exquisite but often more functional models. The type of phonograph one could display in a family room or parlor would serve as an indicator of personal success. Predictably, the same social significance came to be attached to radio receivers. Certain brand names were known to be more elaborate and hence more expensive than others, and these too could serve as a sign of social prominence and personal success. The same attitudes prevailed in the selection of a piano for the home and an automobile for family use—brand names became all important.

When television sets were first marketed on a large scale in the 1940s, their designs were all rather similar, with cabinet styling being, for the most part, inconsequential. But by the mid 1950s, when wide-screen receivers were being marketed in elaborate cabinets, brand names again became a matter of prestige, as did viewing-screen sizes: a twenty-one or twenty-four inch screen was known to be much more expensive than a ten-inch one, and hence a better indicator of personal success and affluence.

The early telecasts of the 1940s and early 1950s were carried on with the same casualness and spontaneity as the first radio broadcasts had been some thirty years earlier. All telecasts were aired live until the later 1950s when videotaping began to see widespread use even though the occupational hazards of live television were sometimes even more serious than those of radio's earliest days. A wrongly calculated fall during a fight scene would sometimes send scenery crashing to the floor of the studio, revealing scurrying technicians and different stage props to the viewing audience. Performers sometimes forgot their lines and props such as revolvers and cigarette lighters either failed to work or sometimes fell apart during live telecasts. Yet when videotaping eliminated these problems, it also deprived the medium of some of the spontaneity that characterized its earlier years.

Television, radio, and motion pictures were not well received by the established arts, in spite of their immediate acceptance by the general public. Each of them passed through what might be called a "novelty stage" in which public interest in them rose and fell with equal rapidity. Motion pictures were first shown to immense crowds of people eager and content to see anything that moved on the screen. But, as public interest waned, films were shown to limited audiences in circus side-shows and were also shown in vaudeville houses, where they were called "chasers," intended to clear the theater for a new audience.

Radio experienced no such rise and fall, although it clearly went through a novelty stage. Just as the first motion picture audiences were content to see anything which expressed motion, the first radio listeners seemed content to receive almost anything audible. However, after this novelty period, the quality of programming became progressively more important, as networks vied for the attention of the public. Much of the explanation for these novelty periods can be attributed to the public's first fascination with the invention itself; the fact that motion pictures and radio broadcasting actually worked perhaps made quality seem initially unimportant.

The reaction of the critics to these novelty periods was often one of lordly disdain. Many critics were unable to understand the public's fascination with the inventions the media comprised. They often wrongly concluded that the viewing and listening public had no conception of artistic quality, being satisfied with anything purporting to be entertainment, however banal it happened to be. The same critical reaction was expressed toward the first network television broadcasts, although telecasting passed through its novelty stage much more rapidly than any of the other media.

Of all the media of this century, only the phonograph was given the blessings of the established arts early in its novelty period. The entertainment industry seemed to rejoice at the invention of the phonograph, since the voices and instrumental artistry of great performers could at last be preserved. But the quality of reproduction which the early phonographs afforded hardly warranted this attitude. While imaginative copywriters were heralding the possibility of preserving the voice of Adelina Patti, the famed Italo-Spanish soprano of the last half of the nineteenth century, more realistic appraisals of the new medium were being issued by those who had seen it demonstrated:

> The instrument has not quite reached perfection when the tones of a Patti can be faithfully repeated; in fact, to some extent, it is a burlesque or parody of the human voice.... Hence, it is extremely difficult to read what is said upon the instrument; if a person is put out of the room and you speak into it, he can with difficulty translate what it says.[2]

Unfortunately, the instrument did not reach the perfection the author speaks of until the early 1900s, and Madame Patti, who began her professional career in 1859, did not make commercial records until 1905, after much of the beauty of her voice had gone.

Perhaps the most singularly lamentable feature of all the twentieth century media is that much of what they presented is lost to us completely. Highly acclaimed silent films were often destroyed after their box-office appeal had waned, and many of those that did survive could not be preserved because of the gradual dissolution of the film emulsions. Similarly, many valuable copies of phonograph recordings were lost to the scrap drives of the two world wars, and many of the master discs from which they were pressed were lost or destroyed.

The bulk of radio and television programs which have been

aired are not preserved. Much of what is available to us of early radio programs has been preserved in the form of air checks, or electric recordings of parts of programs transferred onto metal or lacquered discs. The metal air-check recordings are seriously flawed by surface noise and are often highly unreliable indicators of musical programs. A number of early television programs were preserved by the "kinescope" film technique, although their quality is markedly inferior to that of the original telecasts. Regardless of the quality of what has come down to us, what is important is that something of the immediate past has been preserved. What has been preserved gives rise to the wish that more had been saved.

Part Two

Popular Music On Records, 1900-1975

Colored singing and playing artists are riding to fame and fortune with the current popular demand for "blues" disk recordings and because of the recognized fact that only a Negro can do justice to the native indigo ditties such artists are in great demand.

Variety, July 26, 1923

3.

The Red Seal Era

"A Wonderful Invention—Speech Capable of Indefinite Repetition from Automatic Records," read an editorial headline in a November 1877 issue of *Scientific American* announcing the invention of the phonograph by Thomas Edison. Similar announcements were to appear in *Harper's Weekly* and other magazines throughout the year 1878. As the first tinfoil phonographs were being marketed for exhibition purposes, scientists and laymen alike were speculating about this "miracle of the nineteenth century" and its future. "It will henceforth be possible," Edison wrote in June of 1878, "to preserve for future generations the voices as well as works of our Washingtons, our Lincolns, and our Gladstones, and to have them give us their greatest efforts in every town and hamlet in the country."[1] In the hundred years that have passed since Edison issued his prediction, the phonograph has had an immense effect upon the diffusion of values and the reinforcement of social roles in American popular culture.

During its novelty period before the emergence of the recording industry in the 1890s, early recording machines were put to a variety of experimental uses. Often eminent voices were preserved, such as that of Pope Leo XIII, Gladstone, Bismarck, Franz Joseph, and Wilhelm II, all of whom were recorded by Edison's European agents in the late 1880s and early 1890s. Recordings were also made of obscure European dialects and African tribal languages, and in the United States a few cultural anthropologists secured recordings of the languages of the vanishing Indian tribes of the West. The phonograph was even put to scientific uses during its infancy when it was used to record wildlife sounds. A recording entitled "Song of a Nightingale," one of several issued domestically by the Victor Talking Machine Company, and assigned catalog number 64161, has on its label the caption, "Made by a Captive Nightingale in the Possession of Herr Reich, Bremen."

With the emergence of an industry in the 1890s these experimental uses were superseded by the phonograph's attraction as a medium of musical entertainment. It was not the first mechanical device to be employed for a musical purpose, for calliopes, music boxes, player pianos, and mechanically played instruments had been in use before the phonograph's inception. But the phonograph represented the first mechanical entertainment medium which could reproduce a musical performance just as it had been originally given.

By 1910 the phonograph record had become the dominant medium of home musical entertainment, and its inventor had become a national hero. Edison had invented not only the phonograph, but also a host of other twentieth century marvels including both the incandescent lamp and the "electric pen," from which the mimeograph process was developed. "The Wizard of Menlo Park," as he was called, had unquestionably become an American folk hero. He had also become the motivating force behind "Thomas A. Edison, Incorporated," the title under which the many Edison interests, including the production of phonographs and recordings, had become consolidated. This company along with the Victor and

Columbia companies came to dominate the recording industry well into the 1920s. But Edison's company, at least from a musical standpoint, had been pursuing a slightly different course from that of its two largest competitors. As phonograph historian Roland Gelatt succinctly put it, "While Victor was courting the public with Caruso and grand opera, Edison was holding forth with Arthur Collins and 'coon songs.' "[2] Unfortunately, one of the first entertainment uses to which the phonograph was put aided in furthering a racial stereotype.

Ironically, the phonograph became an instrument which promoted a stereotype of black Americans which was deeply rooted in the American mind. Much can be gathered from an analysis of this genre of popular music—the so-called coon song—not only about early recordings and the industry and persons who produced them, but about the culture in which they flourished as well.

Immediately before the United States entered the First World War, the Victor Company issued a series of recordings entitled "Songs of the Past" in which its own choral group sang the refrains to what were advertised as the best loved songs of the days preceding the turn of the century. The record labels contain the titles of such well-remembered songs as "The Old Folks at Home," "When You and I Were Young, Maggie," and "Silver Threads Among the Gold," as well as "Little Alabama Coon" and "All Coons Look Alike to Me." The latter songs, which were every bit as popular as the former mentioned, were originally called "darky songs," and were considered refined in comparison to the coon song:

> By "coon songs" are meant up-to-date comic songs in negro dialect. The humor of these songs cannot be called refined, and for that reason we have distinguished them from old-fashioned darky humor.[3]

This definition appears in the Victor Records catalog of 1914. While it is difficult to imagine how one form of songs ridi-

culing blacks could be more refined than another, the definition does at least reflect the use of the term "coon song"
prevalent at that time.

While characterizations of the black man had been employed for some time in other forms of entertainment, notably
in minstrel shows for a supposed comic effect, early recordings of coon songs employed the most racist, abusive language possible for the sake of a greater effect. Consider, for
example, the lyrics to this popular coon song of the pre-World
War I period:

> Oh, I know a little nigger
> Who would whistle in the square,
> "Dum-dee-dee-dee-dee-deedly-dum."
>
> Oh, you're bound to hear him comin'
> Round the corner every day,
> "Dum-dee-dee-dee-dee-deedly-dum."
>
> He'd whistle night and day,
> In his own peculiar way,
> Indeed he was as happy as a loon!
>
> And it made him feel so proud
> When he whistled out so loud,
> "Dum-dee-dee-dee-dee-deedly-dum."[4]

The title of this piece of entertainment—or so it was called
in early record catalogs—is "The Merry Whistling Darky,"
and it was recorded on the Edison label by S. H. Dudley, one
of many names which came to be identified with coon songs
and "darky comic specialities." Like all such songs, the lyrics
were meant to be spoken or sung in the stereotypical speech
attributed to Blacks, and its effect was meant to be a comic
one.

This particular recording centers on one element in the
stereotype, the animal-like happiness often attributed to
Blacks; other elements are to be found in similar recordings:

Erastus Henry Johnson am
Forgiven for them sins;
But he thought the Wicked Coon
Had put the hoodoo onto him.

So he went to seek a voodoo
Who would drive the spell away,
"Ah-hoo," "ah-hoo," so the niggers say!

The voodoo said, "The rabbit's foot
Can lead the path aright,"
So he took it to the graveyard
In the middle of the night.

The bells of de clock was strikin' twelve,
The bats flew 'round his head;
"Ah-hoo," "ah-hoo," so the nigger said:

"Can't you hear dat plinky-plunky tune,
Played by the Ghost of the Banjo Coon?
Redbirds call, and the sleeping whippoorwill,
As soon as the moon goes behind the hill.

Two of our goats and the dogs begin to howl;
In the steeple of the church starts the hootin' of de owl
Who flies up, and all begin to croon,
'Cause they know its the Ghost of the Banjo Coon!"⁵

These lines constitute the verse and refrain of an Edison recording entitled "The Ghost of the Banjo Coon," which was
recorded by Arthur Collins, who with his partner Byron G.
Harlan came to be identified with the coon song genre.

If the superstition, fear, and hints of witchcraft which this
recording plays upon are part of the Black stereotype, two
other elements are mockingly stressed in another Edison recording entitled "A Coon Wedding in Southern Georgia," performed on the recording by the vaudeville group MacIntyre,
Heath, and Company:

> Brothers and sisters, I would like to request the unfortunate
> couple which am about to participate in this here catas-
> trophe to stand up before me.

George Washington Abraham Jackson, does you promise
to shelter and feed this lovely female froo-line [*fraulein*] to
the best of your a-biliousness? (Response: "I does!")

Lucinda Martha Mathilda Jones, am you willin' to run
the awful risk of takin' this here black man for better or for
worser? (Response: "I'se gwine to take de chance,
Parson!")

Then accordin' to the law that am confest'd in me, I
denounces you as tied hand-and-foot, and what De Lawd
his j'ined asunder, let no man separate together![6]

This characterization is quite moderate when compared to
other coon songs and darky comic specialties, in which the
negroes of the lyrics are assigned speech impediments for an
enhanced comic effect.

Two such recordings, both made by the Edison Company,
were entitled "Possum Pie (or, 'The Stuttering Coon')" and
"Stuttering Dick." The last-mentioned of these was recorded
by Edward Meeker, and contained the following lyrics:

> Dick Alexander Simpson was
> A great big, tongue-tied coon!
> He stutters and he mutters
> Every morning, night and noon.
>
> If you would stand and talk to him,
> You'd get a shower-bath;
> You'd have the hardest time in life
> A-tryin' not to laugh!
>
> Dick's sweetheart she was tongue-tied, too,
> And her first name was Sis;
> And in the parlor they would coo
> And sit and talk like this:
>
> "Sis-a-Sis-a-Sis-a-I-love-you,
> Do y-y-y-y-y-you love me, too?"
> "Y-y-y-y-yes, oh, quick—
> "Y-y-y-y-yes, I love you, Dick!"[7]

These and similar lyrics constituted "comic effect," and many additional elements of the black stereotype are found on other recordings made during the same period.

The pioneer recording artist Billy Golden, in the company of several partners in duets labeled "darky comic specialties" and recorded by the Edison Company, relied upon several elements of the black stereotype. In one of his recordings, entitled "The Coon Waiters," one of the characters is asked at what time he had arisen that morning. When he replies, "Seven, L. N." he is asked about the meaning of the letters— and jubilantly replies, "Lazy Nigger!" In another Golden record of the same period, "The Colored Recruits," a black enlistee asks the white recruiting officer if he can take his "rozzer" with him to fight the enemy. One recording popular during this period makes no attempt to depict the entire black culture in anything but abusive, stereotypical language:

Brothers and sisters, Adam and Eve in the Garden of Eden —what a beautiful sight until the serpent come! Then when Eve done eateth the apple and give Adam a bite, the Lawd done come and said, "Look here, you triflin' niggers, you done eat my apples! I reckon you'se a-fixin' to steal my chickens next! Get outa here!"

Then Adam and Eve was so scared they turned white— and dat's how the white man come about! 'Cause of the meanness of Adam and Eve! Adam and Eve were throwin' away the beautiful Garden of Eden for a apple. Now, then, if it had a-been a watermelon . . .

Then come the Fall, and it was a mightly cold day for Adam and Eve, and they put on their clothes! That's about all you niggers have done ever since, is put on clothes. Am seein' you women down yonder dressed up like peacocks on this here beautiful Sunday—nobody would ever believe that you had to go out and work for your husbands on a Monday.[8]

This monologue is excerpted from an Edison cylinder recording entitled "Parson Spencer's Discourse on Adam and Eve," made by the veteran recording star Len Spencer in the early 1900s.

Not only do the lyrics portray blacks as thieves and slothful creatures, but they also reflect the then-prevalent white view of the black man's versions of Christian teachings. Even the prestigious Fisk University Jubilee Singers merited this description in the Victor catalog:

> The Jubilee Songs, collected and introduced to the world by Fisk University, and which might be called Negro Folk Songs, are quaint and interesting numbers. Some touch the heart with their pathos; and some excite to laughter by their quaint conceptions of Biblical facts.[9]

The wording of this description, like the recordings listed here, presents one with an unfortunate and cruel, but nevertheless pervasive and longstanding portrait of black people: musical, happy, at once religious and superstitious, snappily-dressed, fond of watermelon, often thieving, and always lazy and stupid.

Only eight "coon songs" are either mentioned or excerpted here, although it would have been easy to list eighty, or even one hundred and eighty such recordings, all recorded between the years 1891 and 1917, mostly by the Edison Company. To be accurate, Edison was not alone in recording coon songs for large-scale distribution. Both the Victor and Columbia interests had similar listings in their catalogs, although neither company recorded or distributed them in the quantity that Edison's did. Of the two, Victor paid the least attention to the genre, limiting its major catalog entries to well-established vaudeville routines; among others, Victor listed recordings by May Irwin ("May Irwin's Bully Song" and "The Frog Song"), and "The Virginia Judge" by Walter C. Kelly. Both Irwin and Kelly were nationally famous performers. At the same time, the Victor catalogs also featured choral recordings of most of black composer James Bland's works, along with the spirituals of the Fisk and Tuskegee Singers, both of which remained staples in the Victor offerings.

The Columbia Company had featured in its early years a large number of coon songs and darky comic specialties and since exclusive contracts prohibiting performers from making recordings for other companies had not yet been adopted at that time, it was not uncommon to see the same listings in both the Columbia and Edison catalogs. In 1903, however, Columbia made a series of operatic recordings which became known as the Columbia Grand Opera Series. Although this first series was not very successful, the company gradually moved in the direction of opera and concert selections, as well as to recordings by brass bands and vocal renditions of popular songs. By 1915, the number of coon songs listed in the Columbia catalog had diminished and had been replaced by the recordings of Bert Williams, the most successful black showman of his time.

Aside from their individual catalog listings, the Victor and Columbia Companies differed from the Edison Company in at least one noteworthy way. Edison maintained firm personal control over his company, to the extent that he had ultimate control over the artists and their repertoires:

> Edison was incapable of utilizing this talent to anyone's satisfaction but his own. He was continually interfering with the choice of repertoire and would stubbornly refuse to issue recordings that bore the approval both of his own recording directors and the artists themselves. His head teemed with half-baked notions about music. He preferred "melody" and "heart songs" to "the opera type." He had no use for accompaniments. "Every accompanist," he said, "tends to spoil the song. Accompanists should only be heard between the parts." His favorite song was "I'll Take You Home Again, Kathleen." All this resulted in a chaoti-

cally organized catalog in which certain areas of music were totally ignored and where miscasting of accomplished musical artists was painfully apparent.[10]

Edison often referred to the phonograph as his "favorite invention." Judging from the many incidents in the history of his company in which his own musical preferences were imposed upon artists and directors alike, it appears that he wished to maintain complete control over its use, at least within the confines of his own company.

Edison's personal control over the interests and, more importantly, the repertoire chosen for recording may account for the quantity of coon song records marketed by his company. The greatest market for these recordings was in the rural Midwest and the deep South, and Edison depended upon this trade for his profits. But, the Victor and Columbia companies had clearly demonstrated that they did not have to depend upon this genre for their livelihood; a great demand existed for vocal and instrumental recordings of a "classical" type. Considering Edison's musical tastes and the unlimited power he had within his company, it is not surprising that opera records and classical selections were featured only in a minor way in his catalogs.

When Edison did feature such recordings it was only to try to appeal to a segment of the public which would not have been interested in the coon songs of Arthur Collins and Billy Golden. Shortly after he had introduced a new phonograph— the "Amberola"—and a new line of operatic recordings to be marketed with it, many featuring the renowned *heldentenor* Leo Slezak, the Edison Company provided this rationale for its dealers:

> Now that you've got Slezak and the Amberola to take care of one class of your customers, and all the other styles of Phonographs and all the other records, both Standard and Amberol, to take care of the other classes, you're equipped to take out all the profit there is in the business. . . .

Because while the Amberola class is resting and the
Grand Opera lovers are saving up to buy more records, the
good old "ragtime-coon songs-Sousa-Herbert-monologues-
sentimental ballads" crowd will still be on the job buying
Phonographs of other styles, and Standard and Amberol
records, until there's frost on the sun.[11]

Whether or not the Edison dealers accepted the reasoning
and consequent optimism of this appeal, the fact remained
that the public showed no interest in the Edison opera issues,
primarily because he had made it clear through his catalogs
what sort of "class," as the rationale termed it, he was appeal-
ing to with his music. By the time he elected to make recordings of a different kind, his company had become identified
with a segment of the population that showed no interest in
grand opera.

Coon songs remained a staple in the Edison catalogs, and
as new songs and performers emerged, they were often fitted
into this classification. When Sophie Tucker made her first
cylinder recordings for the Edison Company, she was billed
as a "coon shouter" in publicity releases, and when Irving
Berlin's "Alexander's Ragtime Band" was recorded by Billy
Murray on the Edison label in 1912[12] the label bore the description "coon song," even though the lyrics and the brass
band which served as the accompaniment in no way fitted the
description.

In the 1920s a new series of recordings and another type
of music became popular. The career of one artist, Enrico
Caruso, dominated the musical scene during this era. The
level of artistic achievement and public esteem which Caruso
attained can be seen by the fact that today, more than fifty
years after his last public performance, his name is known to
many who never saw or heard him, and who have little association with grand opera, the musical form which he established so firmly in this country.

The relationship between the public's esteem for Caruso as

a singer and the following his recordings generated is important to the emergence of grand opera as a form of popular music in this country. Ironically, his recorded voice was heard at the Metropolitan Opera House in New York before he actually sang there. This was by means of one of the ten records he made for the Gramophone and Typewriter Company of London and Milan in April of 1902. One of these records was sent to Heinrich Conreid, then general manager of the Metropolitan, who was conducting a search for the best Italian tenor voice available for the opera company at that time. In this search Conreid is said to have asked an Italian bootblack who Italy's greatest tenor was; Caruso's name was given in reply. Whether the story is apocryphal or not, Caruso's European reputation, combined with the record which Conreid heard, earned him a contract with the Metropolitan Opera Company. He made his American debut with them on November 23, 1903.

The following year, the Victor Company, which had issued his Gramophone and Typewriter records under their label by a special arrangement, signed him to an exclusive contract. This has been described both by historians and the Victor Company itself as the most important event in Victor's financial history. Caruso's artistic reputation grew with each year and with the new roles he assumed—culminating in his Eleazar in Halevy's opera *La Juive* opposite the American soprano Rosa Ponselle. At the same time, the number of Victor records he made increased, and as they were purchased by people who would not otherwise have heard him, his reputation became a national one. In the process he established the Victor Company's Red Seal celebrity records as the epitome of recorded entertainment.

The term "Red Seal" stemmed from the stratification of artists and repertoire practiced by the Victor Company and other companies as well. Certain colors or designs of the record labels were used to differentiate types of entertainment and artists as well as the price of the records. A black label was used on band recordings and on what Edison would have termed melody and heart songs. The black label record was the lowest in the Victor Company's stratification system, with most of the records selling for seventy-five cents. Above it, both monetarily and artistically in the catalogs, were the purple and the blue labels, both of which were reserved for performers of a "higher" stature. Nationally known vaudevillians such as Harry Lauder, George M. Cohan, and the team of Nora Bayes and Jack Norworth recorded on the blue and the purple labels, as did a number of opera and concert singers whose reputations were not great enough to warrant an elite Red Seal contract.

The blue and purple labels were priced variously from seventy-five cents to two dollars, depending upon the professional stature of the artist. Red Seal records on the other hand sold for an average of two dollars, and unlike the blue and black seals, were pressed on one side of the record only; the other side of the disc was either left entirely blank, engraved with the name "Victor," or had English translations of the librettos of operas sung in foreign languages. Even among the artists in the Victor catalogs a stratification system existed; singers were differentiated by the price of their recordings.

Dame Nellie Melba, whose reputation as an operatic soprano rivaled Caruso's as a tenor, made Red Seal recordings which sold at three dollars each, and when she and Caruso recorded the duet "Osoave fanciulla," from Puccini's *La Boheme,* the record sold for five dollars. In some instances the recordings of one performer alone would be granted the five-dollar price; Adelina Patti, perhaps the most renowned soprano of the late nineteenth century, made a series of Red Seal records which sold at this price.

In terms of selling price alone, the Victor Red Seal reached its zenith in 1908, when the sextet aria "Chi mi frena in tal momento?" from Donizetti's opera *Lucia di Lammermoor* was released at the price of seven dollars. This recording, made on February 7, 1908 and assigned the catalog number 96200, featured the voices of Caruso, soprano Marcella Sembrich, baritone Antonio Scotti, and basso Marcel Journet; at the price of seven dollars it was not intended to make a great deal of money. It was to be regarded more as an unusual bit of publicity, as the Victor Company told its dealers in a memorandum:

> Do not underestimate the value of the Sextet as an advertising medium. This feature of the record is very much more valuable to the average dealer than the actual profit he may make on its sales. Not all of your customers can afford to purchase a $7.00 record, but the mere announcement of it will bring them to your store as a magnet attracts steel.[13]

With the release of the *Lucia* recording the reputations of the performers were enhanced in that more people become aware of them. Perhaps more importantly, possession of the record became a means of identifying with the Fifth Avenue "Gold Coast" upper class, and a means of separating oneself from the common man.

The Red Seal record became a sign of cultural taste as well as an indictor of personal success. As Roland Gelatt wrote in *The Fabulous Phonograph*:

> In this prosperous and receptive atmosphere, Red Seal Records throve magnificently. Across the land, in towns where opera companies had never set foot, a growing clientele for standard arias and ensembles was found to be patronizing Victor's ten thousand dealers. It would be hard to say how much of this trade derived from a genuine desire for good music. There was, aesthetic satisfaction aside, a redolent snob appeal attached to Red Seal Records. They were expensive, and expensive in an autocratically stratified way.[14]

Paradoxically, upper-class aspirants who might have cared nothing about grand opera often owned Red Seal records, especially those of Caruso. Either played or displayed at appropriate social moments, they might become instrumental in helping their owners gain in-group acceptance.

Not every purchaser of Red Seal records was interested in them for their snob appeal, nor, perhaps, for the operatic arias of Verdi, Donizetti, or Puccini. To meet the musical tastes of another segment of its trade, the Victor Company issued popular compositions performed by its Red Seal artists. Such vocalists as Marcella Sembrich and Geraldine Farrar recorded popular songs of the "Home Sweet Home" and "Mighty Lak' a Rose" variety in addition to their purely operatic releases.

Two Red Seal artists in particular forsook opera and operatic recordings for the more popular market and enjoyed record sales which on several occasions exceeded even Caruso's. One of these was soprano Alma Gluck, whose recording of James Bland's "Carry Me Back to Old Virginny" (Victor record 74420) had the distinction of becoming the first Red Seal to exceed the one million mark in total sales. With her husband, violinist Efrem Zimbalist, Madame Gluck made a number of duets which were also best-selling catalog entries for Victor. Like Alma Gluck, Irish tenor John McCormack left opera for the more intimate concert stage and also came to enjoy one of the largest followings in the history of recording. Often called "Ireland's Caruso" because of the public esteem in which he was held, McCormack's Red Seal recordings of Irish ballads and folk songs quickly established him as one of the most popular singers in the Victor catalog.

Part of John McCormack's following provides us with an insight into another dimension and role of the Victor Red Seal, one which is particularly important to the study of subcultural assimilation in the early part of this century. Irish immigrants, who by virtue of their economic status could only have dreamed of success like McCormack's, purchased his records whenever their limited means would permit it. They seem to have done so partly because the more traditional

songs evoked memories of more secure times and partly because John McCormack may have provided them with a
means of cultural identification. He was looked upon favorably by the dominant culture in which they were a minority.
The same may be said of the Italian immigrant's role in
Caruso's successful career. Stanley Jackson, his biographer,
wrote,

> To New York's Little Italy he was far more than a voice;
> he had become a symbol of hope and laughter in adversity.
> They identified fiercely, patriotically, with the chubby little
> man who had escaped from a Neapolitan slum to win story-
> book success on alien soil but still spoke broken English
> and remained as Italian as macaroni.[15]

The inference that an immigrant's ability to identify with
Caruso or McCormack may have helped assimilation into the
larger culture seems warranted, although it may be difficult
to demonstrate.

The assimilation process is certainly made easier when the
minority group can lay claim to accomplishments and values
which are favorably regarded by the dominant culture. The
fact that Italian opera and the singing of Caruso and McCormack were so regarded by Anglo-Americans may have ex-
pedited the assimilation of Italian and Irish immigrants. The
converse may be seen in the case of black Americans whose
cultural heritage was regarded as primitive by the larger culture. This, in combination with a host of other factors, made
their assimilation immensely difficult.

Caruso and McCormack were what might be termed ethnic
performers in that a substantial part of their following was
composed of people from their own ethnic groups. Like
John McCormack, Caruso recorded a number of popular
songs which were directed to members of his own immigrant
group. Some of these songs were Neapolitan in origin, such

as Nutile's "Mamma mia che vo sape," which Caruso sang in his native napuletan' dialect on Victor Red Seal 88206. Others were equally well known outside the Italian communities, folk songs such as DiCapua's "O sole mio," and Paolo Tosti's "Addio." As his fame grew, the Victor Company urged him to record standard concert songs and hymns, such as Bartlett's "A Dream" and Geehl's "For You Alone," both of which Caruso sang in English to widen his appeal to purchasers of nonoperatic records.

Other ethnic groups could also identify with various Red Seal artists, some of whom gathered immense followings. One of these was Welsh tenor Evan Williams, whose popularity steadily rose from 1907 until his death in 1918. Although American born, his parents had been Welsh immigrants, and Williams had worked as a youth in the coal mines of Ohio and Pennsylvania. Unlike John McCormack, whose career his somewhat resembled, Williams was not an opera singer, but limited his singing to concert appearances and phonograph records. His repertoire consisted mainly of hymns and English renditions of standard tenor operatic arias.

Apart from the Victor Company, recordings of other singers who had special ethnic appeal were being marketed. In Jewish communities the cantorial records of Josef Rosenblatt frequently outsold those of any other performers, as did those of the cantors Sawel Kwartin, Gerson Sirota, and Mordecai Hershman. Many of these were issued on special labels reserved for what the record companies often termed "limited appeal audiences," which referred mainly to immigrant groups. The Columbia Company, for example, issued a number of songs and comic selections under the heading "Foreign Series," many of which were performed in Slavic languages. Whether the record companies intentionally sought out ethnic performers, or whether the connection between them is more accidental than intentional, they eventually recorded all sorts of ethnically diverse performers, perhaps indicating the assimilation of the ethnic groups themselves. What made possible the widespread appeal of most of the ethnic singers mentioned here was the Red Seal line of records. It began in 1903 and dominated all other lines of recordings until the late 1920s.

4.

The Big Band Era

The aftermath of World War I brought about significant changes in musical tastes, changes which gradually brought about the demise of Red Seal records. What became publicly accepted as Jazz first came into wide popularity just after 1917, when the Original Dixieland Jazz Band made its first Victor black-seal recordings. The success of the highly derivative Dixieland group led to the rise of others who played in an extremely uncreative way, at least in comparison to a black jazz band like Joe "King" Oliver's, with whom Louis Armstrong's recording career began.

The popularity of jazz, with its driving rhythm, unrestricted melody line, and often dissonant note combinations, was perhaps symbolic of the effects of the war itself upon the public—a public which a mere two years earlier had seemed content with the Red Seal records of Evan Williams and Alma Gluck. Evan Williams' sudden death in 1918 itself contributed to the Red Seal's decline, as did the untimely death of the one artist who had long assured its success; Enrico Caruso, whose career the *New York Times* called "a long crescendo," died in Naples on August 2, 1921, creating a void in the Red Seal catalog which was never to be filled.

A development within the recording process also contributed to the decline of the Red Seal in the mid-1920s. When recording became electric in 1925 the phonograph recording ceased to be primarily a vocalist's medium. Since the elite Red Seal line was almost exclusively a line of vocal recordings, they were slowly replaced in popularity by orchestral recordings, both symphonic and popular. Too, the advent of a great number of record companies, among them Brunswick, Vocalion, Perfect, Okeh, and Gennett—all of which capitalized on the popularity of jazz and dance band music—added to Victor's competition. Prior to World War I, Alma Gluck's Red Seal record "Carry Me Back to Old Virginny" had sold over one million copies; after the war, a double-sided black seal featuring "Whispering" on one side and "The Japanese Sandman" on the other also exceeded the one million mark. This record, listed in the Victor supplements as black label recording 18690, featured the dance band of Paul Whiteman, whose name is still the one most often associated with the popular band music of the 1920s. His recordings were usually classified under the jazz heading in the Victor catalogs, although the records he made between 1920 and 1925 hardly merit this description. In the late 1920s, when he employed famed cornetist Bix Beiderbecke, the term jazz was perhaps appropriate. But the first Whiteman records, well orchestrated as they were, suffer notably when they are compared to black efforts of the same period.

The style of the Whiteman band clearly passed through different evolutionary stages, beginning with acoustic recordings in 1920–1924 such as "Whispering," "Carolina in the Morning," and "I'll Build a Stairway to Paradise." Though they do not represent true jazz, the arrangements which Whiteman utilized during this period were innovative compared to some of the "society" orchestras then prominent. The list of records Whiteman made during this period is also a list of the popular songs of the period, including many of the songs of Jerome Kern, George Gershwin, and Irving Berlin.

The playing style which superseded his acoustic recordings can be traced to the evening of February 12, 1924, when Whiteman personally conducted the first public performance of Gershwin's *Rhapsody in Blue* at New York City's Aeolian Hall. A double-sided Victor black seal recording of this work made by the new electrical process was issued late in 1927. It featured Gershwin as lead pianist. In 1926 Whiteman began a series of new recordings with the Paul Whiteman Concert Orchestra and thereby entered into the second stage of his style's evolution.

The sequence of the refrain in his best-selling 1927 recording of "When Day Is Done" typifies the band's style during this period. The first half of the record is composed of string and piano ensembles playing the verse, a first chorus of the refrain, and then the verse again. This is followed by a solo jazz-like interpretation of the refrain played by cornetist Henry Busse, after which the record concludes with the entire band playing the melody line in unrestrained double time. This style was eventually displaced by the one the band adopted in 1927 and 1928, which is treated in chapter 8.

Just as the success of the Original Dixieland Jazz Band led to imitations of its style by other, less creative groups, Paul Whiteman's success soon gathered him competition, although the volume of his record sales remained the largest of any dance band through the late 1920s. Early in Whiteman's recording career, the Columbia Company had offered the Ted Lewis Dance Band as a competitor, and for a time the title "King of Jazz" was being claimed by both of them. This must have been at once comic and tragic to a player like Louis Armstrong, whose earnings were probably less than one-tenth of either man. The Brunswick Company, under the aegis of Gustave Haenschen, also offered its recordings of the Isham

Jones Orchestra, which played many of the songs that Jones had written in collaboration with composer Gus Kahn— among them "It Had to Be You," "I'll See You in My Dreams," and "Swingin' Down the Lane."

Dance orchestras continued to account for most popular record sales through the mid-1920s, when the bands of George Olsen and Jean Goldkette continued in the stylistic pattern Whiteman had established. The Goldkette Orchestra, which was the first major band to feature the cornet playing of legendary Bix Beiderbecke, recorded arrangements in which several sections of the band were adapted to Beiderbecke's personal style. And the George Olsen orchestra contributed inadvertently to the type of recorded entertainment which came to displace dance orchestras in the late 1920s. When Olsen recorded "Who," from the Jerome Kern musical *Sunny,* he employed a vocal trio to sing the melody line on one of the refrains. The success of this record prompted other bands to hire vocal trios, and by 1927, a year after the "Who" recording, both the Goldkette and the Whiteman bands also featured trios. The members of the Whiteman trio are particularly noteworthy because of the importance one of them had for the music of the next decade; along with Harry Barris and Al Rinker, who played piano and also sang, was the group's occasional drummer and third voice, Bing Crosby.

Throughout the late 1920s Crosby was featured on many Whiteman recordings, although he was not named on the labels. With Barris and Rinker he made several Okeh records under the name of "The Rhythm Boys," and he continued with the Whiteman band until 1931, when he made a few Victor recordings with the Gus Arnheim band, a West Coast dance orchestra which was then engaged at the Cocoanut Grove. In the summer of 1931 he made a series of Brunswick records, one of which, "Where the Blue of the Night Meets the Gold of the Day," came to be identified with him throughout the rest of his career.

The gradual movement from dance band records to those of individual vocalists was not initiated by Crosby, but by Gene Austin, whose 1927 recording of "My Blue Heaven" was for many years a bestseller. Austin's total record sales for the late-1920s numbered more than 80 million, according to Victor sales figures. His warm, rather casual singing style reflected the country and western influences upon his youth and early career, much of which was spent in the South and Midwest. As Austin's vocal recordings began to displace dance band records in popularity, other popular music genres were also beginning to be recorded. Country and western songs were first recorded in the late 1920s, although some country ballads and composed "folk songs" had been recorded by Vernon Dalhart, whose rendition of "The Prisoner's Song" was recorded by almost every phonograph company in existence, with Dalhart often using assumed names on the labels.

Although music historians have claimed Dalhart as one of the early country and western stars, his career was most associated with another popular music form, the so-called novelty song, which usually drew upon some recent historical event or national tragedy. When Caruso died in 1921, Dalhart recorded one such song called "They Needed a Songbird in Heaven (So God Took Caruso Away)." He entered the studios again in 1926 when Rudolf Valentino died suddenly, this time to record for the Regal Company a novelty song entitled "There's a New Star in Heaven Tonight—Rudolf Valentino." And when Lindberg crossed the Atlantic in 1927, one of the first recorded versions of the novelty song "Lucky Lindy" was Vernon Dalhart's.

To most country and western historians, it was not Dalhart but Mississippi-born Jimmie Rodgers who was the first commercially successful country balladeer. Rodgers, who had learned to play the guitar from black railway hands while he was working as a brakeman in Mississippi, made his first records in Bristol, Tennessee, in August of 1927. The recording sessions took place in an abandoned warehouse which had been crudely made into a recording studio. But, Rodgers' association with black musicians did not end with his railroad days; in his Regal Company recording of "Blue Yodel No. 9," Louis Armstrong on the cornet forms part of the accompaniment. A host of prestigious country and western singers followed Rodgers' recording success; among them were Ernest Tubb, whose recording of "Walkin' the Floor Over You" was a best-seller in 1941, and Hank Williams, whose death from an overdose of drugs and alcohol at age twenty-nine ended a songwriting career which produced "Your Cheatin' Heart," "I'm So Lonesome I Could Cry," "Cold, Cold Heart," and "Lonesome Whistle," some of the most popular songs of the country and western genre.

Jimmie Rodgers' performing style on his records of the late 1920s was not a popular one, taking popular in the Gene Austin sense of the term. Like the jazz playing of Joe "King," Oliver or Fletcher Henderson, Rodgers' singing was not accepted by the middle and upper classes, who could neither identify nor sympathize with the lyrics of his ballads. The accepted popular singers of this period were Gene Austin, Arthur Tracy ("The Street Singer"), "Whispering Jack" Smith, and Nick Lucas. As of 1929 Rudy Vallée joined this select group; with his Eastern roots and Yale baccalaureate degree, Vallée was the antithesis of Jimmie Rodgers.

Like Gene Austin, Rudy Vallee (for whom the term "crooner" was reputedly coined) enjoyed an immense following on both records and radio. His singing career eclipsed Gene Austin's in the years 1929 to 1932 and was itself eventually overshadowed by those of Bing Crosby and his baritone rival of the early 1930s, Russ Columbo. Crosby and Columbo were enjoined in what became popularly known as "The Battle of the Baritones," a somewhat mythical encounter from which Crosby, by a quirk of fate, emerged the victor; on September 2, 1934, Russ Columbo died at the age of twenty-six in a freak accident involving the unintentional discharge of an antique pistol in the studio of a photographer-friend.

Two years after Columbo's death a new musical trend which rivalled the style of Gene Austin and Rudy Vallee emerged. A return to band music began in 1936 and lasted until approximately 1945, when individual vocalists again came to dominate the record business.

The music of this period grew out of black jazz forms, but it was also much influenced by other popular music styles. Fletcher Henderson, for example, was responsible for many of the well-known Benny Goodman band arrangements. In the 1920s Henderson led one of the most successful black bands in the country, one in which Louis Armstrong played for a time. Many of the "swing" movement's players and leaders had served as members of studio bands for recording sessions at Victor, Columbia, Brunswick, and some of the smaller record companies. For example, Tommy and Jimmy Dorsey are listed in the studio bands of two blues recordings by Ethel Waters made in the 1920s, "Black and Blue" and "Am I Blue," Columbia's 2184–D and 1837 respectively.

Most of the musicians of the big bands had recorded for the major companies, sometimes in bands having the same people using different names. This was a common practice in the industry, as Brunswick's Gustave Haenschen stated in a recent interview:

> We listed several bands in the Brunswick catalogs, although many of them had exactly the same personnel. This was a common practice then. We employed a number of "regulars," all of them excellent musicians, and we tried to develop a certain style for each of the names we recorded under.[1]

The same practice was revived to some extent in the 1950s when rock-and-roll groups often recorded under pseudonyms for various record labels.

The Brunswick organization, under Gustave Haenschen, provided several of the swing players and eventual leaders with some of their earliest successes when the "Five Pennies," led by cornetist Red Nichols, made their first Brunswick recordings in 1929 and 1930. At various times in these recording sessions Benny Goodman, Glenn Miller, the Dorseys, and Gene Krupa backed up Nichols' own playing. They recorded swing-style versions of such diverse songs as "Back Home Again in Indiana," "Tea For Two," and "The Shiek of Araby."

While the beginnings and triumphs of the Nichols group have been considerably romanticized both on film and in popular literature, the somewhat less glamorous but factual details of the group's origins were recalled recently by Gustave Haenschen:

> As you know, our company, Brunswick, was the source of the Five Pennies' success on records. And as I was then the recording director for popular releases, Red Nichols came to me a number of times asking us to give him a chance with some of his arrangements. Well, I got together what became a staple group for the sessions, and we put up a suggestion box outside our offices so that we might get a catchy name for the band. It wasn't long until someone— it may have been one of the secretaries—came up with the logical name, Red Nichols and His Five Pennies.[2]

Nichols' arrangements, like those of many other leaders and players in what later became the Big Band Era, was greatly influenced by the genius of his contemporary, Bix Beiderbecke. In a recent interview jazz guitarist Eddie Condon said of Nichols:

> Most everything Red himself did was taken directly from Bix Beiderbecke's arrangements. At that point in his life, Bix was pretty well mixed up, and didn't seem to mind someone else getting all the credit for what he worked out himself. This is nothing against Red Nichols' playing, which

was technically good, but he got all of his inspiration from Bix.[3]

Benny Goodman, who recorded a number of releases for Brunswick under his own name, became the progenitor of the swing movement in the Big Band Era, following a highly successful engagement at the Manhattan Room in New York City's Hotel Pennsylvania in the autumn of 1936. The era is said to have begun not with the Goodman band, but with the "Casa Lomas" led by Glen Gray. The Casa Lomas had been booked for two weeks in December 1935 by Robert Weitman, the managing director of the Paramount Theater in New York City. After the band set attendance records during its first week, the engagement was extended to four weeks; thereafter other bands were featured in ballrooms and showrooms across the country. The Benny Goodman 1936 engagement at the Manhattan Room followed in the wake of the Casa Loma success.

The Big Band leaders and their sidemen, or lead players, often used a threefold division among playing styles to describe the musical scene of the late 1930s and early 1940s. Swing, the style in which Benny Goodman, Artie Shaw, and the Dorseys played in the late 1930s, was characterized by jazz influences in its tempo and arrangements, and was set apart from the sweet style played by such bands as Hal Kemp's, Eddie Duchin's, and Guy Lombardo's. A third category was originated by the musicians themselves and bore the pejorative title Mickey Mouse Music. The list of candidates for this category varied, depending upon whether the electors were swing or sweet. Stylists like Guy Lombardo seemed to fit the category well. To others, the tick-tock rhythms of the Ozzie Nelson, Jan Garber, and Shep Fields bands seemed better suited to the title. Shep Fields, like Guy Lombardo, tried to create a sound which could immediately be identified with his band, and he eventually arrived at an instrumental combination which featured a saxophone and accordion lead. To further differentiate himself from other bands, Fields blew bubbles into a bowl of water when recording to create what he called "rippling rhythm."

The popularity of the Big Bands, whether swing, sweet, or otherwise, was reinforced by their recordings (many of which were made on the Decca and RCA Victor Bluebird labels) and by their film appearances and radio broadcasts. The first swing broadcasts began in June 1936 when a radio series called "The Saturday Night Swing Session" devoted an hour's program to swing arrangements of popular songs. In combination, the records, film appearances, and broadcasts made the bands' personal engagements immensely successful. When Benny Goodman first appeared at the Paramount on March 10, 1936, ticket lines began to form at sunrise. Even the candy counter set a record, taking in more than $900 in one day.

The swing movement increased in momentum through 1938, a year in which there were a number of recording innovations. Artie Shaw, who had begun his swing career with a band featuring his clarinet played against a string quartet background, recorded Cole Porter's "Begin the Beguine" in the summer of 1938 in an unusual arrangement which seemed to capture both the swing and sweet styles. During the same year Benny Goodman combined swing playing with Baroque music on his RCA Bluebird recording, "Bach Goes to Town." Glenn Miller, who had been unsuccessful as a swing leader, began late in 1938 to play in a new "sweet" style; between January and June of 1938 his style became so popular that it eventually displaced swing altogether. Glenn Miller had more than a purely musical effect upon the Big Band Era, even though his popularity between 1939 and 1942 was one of the greatest of the entire period. In 1942, Miller enlisted in the U.S. Army Air Force to form an overseas group; the Miller Air Force Band broadcast weekly in the United States until 1944, when the band toured England. The broadcasts were continued until December 1944, when a plane in which

Miller was a passenger was lost over the English Channel. The death of Glenn Miller, in combination with a devastating recording strike from 1942 to 1944, marked the official end of the Big Band period.

The recording strike did considerable damage to the bands' continuing popularity, for between August 1, 1942, and November of 1944, the use of instrumentalists in recording sessions was effectively stopped. The strike resulted from an agreement among the American Federation of Musicians not to accept recording offers from RCA Victor, Columbia, and Decca, the three major producers of phonograph records, until they agreed to royalty payments for records sold for use in juke boxes and radio broadcasts. The Decca interests soon agreed to the terms of the new Federation contract, but RCA Victor and Columbia refused to sign the contracts until November, when they could not sustain further losses. In the interim both companies had drawn heavily upon unreleased records and had also recorded some of the Big Band vocalists, who were not affected by the strike and who were accompanied on the recordings by large choral groups.

One of the major difficulties the large companies faced during the recording ban was that of capitalizing on new songs which were being introduced regularly in films. When the song "As Time Goes By" became popular after being featured as the theme song of the Humphrey Bogart-Ingrid Bergman film *Casablanca,* RCA was forced to reissue an early recording of it by Rudy Vallee, who recently recounted what transpired:

> "As Time Goes By" . . . I recorded in 1931. Unfortunately I chose a key much too high for my voice which was already tired from overwork. The song originated in a Broadway show called *Everybody's Welcome* starring Frances Williams. It was not a success and our record also proved unpopular. Nevertheless, by a strange fluke, the number was included in the film *Casablanca* (with Humphrey Bogart

and Ingrid Bergman) and became an overnight hit in the early forties. As the American Federation of Musicians was on strike against the recording companies, no new records were being made. Therefore, Victor dug my disk out of the files and the reissue sold beautifully even though I detest my rendition of it.[4]

Among the rising band vocalists who profited from the ban was Perry Como, who had been featured on the band recordings of Ted Weems; he made his first RCA record, "Goodbye Sue," while the strike was in effect, though he too was backed by a choir rather than an orchestra. Less than a year after the ban was lifted his RCA recording of Russ Columbo's composition "Prisoner of Love" sold more than one million copies, and signaled a return to the popularity of individual vocalists.

The war undoubtedly helped the rise of vocalists like Perry Como. To young couples separated by the war, vocal music seemed more personal than the music of a large orchestra or dance band. Like the recording strike, this factor contributed to the rise of such singers as Como who, after the war, achieved wide success on records.

The singing styles of the postwar vocalists, like the playing styles of the Big Bands, varied considerably. Perry Como's style closely approximated that of Russ Columbo and even more closely resembled the style Bing Crosby had adopted in the late 1930s. By 1946 Como had duplicated their earlier successes, having recorded "Temptation," an earlier Crosby recording, and Columbo's successful "Prisoner of Love," both in 1945. According to RCA Victor sales figures, four million copies of Como records were pressed in one week during 1946.

Tony Martin, in contrast to Como's rather relaxed style, was considered a "big voice," a term that came to refer to singers who had "trained" or operatic voices. Martin sang in a tradition which included in the late 1920s and early 1930s radio tenors Arthur Tracy and James Melton, whose individual repertoires included a number of operatic arias. During the 1950s, when Martin's career was at its zenith, Mario Lanza also became part of this "big voice" tradition. Inadvertently perhaps, the Metropolitan Opera Company itself contributed to popular music in the immediate postwar years. In 1945 Metropolitan tenor Jan Peerce recorded a song called "Bluebird of Happiness" for RCA Victor; on the recording he not only sang but also gave a poetic recitation. The record became one of the best-selling issues of the year. Peerce's venture into the popular market was soon followed by that of Lauritz Melchior, who had dominated Wagnerian *heldentenor* roles at the Met. In 1946 Melchior recorded the "Serenade" from Romberg's *The Student Prince,* which also enjoyed wide popularity. Singers Robert Merrill, Gladys Swarthout, James Melton, and John Charles Thomas—all of whom were principally opera performers—made a number of wide-selling popular records between 1945 and 1950. In 1949 they were joined by basso Ezio Pinza, whose following among critics and public alike nearly rivaled Caruso's and who left the Metropolitan after a twenty-two year career to become an equally successful Broadway star. Pinza's 1950 recording of "September Song," from Kurt Weill's *Knickerbocker Holiday,* is one of the best-remembered recordings of the postwar period.

5.

The Postwar Years

Of all the stylistic periods through which recorded music has passed in this century, the period of Red Seal's domination has been the longest. It lasted almost twenty years, from 1903 until the early 1920s. At that time, electric recording was introduced and what passed as jazz among white bands became popular. Between the Original Dixieland Jazz Band's records of 1917 and Gene Austin's "My Blue Heaven"—which marked the end of the dance band's dominance—only ten years had passed. Only eight years separated Gene Austin's first popularity and the appearance of Glen Gray's Casa Lomas in 1935. These years when Rudy Vallee, Bing Crosby, and Russ Columbo enjoyed immense popularity also see the beginning of the Big Band Era which the Casa Lomas originate. The Big Band Era itself, it spite of the intensity of its first years, lasted only nine years, after which the American musical scene began to change even more rapidly.

Between 1950 and 1960 the pace of this stylistic change quickened substantially, and widely divergent musical forms became intertwined in popular music. Individual vocalists continued to be popular throughout the decade, beginning with Perry Como, Tony Martin, Don Cornell, and others in the early 1950s and continuing with Nat "King" Cole and Tony Bennett, and in the last part of the decade, Andy Williams and Johnny Mathis. Purely instrumental recordings also flourished throughout the 1950s, among them Pee Wee Hunt's "Oh!" and Nelson Riddle's "Lisbon Antigua." The piano solos of Roger Williams and (Lee) Liberace were also immensely popular in the 1950s, as were the duets of Ferrante and Teicher in the early 1960s. What came to be termed progressive or modern jazz also enjoyed a great following, as in Stan Kenton's LP albums of the mid-1950s. Long-standing organizations like Fred Waring's Pennsylvanians, Guy Lombardo's Royal Canadians, and the Lawrence Welk Orchestra (whose roots were actually in the Big Band period) enjoyed equally large followings on records during the 1950s.

But the musical form most often associated with this decade is rock-and-roll, a term which came into national use after two popular recordings, "Rock Around the Clock" by Bill Haley and His Comets and "The Rock and Roll Waltz" by Kay Starr, both recorded in 1955. For a time the term rock-a-billy was used to describe the new music, and it reflected part of the roots of rock-and-roll, namely "hillbilly" and country and western music. Kay Starr, for example, was billed as a "rock-a-billy" star, which reflected her Memphis, Tennessee, performing background; she had sung hillbilly songs there in amateur programs when she was a teenager. Her "Rock and Roll Waltz" had its own country and western roots; it was composed by Shorty Allen, a widely respected songwriter in that genre.

In the late 1940s, country and western music gradually entered the million-selling category in the recording industry through the efforts of a number of postwar performers. "The Sons of the Pioneers," a group which had been seen in Gene Autry's cowboy serials, recorded a ballad called "Cool Water" in 1945, the same year in which country and western singer

Eddy Arnold sold over a million copies of his "Bouquet of Roses." In 1947 their successes were followed by film cowboy Roy Rogers' RCA recording of Cole Porter's "Don't Fence Me In," which also helped to secure the place of country and western music in the popular spectrum.

As the origins of rock-and-roll can be traced in great part to hillbilly and to country and western music, so its characteristic instrumental sound can be traced to the popularity of the electric guitar, an instrument which had been used chiefly for American conceptions of Hawaiian music prior to the popular records of Chet Atkins. In 1949 Atkins gave RCA Victor a best-selling record of one of his own compositions, "Gallopin' on the Guitar," which featured his extremely innovative playing. Although his first experience was with an acoustic guitar, Atkins recorded "Gallopin' " with an electric instrument and thereby showed its recording potential. The instrument was also popularized by the recordings of Les Paul and Mary Ford, whose popular early-1950s recording of "Vaya con Dios" actually belonged to rock-a-billy genre, in spite of its title. The Paul-Ford records relied heavily upon a technical development in record engineering called multiple track recording, through which Mary Ford was able to sing duets with herself and Les Paul to create guitar solos which exceeded any known human ability.

Multiple-track recording, along with remodeling techniques, so called because they enabled recording engineers to remodel a voice, enhanced and in some cases made possible the careers of a number of rock-and-roll singers in the late 1950s. Early in the decade, critic Irving Kolodin lamented their use in the RCA Victor recordings of Mario Lanza, taken from the M–G–M motion picture *The Great Caruso.* In June 1951 Kolodin wrote:

> As most everyone knows, M-G-M is offering a film called *The Great Caruso,* in which Mario Lanza, Philadelphia-born tenor, is impersonating as much of Caruso as the film

ventures. The question naturally arises: Will anyone ever make a film called "The Great Lanza?" To judge from this sampling of his talents, the nays have it.

Lanza's normally robust and fine-textured voice has been tricked up by every device known to the acoustic trade— open, echoey hall, built-up volume level, uncommonly close microphoning—to make him more Caruso-like.[1]

Kolodin ended the review by saying, "It's hardly possible to turn down the record to a point of ordinary audibility, which makes it fine for tracing down rattles in a speaker anyway." What he was objecting to was not, of course, Lanza's vocal ability, but rather what happened to this ability between the time Lanza produced a ringing high-C and the time the recordings of it were pressed. His objections perhaps turned to lament when in 1960 more extensive techniques were used to create an acceptable voice for Fabian Forte, one of the many rock-and-roll performers who followed in the wake of Elvis Presley's success and who by his own admission had much less ability than Mario Lanza.

In the late 1950s, however, a performer did not necessarily suffer from the recording engineer's improvement of his or her singing. Personal appearances were of less importance than the success of one's records, particularly during a time when disc jockeys formulated "Top Forty" lists of the most popular releases during a given week, and when new recording companies were being formed almost overnight, many being subsidiaries of the established ones. Unlike almost any other genre of popular music, the phonograph recording was the central medium through which rock-and-roll music reached the public, either directly, when the records were played at high school parties and dances, or indirectly when they were heard on pocket-sized transistor radios. It was not until the 1960s with the Beatles' appearances in this country that personal appearances again became important; this phenomenon can be traced to a renewal of interest in the performers themselves. In 1956 most people could differentiate only with some difficulty between the respective sounds of the "Four Knights," the "Four Aces," the "Four Tunes," and the "Four Coins," and very few of even their most ardent followers could have named the performers in each group. Their records alone were important, and if they failed to follow one million-selling release with another, they were simply forgotten.

As the phonograph recording was the primary medium of rock-and-roll, so the established record companies and their subsidiaries were an important factor in assuring the success of a particular release, performer, or group. Small companies with limited circulations rarely equaled the sales figures of an RCA, Decca, or Columbia release, where an LP album was not considered profitable until its sales surpassed the seventy-five thousand mark.[2] But an examination of some of the better-selling recordings of the small, independent recording companies of the 1950s shed new light upon the subcultural —especially black—origins of rock-and-roll music.

In 1956, for example, Elvis Presley's recordings of "Heartbreak Hotel," "Blue Suede Shoes," and "Hound Dog" led to his billing as the "foremost exponent and creator of rock-and-roll." But, this sort of billing was just as misleading as the Original Dixieland Jazz Band's "Originators of Jazz" had been some thirty years earlier. A rock version of "Hound Dog" had been recorded by black singer Willie Mae Thornton in 1953 and had enjoyed considerable success in the South, primarily in black communities.

Just as the records of Bessie Smith or Ethel Waters had rarely reached the white public in the mid-1920s, Willie Mae Thornton's version of "Hound Dog" never enjoyed the large-scale distribution given to Presley's record, largely because it was recorded and marketed by the Peacock Record Company. This Texas-based independent firm specialized in spirituals and gospel-song recordings. As rock historian Charles Gillett has pointed out, the divergent musical tastes of the black and the white communities tended to be reinforced by the record companies:

> Before 1955 Negro singers had to make a deliberate choice between white and Negro Markets because the divergent tastes of the two audiences prohibited all but the most versatile singers from appealing to both. The difference in tastes was reinforced by an "institutional discontinuity" between the two markets—different companies supplied records to each of them. The white market was dominated by six recording companies before 1955 (Columbia, Decca, Victor, Capitol, MGM, and Mercury) to such an extent that they shared seventeen or eighteen of the twenty bestselling records throughout the ten-year period following the end of the war. In the Negro market these companies played a minor but predatory role. Because they so little understood the tastes of the Negro audience, they allowed the independent companies to field performers. . . .[3]

The carefully arranged, closely harmonized styles of the Mills Brothers and the Ink Spots came to be imitated by a number of black groups who enjoyed regional popularity in the late 1940s and early 1950s. One of them, the Orioles, became nationally successful after their 1956 recording of "Cryin' in the Chapel" exceeded the one-million mark in sales. The Orioles became the first black group to be recorded by an independent company—Jubilee Records in New York City—to attain such success on records. Their success was a major factor not only in the success of other black groups, but also in the success of the smaller, independent record companies, who previously could not compete with the industry's dominant corporations.

As the social and political events of the 1960s brought value conflicts and polarization, moral issues found their way into commercial recordings. The Vietnam War and the United States' deepening involvement in it gave rise to such political songs as Stonewall Jackson's "The Minute Men Are Turning in Their Graves" and Merle Haggard's "The Fightin' Side of Me"—both of which were super-patriotic. Bob Dylan's "World War III" and Barry McGuire's "The Eve of Destruction" were critical of war in general, and notably the war in Vietnam. Before the war and before the bitterness of the ghetto riots, political assassinations,and campus violence, the youth culture had indulged in such trivialities as "Teen Angel" and "The Flying Purple People Eater."

The turmoil of the 1960s permitted no such indulgences, or so it seems when we examine the emergence of folk ballads and protest songs of that time. But it must be recalled that while the Beatles headed the charts in the 1960s, variations on Chubby Checker's "Doin' the Twist" theme were also popular; and while the late 1960s heard many protest songs, "Winchester Cathedral" and Tiny Tim's "Tiptoe Through the Tulips," which had been recorded by Nick Lucas in 1929, were popular. Also, some of the Beatles' songs were rearranged and recorded by such "establishment" orchestras as Lawrence Welk's and found great popularity among the non-electric generation.

But, while all these songs were undoubtedly part of the popular record market, and while they were featured prominently on radio stations whose followings consisted largely of the youth culture, these were not rock recordings. Nor were the rock records of the late 1960s reminiscent of those of the late 1950s. Among the numerous, difficult-to-verify hypotheses one can make about the popular recorded music of the 1960s, it is safe to state that rock music had definitely changed between 1960 and 1970.

One of the most obvious changes concerned the relative importance of the melody line and lyrics of songs recorded in the late 1960s vs. those of the early 1970s. On first examination, the lyrics to the recorded rock songs of the late 1960s and early 1970s assume far greater importance than their melody lines. In no other popular music genre does this seem to be true to such an extent. Many of the songs which were popular at the turn of the century, for example, contain lyrics which take a back seat to their melody lines in whatever lasting popularity they have achieved. Such songs as "In the Good Old Summertime" and "Bicycle Built for Two," are in this category. During the rest of the century prior to the late 1960s, a harmonious melodic line has always been necessary, if not sufficient, to insure the success of most songs. In some instances, a sweeping melodic line might compensate for a rather purple, moon-June lyric, as in the case of the title songs from Sigmund Romberg's *The Desert Song* and *Maryland, My Maryland*. When in other instances a sweeping melody is combined with intricate lyrics, as in Cole Porter's "You're the Top," Irving Berlin's "What'll I Do," and Kurt Weill's "September Song," the effects of the songs seem enhanced.

By contrast, in the later 1960s, notably in the rock, folk ballad, and protest-song genre, neither sweeping melody lines nor intricate, rhyming lyrics were regarded as either necessary or sufficient to insure the success of a particular composition. The lyrics alone seemed important and not in a mere poetic, imagistic way.

Reactions to the lyrics of these songs were as varied as the lyrics themselves. Some analysts expressed alarm over the allegedly subversive character of the messages of various songs. In a speech in 1970, then Vice President Spiro T. Agnew remarked,

> I do not suggest that there is a conspiracy among some song writers, entertainers, and movie producers to subvert the unsuspecting listener. In my opinion, there isn't any. But the cumulative impact of some of their work advances the wrong cause. I may be accused of advocating "song censorship" for pointing this out, but have you really heard the words of some of these songs?[4]

Others have openly declared this new music to be a Communist propaganda tool, intended to sow the seeds of revolution. In an article entitled "That Music, There's More to It

Than Meets the Ear," writer Gary Allen said of the Beatles:

> The new Beatles album containing "Revolution" and "Back in the U.S.S.R.," is, according to a Capitol Records spokesman, "the fastest selling record in the history of the record industry." No wonder the Communists have had some very good things to say about The Beatles, who rated a feature article in Volume 1, Number 1, of *Insurgent*—the Communist DuBois Clubs' official magazine.[5]

Both Allen and the former vice president maintain after the fact that the major record companies and also radio stations which prominently feature acid-rock music must be held accountable for the commercialization of the revolutionary message.

Whether or not their concern for the record companies' roles in spreading the message of rock, folk, and protest music is at all warranted, it is at least clear that many of the major record producers have gone beyond the mere support of teenage fan clubs, which characterized their activities in the 1950s and have attempted to ally the values of the companies with those of their youth-culture customers. Columbia's advertising slogans "The man can't bust our music" and "Know your friends," which have appeared in a number of underground newspapers, are by no means atypical of the major companies' advertising campaigns. To some analysts, such slogans tend to reinforce the Communist revolutionary hypothesis. To others who see the motives of the record companies as simple profit-seeking, the notion that money from establishment business enterprises has been given to and received by anti-establishment underground newspapers, seems incongruous and paradoxical. But, whatever the range and the intensity of the responses to the popular music of the late 1960s and early 1970s, one hypothesis may prove to be the most tenable of all—that what may have begun as a revolutionary style eventually became largely amoral, apolitical, and faddish.

Part Three

Jazz —
Louis and Bix

"J" is for jazz and our plump Prince of Whales
Whiteman, who staggers the musical scales!
—*Time Magazine,* 1925

6.

Myths and Beginnings

Jazz music as a popular culture phenomenon presents a complex problem. In one sense it has never really been part of a popular culture, since its appeal has always been to subgroups of varying kinds. Those in the know—initiates who would not have had to ask Fats Waller what jazz was nor experience his famous reply "If you have to ask, you'll never know"[1]—have been few. "Inside" jazz lovers have been those who exclaim to one another over the performance of some great jazz figure. Performance is the key word, because jazz is preeminently a performer's art-form. Unlike other concert musicians, jazz performers are at their most creative while improvising their own lines. Thus, in jazz, composer and performer are combined into one, and most of the great jazz musicians have been great improvisers.

In the 1920s, "race" label record companies flourished. The jazz and blues music they recorded was at once an evocation, a solace, and a cry of indefinable hope and joy in the face of despair. How else to describe the outpouring of creativity which came from Louis Armstrong, for example?

Though jazz was predominantly black music, there was a

white audience for it too. This audience was made up of the educated, urban elite, often college students, who would travel miles to hear Bix Beiderbecke, little realizing that they were present at the creation of a legend. As LeRoi Jones has pointed out, what was in the natural African tradition for Louis Armstrong was an expression of rebellion for Bix Beiderbecke, a rebellion against the values of a commercial society.[2]

The interaction of white and black in the interstices of American culture, far from the centers of power or the foci of popular culture, is an important element in the history of jazz. While various subgroups were revelling in true jazz, some members of the older generation were being enthralled by a derivative jazz exemplified by the music of George Gershwin and the arranged performances of large white bands like Paul Whiteman's. This is not to say that Gershwin's songs and Whiteman's band were not jazz inspired; Gershwin's tunes for years formed the basic structure of many jazz performances, and from the mid-1920s on, Whiteman's band contained some excellent white jazz players. The point is that their work was taken for true jazz while the work of the real jazz pioneers remained little known. Louis Armstrong was an obscure figure to the mass society until the very end of the 1920s, when he was featured in a Broadway show. He later became a national figure as the leader of a mediocre swing band and as a performer in stereotyped roles in films, but by that time his major jazz contributions were behind him, and he had become a packaged commodity of American commerce and show business. By the time Louis was popular he was playing Uncle Tom roles in films, calling famous white performers "Mister," and using his trumpet high notes as sensational props to his eye rolling and mugging.

The history of jazz is full of myths, and one of the best known is that it originated in New Orleans, moved north to Chicago after World War I, and came of age in the speakeasies of New York in the 1920s, where the flaming youth of that era converged. There is enough in the tale to make it appear accurate, but as LeRoi Jones and Leonard Feather, among others, have pointed out, it is a drastic oversimplification. Afro-American culture was widespread, and there were other centers of origin than New Orleans.[3]

Research on the origins and development of jazz has become quite sophisticated in recent years. Studies based on historical, sociological, and anthropological data have contributed important insights. The work of Albert McCarthy, Nat Hentoff, and Marshall Stearns has been helpful, but LeRoi Jones and Gunther Schuller have contributed major syntheses. LeRoi Jones' *Blues People* discusses the historical context of African bondage in white America and points out that it is in the African tradition of music that jazz finds its polyphonic, polyrhythmic roots, the structure of blues notes, its call and response patterns, and emphasis on improvisation. The dance patterns and folk melodies in the work songs of the second generation of African slaves and the strains of religious music exemplified the role of music in the Afro-American experience.[4]

Many cultural and social influences affected the development of jazz into the polyrhythmic musical expression which came to fruition in New Orleans. New Orleans was a Southern city with a difference. Here grew a complex class-caste system. The presence of free blacks, Creoles, and whites produced a hierarchical social structure with various taboos. That this was the only predominantly Roman Catholic city in the South, and that black musical performances were held in Congo Square in New Orleans long before the Civil War, may have had something to do with the crystallization of New Orleans jazz. The Catholic church provided a certain space for black musical expression, enough for the preservation and development of a musical heritage. Yet, as Marshall Stearns pointed out, European structures and styles were synthesized with the music of the African almost from the beginning. Nowhere is this more evident than in the history of ragtime music.[5]

A French marching band tradition existed in New Orleans and was adapted by black musicians who came into possession of band instruments during reconstruction, when Confederate bandmen pawned their instruments in the city. In a persistent translation of African social structure into New Orleans society, secret societies staked out their own territories in the city and guarded them zealously from intruders. Ceremonial events such as funerals would occasion parades during which the Old Testament injunction to "Weep at the birth and rejoice at the death" would be obeyed. Prominent in these parades were the brass marching bands of the secret societies. They played both memorized and improvised performances of band tunes adapted from themes from both European and African folk sources. In funeral parades, they marched to the cemetery playing slow dirge-like tunes like "Flee as the Bird to the Mountain," but returned marching to rousing traditional melodies like "High Society." This was prelude to an elaborate wake complete with food, drink, and music, affirming life itself following the sorrow, and celebrating the release from the travail of this life. The bands were accompanied by a second line of active marcher-dancers. From both groups came scores of both black and white musicians who would gain local and national reknown as jazz players. But, as LeRoi Jones points out, the blues were the basis of jazz development. Without the slave condition, there would have been no blues. Africa remained alive in the music of the slaves, as so much else in their culture was suppressed. The fusion of African and European musical forms took place in many places throughout the South, but it was the New Orleans synthesis of the process that led to instrumental band jazz.[6] Here French and Spanish traditions mixed with the Anglo-Saxon and African. All contributed to the rich fabric of jazz. Jelly Roll Morton demonstrated to Stanley Lomax, during the famous Library of Congress recordings, how French quadrilles had been transformed into the old New Orleans jazz standard, "Tiger Rag."[7]

Canal Street in what is now the French Quarter was the old dividing line between the so-called downtown and uptown citizens of African origin. The downtowners were lighter-skinned Creoles, people of mixed Spanish, French, and African ancestry. They constituted a special group of freed slaves, for it seems that some of them, at least, owned plantations, held slaves, and had their children educated abroad in France. Jelly Roll Morton, the Creole pianist whose name was originally Ferdinand LaMenthe, insisted that his family were in America long before the Louisiana Purchase, and that they had come "directly" from the shores of France. He also recalled that members of his family were patrons of the French Opera House on Royal Street, and he played the "Miserere" from *Il Trovatore* for Lomax. For the Creoles, music was a common avocation. The musicians tended to be skilled craftsmen and small business entrepreneurs who had thoroughly assimilated the French tradition of music.

The uptowners, by contrast, constituted a poor working-class group, immigrants from other parts of the South and from the West Indies. Their musical traditions were oriented toward African styles of performance and improvisational; polyphonic jazz became their forte. With the coming of emancipation and the Plessey-Fergusen decision of the 1890s, firm racial segregation came to the South. This policy forced a kind of musical fusion between the two groups of musicians. Black people were forced out of trades they had once practiced, and music became a means of earning a livelihood for Creole downtowner as well as uptown working-class black. Yet, the tradition of working at a job in addition to music remained strong in New Orleans into third and fourth generations. Until he left for Chicago, Louis Armstrong himself sold papers and delivered coal in addition to his musical activities, and in the 1940s, when clarinetist George Lewis was discovered in New Orleans, he was working as a stevedore in addition to playing country dances.

Whatever the true facts of this musicological history may be, it is significant from a popular culture point of view that the New Orleans legend emerged and became widely accepted. The jazz which first became popular through recordings was of New Orleans origin. Ironically, it was a white and not a black band which gained early reknown; there was a derivative white as well as an original black jazz tradition in the city, and two of the early World War I period bands were white, the New Orleans Rhythm Kings and the Original Dixieland Jazz Band.

Early black bands which had ventured forth from the city before the great migration of the First World War period included one led by a legendary Creole trumpet player named Manuel Perez. Perez turned down the opportunity to become the first jazz band to record out of fear of being copied, and he was not the only early musician worried lest imitators steal his technique and ideas. Freddie Keppard, another legendary early trumpet man, led a New Orleans based band which performed in Chicago and New York, even travelling as far afield as Los Angeles in the years between 1912 and 1918. The reticence of these early black leaders let the honor of recording the first jazz go to the all-white Original Dixieland Jazz Band (ODJB).

The ODJB was on a vaudeville tour and had appeared at Reisenweber's Cafe in New York when they cut their first records for the Victor studios. Thus it was a derivative white dixieland jazz band which first attained a wide audience in America. Their music was a jerky, staccato version of black music, and in the opinion of most historian-critics it contributed nothing new to the development of the music; but sociologically it was crucial, and musically it was an important event. These 1917 ODJB recordings first gave young Leon Bix Beiderbecke, struggling with his adjustments to his own white society, a glimpse of an art form that was to set him on the road to creative output and personal disaster. The records found their way into the regular Victor catalog and sold millions of copies. By contrast, when the great black bands recorded, their efforts surfaced on "race" recordings, clearly marked as such on surviving contracts. Subdivisions of major companies like Victor or Columbia issued race recordings intended for the Southern black rural and Northern black urban markets. Yet, it is these records which today are much sought after as collector's items. They also sold widely in Europe. Lotte Lenya attested that when she and Kurt Weill were living in Germany in the pre-Hitler days, she and Weill awaited eagerly the newest releases of Louis Armstrong's records.[8]

The closing of the Storyville section of New Orleans by the U.S. Navy in 1917 is an important sociological event and provides an example of the latent effects of reforms that shut off work opportunities for the poorer classes. More European than American, Storyville was the section of the city where in 1897 dope peddling, gambling, and prostitution had legal status. It was the place both white and black people went for their pleasures. As Jelly Roll Mortan noted, "everything in the line of hilarity" was available. It also became a locus of jazz activity when cafe owners began employing jazz bands and entertainers early in the century. The piano playing jobs in the houses of prostitution were particularly lucrative; players like Jelly Roll Morton could bring in as much as $100 a day with tips. In short Storyville was a tenderloin district. It was also a place where black men could both make a living and meet on some kind of terms with whites. In a similar tenderloin district in Sedalia, Missouri, the white music store owner John Stark and the great black ragtime composer Scott Joplin launched the mutual undertakings which led to frame, ruin, and reincarnation for both of them. That was the pattern for many great jazz artists and composers: work in obscurity, a certain limited fame, degradation, and ruin followed a generation hence by rediscovery. The old cliches about the fate of painters and sculptors apply equally to jazz artists.

Vaudeville circuits, the first true mass media entertainment, sometimes included jazz bands. They spread the word about the new "hot" music before the influence of the phonograph. The early legends of New Orleans—for example, the story of Buddy Bolden—are lost in the mists of uncertain memory. The legends are important like those woven about Washington or Lincoln, not as literal truth but as stories about folk heroes. Thus, Jelly Roll Morton sings, "I thought I heard Buddy Bolden say . . ." in the course of a folk jazz song which retells events of New Orleans in the period between the Civil War and the hardening of Jim Crow.[9]

A striking characteristic of the jazzmen of the pre-1940 era is their propensity for creating a web of myths about the great men who went before. It was King Bolden's trumpet that could be heard far across the lake on clear summer nights. It was Bix Beiderbecke's bell-like tones that made strong men weep. It was King Louis Armstrong who once hit 250 high "Cs" in a row followed by a high "F." These folk tales were given wide circulation by early jazz writers who began to make their mark in the sophisticated magazines of the 1930s. As recollections began to appear in articles by Eastern journalists, the legends took on an added dimension. As a result of the serious jazz scholarship which has gone on in the last few years, and with the coming of fame and serious treatment to older jazzmen, the legends have been somewhat dissipated. When Gunther Schuller of the New England Conservatory writes a serious book about classical jazz, perceptions have changed.[10]

One part of the tradition that is true is that jazz moved up the river to the northern cities as part of the general black movement during World War I. The river itself played a role in seeding jazz along its tributaries; river boats sometimes carried jazz orchestras along with their other wares. The Mississippi was not the only river with a boat culture. The Hudson, for example, was plied by paddlewheelers at least until the 1940s. The Mississippi's distinction was that it was the prime jazz river. There is even a photograph of a youthful Louis Armstrong in a river boat jazz band.

People first began to hear jazz on boats tied up in river ports, or so the oral tradition would have it. One story asserts that Louis Armstrong played on a boat which followed the river tributaries to Davenport, Iowa, and that as a youngster just beginning to play the cornet, Bix Beiderbecke may actually have heard Louis Armstrong during a layover in Davenport.

It is an established fact that Joseph "King" Oliver, originally from New Orleans, settled in Chicago during the early 1920s. His band had been on vaudeville tours that went as far west as California. A picture from that tour shows the King Oliver Band dressed in plantation-type work clothes clowning on stage. Even in the jazz world, blacks performed in the trappings of a stereotype. In 1919, King Oliver's band played in the lower stands of Comiskey Park, establishing that the band was in the city before 1920.[11]

King Oliver and his Creole Jazz Band became the sensation of Chicago in the 1920s. Chicago had become the jazz center of the United States. The city was certainly where it was happening in the early 1920s, and it happened all the more when King Oliver decided that he needed a second cornet in his band and sent to New Orleans for Louis Armstrong. When he arrived in Chicago, jazz began to undergo a revolution which would mark its development forever.

In viewing jazz as a part of popular culture it is important to recognize the relationship between the general culture and values of the society and those of the subcultures attached to the jazz world. This consideration brings us to two significant case studies in jazz history: Louis Armstrong and Bix Beiderbecke. These two jazz careers parallel one another; both extend from about 1923 to 1931, when Beiderbecke died and Armstrong became an entertainer in the show business world of the 1930s and 1940s.

The jazz world was a special aspect of America. Institutionalized on the anomic edges of American life, centered in tenderloins, symbiotic with prostitution and its perennial pianists, and focused in the illegal undercover nightclub world of the 1920s, it afforded opportunities for contact between whites and blacks rare in the rest of American life. These contacts included those between black musicians and admiring young white emulators, those between black musicians and white managers. Paul Whiteman recalled in a television reminiscence how Bix Beiderbecke had brought him to visit Louis Armstrong at Armstrong's apartment. It is hard to think of another area of national life where a comparable meeting might have taken place.

Sad to say, this does not imply that the jazz world exhibited ideal racial relations, as some observers have asserted. The necessary perception was not there on the part of most whites. On the other hand, evidence suggests that in terms of opportunity for black talent the music world often paralleled the rest of America. Most recording sessions were segregated until the 1930s. Jazz-oriented bands integrated gradually and piecemeal, led by Benny Goodman's featuring of black musicians in special small groups within his larger orchestras. The whites retained the lion's share of the attractive jobs and engagements.

It is fitting to consider Louis and Bix together. There seems to have been a mutual respect between them, if one can trust the sometimes vague memories of those who claimed to have been there. They created new conceptions in jazz, and they were widely imitated. Contemporary jazz writers are always trying to tie artists to the influence of Bix or Louis.

The claims for Louis are extravagant yet true. One latter-day trumpet player remarked that every time someone played a note of jazz he was acknowledging a debt to Louis. This somewhat redresses a situation which prevailed in the bop revolution of early and mid-1940. The bop innovators tended to regard earlier forms of jazz with contempt as they struggled to gain acceptance for their own daring innovations. With the rising black consciousness there has been a rediscovery by the post-bop generations of the great early pioneers. Thus, Dizzy Gillespie acknowledged Louis Armstrong, and Albert Ayler paid his respects to Sidney Bechet.

Beiderbecke's contribution has been variously described as white jazz or ballad style jazz, but it was he who first began to extend traditional jazz harmony, playing chords and changes which gave rise to modern jazz playing. His pieces for piano give testimony to his rising sophistication and the search for new expressions.

Louis' life was an expression of isolation from and compromise with the mainstream, even as he and Bix became heroes in their special world. To a large extent they remain so today, and their work is now being subjected to fresh analysis by musicologists, music historians, and cultural commentators.

7.

Louis Armstrong

Louis Armstrong was from New Orleans, and his enculturation there was to stay with him all of his life. A few years before he died, he was interviewed on Educational Television.
When the interviewer played some of his old records, the
mask dropped. As he listened to solos dating back to his
earliest days in the recording studios, his lips pursed and his
body rocked gently back and forth in time to the music. The
show business demeanor lifted and there was a momentary
glimpse of his private self.

Who was the real Louis and what were his thoughts? The
public man could roll his eyes, flash his teeth and announce
that he and his band were going to "beat out another mellow
number for ya' folks." He could respond to Tommy Dorsey
in a television appearance with the admonition that they not
play fast or slow but "half-fast." He could startle smug, self-
righteous jazz critics by asserting that Guy Lombardo was his
inspiration. This kind of nonsense and low comedy marked
his public person while the man beneath was enigma. Leonard
Feather once wrote that only with black people was Louis
able to reveal his true self and his real values. Considering the
fact that adulation of him was almost universal among jazz

players of all generations, black and white, it seems plausible that the real Louis knew more than he gave away. His intelligence was such that television interviewers were among the last who could keep up with his sardonic masks. It was fun to watch him as earnest white interviewers struggled with the legend of Louis as he twisted their sense of reality.

His origins remain somewhat obscure despite all that has been written by him and others. What is known of his early life may explain the enigmatic Louis, the hiding of his real self behind the entertainer mask. His parents were ex-slaves, and he lived in "back o' town," the poorest, most heavily black section of the city. His childhood has been documented in different ways, and there has been the suggestion that his mother, whom he loved and respected, had resorted to extreme measures to support her family. Certainly, Louis knew a succession of stepfathers. Proof of the early years is a serious family portrait of Louis, his sister, and his beloved mother in Sunday best, posing in stiff dignity.[1]

For the rest there was the New Orleans Colored Waifs' Home to which he had been sent for firing a pistol on New Year's. There a professor taught him cornet; a surviving photograph shows little Louis in the band. Then there was hawking from a coal cart, errand-running for prostitutes, and peeking into the great jazz cafes of the black world. He listened to King Oliver, Buddy Bolden, Fred Keppard, and Bunk Johnson; it was Oliver whom Louis acknowledged as his mentor. He was married as a teenager and played all over the city and on river boats cruising the Mississippi River system.[2]

His values seem to have been those of a rural youth reluctant to leave his home. He had had one brief stay in St. Louis with Fate Marable and then returned home again to play in the district. Later he answered the summons of King Oliver to come to Chicago. When Louis joined the Creole Jazz Band as second cornet, jazz history began to be made.

At first he played cornet duets with the King, never attempting to strike out on his own. His teenage marriage of
New Orleans days dissolved, and Louis married Lillian Hardin,
a pianist with the King Oliver group. A sophisticated music
graduate of Fiske University, Lil Hardin Armstrong remained
Louis's life-long friend even after their divorce. It was she
who encouraged him to study and develop his talent. The
crowds flocking to hear the band were soon demanding solos
by Louis, and Willie "The Lion" Smith, the famed Harlem
stride pianist, recalled offering money to encourage the young
man. During Gennett record company sessions, Louis' tone
and power had so developed that he had to stand well back
from the recording horn so that the band could achieve recording balance. He was rapidly outgrowing the company he
was keeping. His breaks on "Tears" and his solo and lead
horn on other Creole Jazz Band recordings such as "Dipper-
mouth Blues" and "Krooked Blues" give evidence of Louis'
developing powers.

Among his fans he attracted a group of white, largely
middle-class youths, many of them students at Austin High
School on Chicago's West Side. They had formed small bands
and played at PTA tea dances. Like young Bix in Davenport,
they could use their phonographs to listen to New Orleans
music, and they were enraptured by the work of the New
Orleans Rhythm Kings. More important, in the city itself
they were able to hear King Oliver's Band with Louis on
cornet when a sympathetic nightclub owner let them come
in without paying. This Austin High group and their friends
formed an important core of the musicians and leaders in the
big band swing era.[3]

Louis and Bix remained dominant influences on this group.
In that seemingly primeval age of race relations in America,
there were some occasions when whites and blacks gathered
for jam sessions, where various combinations of players joined

together for informal improvisations and trading of ideas. Johnny Dodds, clarinetist with King Oliver, often hosted the Austin High group at his home. While there is some evidence that admiration of black music did not necessarily lessen racist attitudes, the jazz world was one of the few places where white and black could meet socially as well as musically. Moreover, there were white players who ignored the general reluctance to record with black artists for fear of hurting their careers by being classified as race performers. Jack Teagarden, Eddie Lang, and Eddie Condon jammed with blacks and pioneered recordings in which whites and blacks played together.

Encouraged by his wife Lillian, Armstrong began to develop as an artist, studying embouchure technique with a German teacher. The changes in his style are reflected in the King Oliver recordings. Certain social factors are important to Louis' subsequent artistic and social development, particularly prohibition, white control of night clubs and entertainment, and racial policies of record companies. Chicago's South Side was a brisk night-club center, and prohibition was flaunted everywhere.

After he left King Oliver, Louis played in nightclubs and theaters under a variety of leaders. At the same time he began to circulate among new musicians with different ideas. In transcending the traditions of New Orleans jazz with its strong beat, tight rhythms, and emphasis on the group over soloist, Louis broke out of the binding structure of collective improvisation. The group performances which dominated early jazz reflected a society which did not as yet foster the emergence of striking individuals. In extending the solo line, Louis revolutionized the jazz experience.[4] Without Louis there could have been no Bix Beiderbecke or, for that matter, Dizzy Gillespie, men who contributed to revolutions on their own. Yet, for all of his pioneer efforts, Armstrong remained a child of

New Orleans. Indeed, it was more than fitting that Dizzy Gillespie wrote the eulogy that appeared in the *New York Times* at Louis' death.[5]

By 1925 Louis embarked on a road trip with the Fletcher Henderson Orchestra that included an engagement in New York's Roseland Ballroom and exposed Louis to the ideas of non-New Orleans black musicians like Coleman Hawkins and Don Redman and whites like Red Nichols and Miff Mole. Louis expressed admiration for the technical skill of the latter two, purveyors of what was called New York jazz. The Austin High group resented Nichols' curbing of their expressive musical tendencies when they worked for him, and some of the Chicagoans regarded Nichols as a pale imitation of Beiderbecke, devoid of originality.[6]

During the New York stay, Louis branched out into new recording ventures, cutting sides with Clarence Williams and Sidney Bechet while enhancing his fame by appearances in battles of music around town. It was the kind of vagabond life most jazz musicians lived at that time. In retrospect it seems that people like Duke Ellington and Count Basie have lived most of their lives out of a suitcase. Bunny Berigan, a great white trumpet player of the 1930s, once wryly remarked that the chief difference between a trumpet and cornet was that the trumpet case held more dirty laundry.

During his travels with Henderson, Louis began to develop as a soloist and as a showman. He can be heard in a variety of these post-Oliver recordings, perhaps most interestingly with Henderson where his solos begin to foreshadow what they were to become. Touring black dance orchestras faced the problem of where to stay and to eat while on the road. Often, admired musicians whose music whites would dance to in hotel ball rooms made their way to work via the service elevator. It seemed as if whites could accept blacks mainly in structured roles which implied services rendered and entailed a certain social distance. For Louis Armstrong to be recognized as a serious artist was not possible during his period of greatest creative output. This state of affairs was to have important personal and artistic consequences for him.

The recording policies of most companies are revealing and ironic. Major companies like Victor and Columbia had so-called race releases. Smaller companies like Gennett and Paramount devoted much of their output to this "race" line. In 1925 Louis Armstrong signed a history-making contract with the Okeh Company. Known as Louis Armstrong and his Hot Five or Hot Seven, the bands were in the beginning drawn largely from King Oliver's Creole Jazz Band and included (among others) Johnny Dodds on clarinet, Lil Hardin on piano, Kid Ory on trombone, and Johnny St. Cyr on banjo. A copy of a surviving contract from November 12, 1925, lists the leader for the occasion, the serial number of the record, and under the heading "remarks" is written one word, "race."[7] The chief commercial pop music output of most of the record companies of the period produced an endless line of pale trivia that has now happily faded from memory. Recordings of the Armstrong Hot Fives and Hot Sevens, on the other hand, are among the most sought-after collector's items in jazz.

Armstrong, while being presented in the race system of marketing, managed to spread his revolution via the phonograph record. He had no choice if he wanted to record. On "Heebie Jeebies" he presents what may be the first example on record of scat singing—the humming and mumbling in improvisational style of nonsense syllables—thus setting off a legend that he had dropped the sheet music during the recording session and carried on as best he could.

During the first period of his Okeh recording activity, Louis again played the Chicago cafés. It is alleged that he could play at full volume for as long as nine hours at a time. When Duke Ellington's elegant trombonist Lawrence Brown retired from the band in 1972, he remarked that he had heard all the great trumpet men from Louis on, and that many of them

could be good for an hour or two, but that Louis was the only
one who could sustain the high quality of his performance
over an entire evening.[8] In May 1927, with "Wild Man
Blues," he emerged as a soloist. Taking his longest extended
solo to date, some thirty-two bars, he reached a high "F"
while keeping that incredible tone and power intact through
his entire range.[9]

May 1927 was significant also because it was then that
Louis began to record with players who were not from New
Orleans backgrounds. Chief among the new associates was
pianist Earl Hines, a major innovator in piano jazz. Some of
the ensembles were arranged now, although New Orleans
improvisation remained. However, it was daring, flexibility,
and individual expression that marked Louis' solos as his art
approached its zenith. He was a young giant, confident and
strong, sure of what he could do and doing what no one else
could. "Chicago Breakdown," "Weatherbird," "Monday Date,"
and above all, "West End Blues" date from this Okeh recording period.[10]

In the winter of 1928–29, Louis came to New York, replacing Duke Ellington at Connie's Inn in Harlem after a stint
at the Savoy Ballroom. With him at this period were Don
Redman, saxophonist and arranger, Earl Hines, and Zutty
Singleton, drummer, in a mixed group of New Orleans and
non-New Orleans musicians. The Okeh recordings from 1925
to 1929 mark Louis' metamorphosis from a participant in collective music to a soloist of the most persuasive power. Now
an inevitable fate awaited him. Louis was a hero, rooted in his
own cultural experience as a black man, a leader, a nonpareil,
one of his culture's greatest creative geniuses. But he was
black, and the majority culture could not accept either his
ethnicity or his jazz talents. Given the values of the commercial entertainment world, Louis became a hot property, and
this preordained his fate. There simply was no place for him
to go as a jazz artist. Instead, he became a show business

commodity, a product to be packaged and presented for profit. His appearance in the 1929 all-black hit musical, *Connie's Hot Chocolates,* opened the path to fame as an entertainer. He stopped the show when he played and sang Fats Waller's tune, "Ain't Misbehavin'."

He began fronting a big, loose-playing dance band, singing, mugging, waving a handkerchief, and screeching out high notes. To be sure, beautiful solos still emerged over the moaning backgrounds provided by the mediocre big bands behind him. Listen to "Blue Again" or "Sweethearts on Parade"; the technique, the ideas, the imagination and the emotion were still very much in evidence. Moreover, there were still glorious moments with small groups, as in the 1929 recording of "Knockin a Jug"; the record included Jack Teagarden, a white trombonist, and Eddie Lang, a white guitarist, along with his black cohorts Earl Hines and Zutty Singleton. Louis' solo comes at the end of a record of solo performances and is a thing of fire and beauty. But it was the end of that sort of thing for a long time. Until the late 1940s, most of his recordings would be with large bands.

What of Louis' consciousness? If he could record "Black and Blue" with its telling lyrics about black feelings of persecution and dread, how could he at the same time sing "Shine" with its dreadful caricatures? Louis suffered a kind of artistic death after he underwent the packaging. To have resisted the compromise might have consigned Louis to the fate of Sidney Bechet, the pioneer soprano saxophonist, who rarely strayed from traditional jazz. Although Bechet continued to work in small groups during the swing band dominated 1930s, he sometimes found it necessary to work in non-music jobs. Only after he exiled himself to France in the 1950s did he find a measure of reknown.

In 1937, Jelly Roll Morton, the endlessly tuneful New Orleans pianist and composer, was eking out a living playing in a Washington, DC nightclub, virtually forgotten. At the same

time, Benny Goodman's Band was attaining fame and fortune
playing Fletcher Henderson's arrangement of Morton's "King
Porter Stomp." Such were the ironies of the time.

When Louis was leaving New Orleans to join King Oliver,
one of the toughest black men in town took him aside and told
him to find a white man to front for him. He did.[11] Other
gifted blacks like Fletcher Henderson and Sy Oliver found
their fronts in white swing bandleaders; they arranged for
their bands while remaining virtually unknown to the record
buying, jitterbugging public.

Yet, something true endured in unpromising places. A Mae
West film of the mid-1930s includes a political parade scene
with Mae riding in a carriage. The camera catches a black
street cleaner in a white uniform topped by a pith helmet. The
street cleaner joins the parade. Suddenly, he produces a
trumpet from somewhere and the screen erupts in gorgeous
sound. It is Louis Armstrong. Later, in the Bing Crosby movie
Pennies from Heaven, he and his band would steal chickens.
On radio Louis would call Crosby "Mr. Bing." Years later
Crosby would profess surprise when told that Louis felt hurt
because he had never been invited to the singer's home.

8.

Bix Beiderbecke

Louis Armstrong was black, Southern, rural, and matured musically in an environment which encouraged his talent. Bix Beiderbecke was the reverse. Louis fit his immediate world, and it nurtured him. Beiderbecke was white, more than comfortably off, middle class, and middle western. In the end, he was worse off than Louis in terms of his art and, indeed, of his life itself; he could not survive in the American culture of his time as a jazz artist or entertainer.

He was the first important white contributor to the development of jazz. Some critics think he was the greatest of all white jazz innovators. However, his involvement with jazz placed him in conflict with his own culture.

Bix's German immigrant family did well in business. His mother was a gifted pianist and organist, and his grandfather directed a German chorus in his home town, Davenport, Iowa. Musical talent and considerable cultural attainment appeared on both sides of his family. He was the kind of boy who ordinarily would have proceeded from high school to college, but Bix fell victim to the phonograph and the cornet. He might have made his mark as a serious composer or as a

tolerably dotty music professor at a progressive college but
he was captivated by jazz via phonograph records as a boy in
his teens. The fascination was to be his glory and his disaster.
Recognized early as a child prodigy, he picked out the
melody from a Liszt rhapsody before he was five. When he
was seven, he was mentioned in the newspaper as a lad who
could play anything he had heard.[1] Early on, Bix exhibited
the incredible ear that jazz colleagues were to notice with
wonderment. However, as is often the case with off-beat
prodigies, his early piano lessons did not take. But, when he
turned to record buying, he fell under the spell of the Original
Dixieland Jazz Band, whose Victor records were in the family
collection. He acquired a cornet, and though he never took
a lesson, he began accompanying the records of the first
white jazz band to record. When the vastly superior New Orleans Rhythm Kings and King Oliver's Creole Jazz Band also
put their sounds on wax, young Bix extended his repertory
by playing along with these bands as well. There was no
Storyville in Davenport, no font of jazz creativity, but the
river boats from New Orleans tied up there from time to time,
and Bix may have heard New Orleans Bands on these ships.
He may even have met Louis and a white cornetist named
Emmet Hardy on the riverboats, but these assertions are impossible to prove.

Legends about Beiderbecke are probably more prolific and
bizarre than those about any other musician. All the materials
for a tragic legend are there, including an early death and a
failure of enormous talent. Perhaps a culture which has en-
shrined success allows its members surcease about their own
shortcomings by glorying in the final failure of the enormously
gifted. Young Bix was enormously gifted.

His ill-fated career exemplifies several aspects of American
popular culture: the commercial encroachments in American
popular music, the ghettoization of jazz music and the jazz life
itself, the self-destructive force within creative artists respond-

ing to a hostile or indifferent society, and the unresponsive-
ness of that all-encompassing institution of popular culture,
the educational system. Institutions meshed in a way which
foreclosed Bix's chances, leaving a fascinating riddle. What
might he have become? There are only tantalizing glimpses,
no more. We know what he became: the greatest white jazz
player of his time and the first jazz musician to bring to this
music elements of modern harmony, anticipating the bop
revolution of the 1940s by more than twenty years.

Prohibition plays a part too, with the ready availability of
liquor during the 1920s and its symbolic value for young
people as a way of flouting established morality. Then, too,
jazz was black music, and in the 1920s America was still
locked into rigid racial outlooks. There is a wonderful irony
about this off-beat youth taking up the music of the most
oppressed of American minorities. LeRoi Jones has suggested
that the music which for Louis was in the mainstream of his
cultural experience was for Beiderbecke an alien art, an expression of rebellion against the values of his own culture.[2]

Like many gifted people, Bix did not do well in his local
high school, and his family sent him to Chicago to Lake
Forest Academy, where he again did not fare well. But, for
his musical development, it was a fateful choice; the South
Side of Chicago was rocking with the sounds of black New
Orleans pioneers, and King Oliver and his Creole Jazz Band
with Louis on second cornet led the way at the Lincoln Gar-
dens. The two cultures met, and Beiderbecke was the fruitful
amalgam.

If one were to draw a historical map of jazz, Chicago in the
1920s would be at its center. Bix met and played with Louis
and Johnny Dodds, King Oliver, and the Austin High group.
One of them, saxophonist Bud Freeman, on BBC television
program, "Jazz 625" in 1965 insisted that Bix was the
greatest jazz musican he had ever heard. As might be expected, jazz was a youth movement. There were groups every-

where, professional and amateur, many with colorful names: the Scranton Canaries, the Original Memphis Five, the Rhythm Kings, the Chicago Loopers, the Original New Orleans Five, and so forth. For Bix there would be the Wolverines, a group made up mostly of college students who played the new music.

As for Lake Forest Academy, Bix didn't fit in there any more than he had in the Davenport public schools. Bix's way was that of Robert Frost, who endured Dartmouth for a semester and left announcing that a man of imagination could not tolerate college. He might well have put it the other way. The fact that Bix was soon dropped from Lake Forest did not surprise his mother; she had not expected him to last as long as he did.[3]

Since Bix had formed a band with some classmates and jobbed around the Chicago area, playing largely for college audiences, the Lake Forest experience was not a total loss. Although he had played in the school orchestra, the teacher-conductor assigned the cornet solo to another, more tractable student player. Bix's life resembles F. Scott Fitzgerald's in that a glorious talent was entrusted to a personality constitutionally unable to preserve and protect it. The exposure to liquor and unstable working conditions and the absence of a secure social life apparently overwhelmed a sensitive young man totally absorbed in his music. Expelled from Lake Forest, Bix encountered indifference to this talent by the established structures of his society. He was to live out his brief life in a vagabond world of contradictions. His life was one of movement; in an enveloping haze of alcoholic deterioration he rarely stayed long in one place.

Cut loose from formal education, he joined the Wolverines and became the star of the group. With them he made his first recordings at the Gennett Studios in Richmond, Indiana in 1924. The sounds are those of a developing genius, the harbinger of a sound that was to bloom in time into a pure golden tone that challenges descriptive language. The Wolverine life meant further restless movement, playing in amusement parks, lake resorts, and dance pavillions, and for fraternity parties and college proms. The band gained a following at Indiana University where Bix befriended the future composer Hoagy Carmichael, then a law student.

After some eighteen months with the Wolverines, Bix was already established as at least a regionally known jazz player, but he sensed a need. During this period when he remained briefly in one place, Bix attended symphony concerts. One friend recalled that, when Bix went backstage at the Cincinnati Symphony, he was greeted warmly by the musicians in the orchestra.

Many of his friends, from saxophonist Frankie Trumbauer to singer Bing Crosby, have testified to Bix's love of modern impressionistic music, particularly Ravel, Debussy, and Stravinsky, as well as the Americans McDowell and Eastwood Lane. Even if the stories about Bix's difficulty in sight reading are true, they in no way indicate shortcomings in musical ability or take away from his fabulous ear, which could reproduce complicated scores after a few hearings.[4]

After the stint with the Wolverines, Beiderbecke sought the technical musical training he needed and, returning to his home state, enrolled at the University of Iowa in 1925. He registered for music courses but also had to take English, ethics, and religion. His attempt to substitute an additional music course for religion was vetoed by his freshman counselor, who also told him he would have to add physical education, ROTC, and freshman lectures. Shortly afterward, he left the university.

So, he returned to jazz or, rather, to the commercial, white, dance-band world. After a short stay with a regional dance band, he ultimately joined the Jean Goldkette Orchestra, one of the most famous white dance bands of the 1920s. There he found some good company to nourish him in the persons of saxophonist Frankie Trambauer and Bill Challis, a sympathetic arranger who often consulted him on backgrounds and designed trumpet section work in his style. But it was a world of demanding dance music and written-out arrangements which left occasional open spaces for the jazzman's improvisational art. As a result, much of Beiderbecke's playing was restricted to score reading. The band may have been one of the best jazz groups of its day, but restrictive recording policies by Victor kept them from putting their best work on wax. The Goldkette legacy of records is interesting today largely as an example of period music, save for Bix's occasional brief solos. The indomitability of his art was such that in any setting Bix's sound was unmistakable.

Goldkette was a shrewd businessman; he packaged popular music, and Bix was one of his highly paid commodities. For all of the money he was able to make in his dance-band days, it is characteristic of Bix that in the end he had nothing.

Despite Goldkette's business acumen, his band broke up, and Bix moved to the Paul Whiteman Band, where he was to become a star performer. Whiteman's performances ran the gamut from arranged big band jazz to florid renditions of light classics. In these surroundings Bix's consciousness of true jazz remained. There are reports of his offering an entire week's salary to blues singer Bessie Smith in Chicago in the early 1920s to keep her singing, and of his admiration for Louis Armstrong and Ethel Waters. Also, Bix continued to play in the night clubs of Harlem, and jazzmen recall battles of music with great black horn men like Rex Stewart, later of the Duke Ellington band. Unlike many white musicians, Bix seems to have been oblivious to racism. He jammed with blacks, and in his last recordings worked with Bubber Miley, the growl trumpeter who played with the Ellington band in the early 1930s.[5]

Record companies maintained strict segregation policies, and mixed sessions of black and white musicians did not occur until the late 1920s and early 1930s, with Armstrong and Teagarden, Bix and Miley, and Fats Waller and Eddie Condon leading the way. Another institutional barrier was the exclusive nature of recording contracts. Most Bix enthusiasts regret that he never recorded with Louis Armstrong, or with the Chicagoans and their like until the very end of his life when his powers were clearly on the wane.

Whatever the case, Whiteman apparently loved this charming, quietly intense young man and appreciated his talent. In a trumpet section which contained several famous lead men, Whiteman chose Bix for the solo cornet on his band's recording of Gershwin's *Concerto in F*. Meanwhile, the sympathetic Goldkette arranger, Bill Challis, had moved over to the Whiteman Band along with some of the more jazz-oriented Goldkette players. To his credit Whiteman showed Bix off in small jamming groups of a band within the band which at times included the Dorsey brothers, Frankie Trumbauer, and Hoagy Carmichael. Bix's extension of the harmonic conceptions of jazz and his lovely tone reached their zenith during his time with Whiteman. During this time he was wearing out a recording of Stravinsky's *Petroushka*.

During the transition from Goldkette to Whiteman he signed to make records for the Okeh Company as Louis had a few years before. His first Gennett records with the Wolverines had revealed an embryonic conception, particularly in the tantalizing cornet solo on "Tiger Rag" and a harmonically interesting if technically jumbled piano solo on "Big Boy." On the Okeh recordings in the spring of 1927, his talent had ripened. The Whiteman records for Victor allow glimpses of his wonderful sound and ideas in songs like "Mississippi Mud," "San," "From Monday On," and "Lonely Melody," but the Okeh sessions gave him space for extended solos for the first time. Bix was perfecting the ballad style of playing, making use of tin pan alley pop material in a jazz way; he thoughtfully and soulfully threaded his extensions

through the chord structures of pop tunes, but he did not
abandon the traditional jazz repertory. In sessions for Okeh
with Trumbauer he soloed on "Clarinet Marmalade," "Way
Down Yonder in New Orleans," "Singing the Blues," and
"I'm Comin' Virginia"—a mixture of traditional jazz tunes
and tin pan alley pop. The sound was lovely, and his tone was
pure, rounded, and bell-like; the changes explored with
broken and diminished chords including ninths, thirteenths,
and flatted fifths. His performances are haunting, but where
Louis Armstrong was exuberant, Bix's emotions were un-
derstated and intropective: he expressed passion by implication.

The Whiteman schedule was grueling, with new arrangements of current hits piling on one another, to Bix's frustration. Perhaps he was seeking a respectability otherwise denied
in Whiteman's light concert music. Perhaps his attitude resulted as much from educational opportunity denied as from
his own forgetful, vague, and eccentric personality. Whatever
the case, symphonic jazz apparently palled on him, and his
drinking assumed disastrous proportions. Whiteman sent him
off for a cure, and there were visits to Davenport, where the
home folks had no idea who he was to the very end.

Meanwhile, the 1929 depression had set in. Whiteman was
in the midst of a contract dispute after switching from Victor
to Columbia and cut down the size of his enormous outfit.
The Whiteman Band with its radio commitments and the
trivial material forced on it by Columbia had no place for Bix,
especially in his deteriorating condition. He returned to New
York, took a small apartment in Queens, drank, ate little, and
seemed to drift into a haze of passivity. Only his recordings
of Stravinsky and his work with Bill Challis on piano pieces
seemed to rouse him from his torpor. Although the evidence
is sketchy it appears that many of his friends visited him at
his apartment in his last months. Some worked to get him
radio jobs, and there was an abortive attempt to get him into
the Casa Loma Orchestra, but he resisted. The only musically

significant work of his last days was with Bill Challis on the arrangement of "In a Mist," which he had recorded a few years before, and a last recording session in which he used mutes, a rarity for him. He died on August 6, 1931, at the age of twenty-eight. The doctor's certificate attributed death to pneumonia, perhaps in an effort to protect the feelings of his family and friends.[6]

It's comforting to talk about Bix not having died unknown and to speak of his art and integrity. Listen, for example, to the Whiteman record of "Sweet Sue"—not a cliché of the period is overlooked. Here is symphonic jazz at its worst, complete with endless introductory passages, violin meanderings, and over-statement. Then, suddenly, something is signaled; the trumpets ring and the lumbering machine stops, and for thirty-two bars there is only Bix with a derby over the horn. In the midst of that turgid orchestration, imbeddded with overt commercialism, there is a thirty-two bar moment of truth.

Yet, an overarching question remains, even as we listen to the haunting recorded phrases of "Singing the Blues" or "I'm Comin' Virginia." It is an ominous one for our society and its popular culture: Are the social, political and economic dynamics of our society and popular culture as fatal to life as they are to art? The history of jazz is littered with personal catastrophes, alcoholism, drug-addiction, and early death. Towering figures have perished ignominiously. The trials which they had to endure led to dissipation and pathos. Bix is by no means alone; the list is far too long—Charlie Green, Pinetop Smith, Bessie Smith, Billie Holliday, Charlie Parker, John Coltrane, and Albert Ayler are only a few of the more famous people on it. Ignored, subjected to the most shattering indifference, often noticed years after their passing, jazzmen have been peculiar victims. Stultified, finding no place for their efforts, they are frequently rediscovered in the shadows and become fetish symbols of a new kind of intellectual elite. Sonny Rollins was making a perfectly honest and elegantly

absurd statement of protest when he retired from active playing and for a time took to playing his saxophone on evening
subway platforms.

For Louis, the catastrophe took a different, perhaps more
insidious form, since he became such a widely accepted figure
in popular culture. He was the ambassador of jazz, who
seldom played his authentic self after 1931. Only rarely did
he let his real feelings surface, jiving America when the opportunities presented themselves. He died a relatively old man
showered with national honors from a people who never knew
him, and Louis had become reluctant to take risks. His
funeral in Queens was attended by white show-business and
political greats, but it was far from what might have been a
fitting farewell—a funeral parade in New Orleans with a
second line to celebrate those fantastic years from 1923 to
1931, years which no other musical artist in American history
could touch. Maybe Louis could only reveal himself to black
people and the few whites like Jack Teagarden who seemed
somehow able to slough off their shackles.

Jazz was a people's music, but the people were a shunned
minority. It developed in its own social and intellectual ghetto,
and its practitioners lived far from the centers of social and
musical esteem. The lives of these two cornet-trumpet players
are instructive. They lived both in and out of popular culture;
perhaps we can appreciate them only in retrospect for what
they truly were and what they achieved. The thousands who
gathered at Louis' funeral looked like the extras on a Fellini
set. The thousands who gathered in Davenport on the fortieth
anniversary of Bix's death merely compound the pathos. The
lives of Louis and Bix become tragedy when we recognize that
their great talents were unfulfilled and subverted.

Part Four

American Vaudeville

Realizing that the permanent patronage of Proctor's Theater is largely composed of ladies and children who can always attend without escort, the aim of the management will be to offer only refined entertainment kept scrupulously free from any gross or objectionable features.

Proctor's Theater,
1894 Handbill

9.

Origins of Vaudeville

If ever there was a mass form of entertainment with important characteristics for value diffusion, it was vaudeville. From the 1870s to the 1930s vaudeville was perhaps the dominant form of mass entertainment in America. An anthropologist from a future civilization, digging into the rubble and finding artifacts from the world of vaudeville, would be able to learn a great deal about the life of the vanished civilization he had discovered. Vaudeville reflected the American experience of its time very broadly, including racial and religious stereotypes, low comedy, sensationalist advertising, ruthless competition, faddism, censorship, classical and oriental architecture, monopolies, itinerant actors, railway depots, hotels and boarding houses, robber barons, trade unions, strikes, blacklists, blue comedy, innocent charm, skill in performance, opportunity for immigrant talent, a hierarchy of performers, and huge organizations.

The term vaudeville is a relatively ancient one, and the notion of a bill of fare containing a variety of acts is even older than the term itself. The term may have originated from the time of the Norman invasion of Britain, or it may refer to certain types of street singing. Whatever the case, it appears that there was a theater called "Vaudeville" in Paris as early as the 1790s. Film buffs may recall the magnificent post-World War II French film *The Children of Paradise*, which depicts an early nineteenth century theatrical family and its various bills of fare, including acts which would have been typical of twentieth century American vaudeville. Especially memorable are the wonderful pantomimes of the great French actor Jean Louis Barrault.

Early acts of variety, as they were at first called, seem to have been squeezed between the acts of more serious theatrical enterprises such as opera. In Europe, vaudeville came to signify a variety show, while in Britain similar purposes were served by what was called the music hall. Film buffs who have seen Hitchcock's 1930s masterpiece *The Thirty-Nine Steps* have a fairly clear notion of how an English music hall with its flowing bar and repartee between audience and performers worked. In America, the audiences were not so involved in the presentations of the performers, although they had obvious ways of voicing approval and disapproval. However, it was easy for an act to die at birth, as Fred Astaire learned when he and his sister were trying out a kid dance act in the early part of this century.[1]

In the first half of the nineteenth century, French vaudeville expanded to include one-act comedies and short plays. This practice was emulated by American vaudeville during its death throes in the twentieth century as it futilely tried to compete with newer forms of entertainment.

The English forerunner was extremely important to the growth of American variety theater, and itinerate English performers coming to the New World seem to have presented the first variety bills. Although there is some evidence that comic entertainers drifted about America even before the Revolution, it was not until the mid-nineteenth century that this continent saw wide exhibitions of the burlesque variant of leg art coupled with low comedy. The term vaudeville itself seems to have been first used in America in the 1880s in the American southwest by a touring group presenting a variety of speciality acts.

Beyond the obvious English influence there were other sources of inspiration for vaudeville, but all of them were shaped by American notions of ethnicity, rectitude, servitude, freedom of movement, and frontier life. Among the indigenous sources of American vaudeville were minstrel shows, traveling medicine shows, circuses, dime museums, town hall and beer hall entertainments, honky-tonks, the legitimate stage, grand opera, and pantomine and musical comedy. But, there would always be something about vaudeville which smacked of the lower forms of life, of earthiness and low comedy. Its purveyors would always have to struggle for respectability.

From English music halls came the staples: comic songs (suggestive and other), acrobatic acts, conjuring acts, juggling, and dancing. These were at first presented in tavern settings with women from the show working the side boxes urging patrons to loosen up and purchase the management's watered liquors. Not until the 1840s were variety bills in America presented in theaters separate from bars. At this time English music hall performers traveled the frontier presenting their acts in the sometimes dangerous surroundings of frontier saloons with stages. Even before this time, American impressarios had presented a formula of variety acts in circuses as they would later in the century on river showboats. As a result of the relatively sparse settlement of the continent, early variety acts and their trappings moved from place to place on a regular route aided by the expanding railroads; this pattern of mobility remained until the end of the medium.

When thinking about dime museums, one of vaudeville's important sources of inspiration, the name of circus master P. T. Barnum comes inevitably to mind. He maintained such an establishment in New York City, but he was not alone in this enterprise; in the 1880s there was a craze for dime museums throughout the country. In addition to Barnum's New York enterprise, museums flourished in Chicago, Boston, Minneapolis, Cincinnati, Pittsburgh, Philadelphia, and some smaller towns. For a dime the customer was able to view exhibits and performances. Buildings often separated the exhibition hall from a relatively small stage. Typical wonders among the exhibits might be a tatooed man, a dog-faced boy, or a three-headed woman. Freaks were a lasting staple of dime museums and can still be seen among traveling carnivals. After viewing the midgets and the wild men of Borneo, patrons would proceed to another part of the museum to enjoy the variety acts. These might include a half-hour to fifty minute format of singers, dancers, minstrels, song and dance teams, magicians, sketch artists, marionettes, and comics, and might sometimes even include a playlet. At times there would be a wax works, a lecturer of the W. C. Fields variety, and platform acts of sword swallowers or fire eaters. Since there could be as many as twenty shows a day, there were often traffic problems, and audiences would be encouraged to leave the theater to make way for new patrons by so-called chase acts which were often merely repeats of performances already seen. This tactic lasted well into the vaudeville era, and early movies were often used for this purpose in the silent days. Even in dime museums, the management discouraged actors from using off-color material because the entertainments were designed to attract a mixed audience. A similar policy was followed in the halcyon days of big-time vaudeville.

Medicine shows were something else, and Hollywood Westerns may not be far from the mark in depicting this kind of entertainment. These parapatetics offered patent medicines to the gullible, with the proprietor often assuming the honorific title of "doctor." To attract patrons he might present an entertainer who juggled, sang, danced, or conjured, and also drove the rig. Often this entertainer would be an Indian or a former slave. Thus, at this early period as later on, the "illegitimate" theater offered a livelihood, if little in the way of self-esteem, to those who were marginal to established society. As late as the 1890s there were well over a hundred medicine shows featuring some form of entertainment while hawking wares touring the American continent.

But more important than either the dime museums or the medicine shows for the development of vaudeville were the minstrel shows. These broad caricatures of black plantation life and manners were performed mainly in "blackface," that is by white men in black make-up. The "comic negro" was a familiar figure on the English stage as far back as the early part of the eighteenth century; black performers were not unknown in America at that time, but minstrels as such seem to have originated with Dan Emmet and the "Virginia Minstrels" in the early 1840s. Moreover, in the South there was ample precedent for whites being entertained by black people. In slave times on isolated plantations, slave entertainment was one of the chief means by which wealthy planters entertained visitors; black "court jesters" would tell jokes, sing, and dance to please the master and his guests.[2] The banjo was known in those days as a musical instrument invented by slaves.

E. P. Christy toured with his minstrel company for many years; he formulated the classic structure of a minstrel show in 1846 when he had an interlocutor in whiteface lead the performance and banter with two end men, Mr. Tamborine and Mr. Bones. The end men were actually just that, men who sat at the end of the full company drawn up in a half-circle. The interlocutor's cry of "Gentlemen, be seated" signaled the beginning of a variegated show which included song and dance teams, comedians, clog and jig dancers, jugglers, and an obligatory sketch. The second half of the show was the so-called olio, a potpourri of relatively unconnected acts which resembled later vaudeville in form. Minstrel shows seem to have hit a peak of popularity in the post-Civil War era, when their style was carried forward by Lew Dockstadter, Al G. Fields, and Dan Bryant. Minstrel music and lyrics often featured so-called coon songs and plantation melodies which perpetrated stereotypes about black life. Not until after the Civil War did blacks participate in these performances, and even then the stereotypes continued.[3]

The most renowned minstrels were white, and some of them like Eddie Leonard, Chauncy Olcott, and Paul Dresser, brother of novelist Theodore Dreiser, later found their way into vaudeville and musical comedy. Sketches like "Octeroon" dealt with surprisingly delicate topics like miscegenation. One widely played sketch depicted an old freed slave returning to his master after an absence of some twenty years. Sitting in a chair the rheumatic old black sang:

> Don't talk of 'mancipation proclamation unto me
> Ah was happier in slavery than Ah been since
> Ah been free.
> The slavery days the happiest days of any unto me,
> In mah good old cabin home in South Ca'lina.[4]

He had come home to die wanting only to see his master again before going off through the pearly gates.

The song set off a sentimental dialog between master and slave, ending with the death of the slave and a heart-felt expression by the master that the old slave had now passed on to his reward. This was a cue for the company to begin softly to sing something like "In the Sweet Bye-and-Bye." Some scholars have insisted that the audience did not take the minstrel goings on as true representations of black life, but it is hard to assess audience impact. This was the key form of stage musical comedy in America during the nineteenth century, at least until it was driven off by vaudeville in the last two decades. Minstrel shows reinforced a pattern of attitudes and perceptions that lasted, though in subtler form to be sure, well into the vaudeville and movie era. Witness, for example, the 1930s movie musical on the life of Stephen Collins Foster, whose tunes had been used by more than one minstrel company during his lifetime.[5]

Changing times and a more sophisticated audience foreshadowed the end of minstrels. The format proved to be too rigid and costly. Audiences chafed at the all-male cast, and concepts of black Americans were changing. While it is true that most professional minstrel companies were gone by the twentieth century, amateur productions lasted well into the 1950s.

From this overlapping helter-skelter of antecedents came American vaudeville. Giving shape to the medium in the later nineteenth century was Antonio (Tony) Pastor. It was a time when one man could by the force of his ideas and personality give shape to a nation-wide expression, and Pastor synthesized the first real bill of vaudeville on October 24, 1881. On that occasion he offered singers, a duet, Irish comics, dancers, instrumentalists, and acrobats. Some of the acts would have seemed familiar in the eighteenth century and earlier. Pastor himself had wide experience in the entertainment world; his background included singing in churches and at temperance societies as a youth, working at Barnum's Museum, performing blackface song and dance, touring as an actor, working as an acrobat, and organizing circus acts. This diversity of experience paid off.

Pastor began his career as a manager by opening a beer garden with entertainment; through various transformations he emerged as the first important impresario of vaudeville with a house on Fourteenth Street in New York. Along the way he originated the traveling company, burlesqued Gilbert and Sullivan, and gave opportunities to performers like Weber and Fields, Nat C. Goodwin, and Lillian Russell. However, his greatest innovation was the introduction of "clean" variety on an October evening in 1881, thus breaking with the tradition of bawdy material that had gone before. His motives were mainly mercenary. He hoped to increase the size of his audiences by bringing women and children into the house; it was a daring policy at the time.

This first official eight-act vaudeville bill included an Irish and a blackface act and was topped off by a rendition by Pastor himself of several old favorite tunes including one called "Lulu, the Beautiful Hebrew Girl." Pastor succeeded in changing the rowdy image of variety; his notion of wholesome performance would be underscored and carried to even greater lengths by succeeding generations of promoters.

Other vaudeville managers followed suit, and gradually the serving of drinks during performances died out in this country. With this change the American public granted much wider acceptance to the medium and the eight-act bill became standard. Pastor's policies may have been motivated by the fact that he was born into an Italian family of Roman Catholic faith. He kept a poor box and a shrine in his theater. By contrast with the big enterprisers who were to follow, Pastor's business organization was simple—most agreements were informal, unlike the driving acquisitiveness that characterized later promoters in show business. In contrast to many of his successors, Pastor was easygoing and personable in his relations with others.

In its golden period from about 1890 to the mid-1920s, vaudeville was a complex kind of organized activity. There were thousands of theaters ranging from small halls over drugstores to the Palace in New York, the dream and goal of every small-time hoofer and quip artist. The organizational patterns of vaudeville emerged as a result of phenomena similar to those in the American business enterprise as a whole. Until the coming of big chains or vaudeville circuits, which tied theater control to talent management and booking, vaudeville remained a highly individual enterprise, with managers of individual theaters doing their own bookings and stamping their own personalities onto their theaters. However, the me-

dium soon succumbed to cut-throat competitiveness and mo-
nopolizing tendencies and became part of the world of robber-
baron personalities. B. F. Keith and Edward Albee, two New
Englanders who followed typical mid-nineteenth century paths
into show business, came to dominance. The very fact that in
America the term used is "show business" is indicative of important motivations. As boys, both ran away with circuses and
became involved in dime museums. They met when Keith
hired Albee as a house spiel artist. Out of this association grew
the fabulous Keith-Albee Circuit, the most powerful and far-
flung of the vaudeville chains. Beginning with a single continuous show in a Boston theater in 1885, they were to run their
string of theaters to more than four hundred by the 1920s.

The idea of continuous performance vaudeville originated
with yet a third pioneer entrepreneur, F. F. Proctor, who began his career as a performer and eventually bought theaters
in upstate New York. Apparently more tender-hearted and
kind than B. F. Keith or E. A. Albee, he built an empire that
rivaled theirs and eventually became locked in a power
struggle with them. Proctor seems to have been a transitional
figure, espousing values that included those of Tony Pastor
while at the same time taking advantage of the changes in
American life and organizing a chain of theaters in the manner of Keith and Albee.

Vaudeville was the dominant form of theater in America
after 1880; it was the first of the mass media with standardized formats, a palpable structure and norms, and large-scale
organization dominated by business rather than artistic values.
It was urban, and its peripatetic nature flowered with the
development of the railroad. Most important vaudeville
theaters were in the heart of a city. Moreover, America was
undergoing vast changes during the flowering of the vaudeville
theater. The idea that the stage was somehow sinful began to
moderate under the growing impact of urbanization and industrialization. The system of chains of theaters and mass

centralized booking gave rise to a managerial class who administered the various activities of the medium. There were receipts to be totaled, tickets to be sold, new attractions to be advertised, theaters to be kept up, and a rigid standard of propriety to be maintained. All of these activities gave rise to a complex organization, many of whose members at the administrative level had gained earlier experience in the newspaper world.

F. F. Proctor seemed to sense the importance of the social changes America was undergoing before other entrepreneurs. He noted the shopping patterns of newly urbanized housewives, observed the availability of a child market, and tailored his presentations to the new realities. He embarked on continuous, all-star vaudeville presentations to bring his entertainments "closer to the hearts of the masses." His announced plan was to "give the masses what they want."[6] To do this, he brought theater stars to vaudeville, took over legitimate theaters, paid enormous salaries, sought out opera singers, and invaded the New York theater district. He marketed something for those with leisure and offered after-breakfast performances; he coined the phrase "After breakfast go to Proctor's; after Proctor's go to bed" to underscore his continuous performance policy.

These three figures, Keith, Albee, and Proctor, reinforced Pastor's policy of clean vaudeville. To attract the widest possible audience, they emphasized their probity and propriety. To attract women and children they made a point of their moral rectitude. To be sure, some artists found the various taboos burdensome and the censorship restricting, but the Keith-Albee threat of blacklisting kept most of them in line. Beginning in the late nineteenth century, Proctor forbade all smoking and drinking in his theaters. In 1894 a handbill for Proctor's theater for the fall and winter season announced:

High class vaudeville in the best and most comprehensive sense of the term embracing novelties of all kinds . . . only first class artists will be selected. Realizing that the permanent patronage of Proctor's Theater is largely composed of ladies and children who can always attend without escort, the aim of the management will be to offer only refined entertainment kept scrupulously free from any gross or objectionable features.[7]

Could there be a more succinct statement of propriety or a more stringent promise to allay the fears and anxieties that attend those who hold such attitudes?

As if to anticipate the drive for novelty that later media would experience, Proctor's ad also promised "always something diverting" and "complete changes every week." To take advantage of the possibilities Proctor instituted a special "Ladies Club Theater." A suggestion that in some ways morality could be relaxed if enough assurance could be rendered was the fact that Proctor offered Sunday concert matinees and got away with it. To be sure, he promised "vaudeville specialties whose offerings are in keeping with the character of the day," as well as souvenirs for the ladies, but he nonetheless offered entertainment on the sacred day of rest, and that was new.

No restrictions were as obvious or as sedulously enforced (by spies if necessary) than those of the Keith circuit. Mrs. Keith was a devout Roman Catholic who deeply influenced her husband's penchant for censorship and barred anything that might be suggestive in the way of materials or gestures. At all Keith theaters the following notice would be tacked up back stage:

NOTICE

TO PERFORMERS

Don't say "slob" or "son-of-a-gun" or "hully-gee" on this stage unless you want to be cancelled peremptorily. Do not address anyone in the audience in any manner. If you have not the ability to entertain Mr. Keith's audiences without risk of offending them, do the best you can. Lack of talent will be less open to censure than would be an insult to a patron. If you are in doubt as to the character of your act, consult the local manager before you go on the stage, for if you are guilty of uttering anything sacrilegious or even suggestive, you will be immediately closed and will never again be allowed in a theater where Mr. Keith is in authority.[8]

This imperative not to offend was deep and long lasting. Long after Keith's death, *Variety* ran a column entitled, "You Mustn't Say That," which warned against such expressions as "hell," "damn," or "Lord Epsom, secretary of the interior."[9]

As late as 1927 in a signed ad in the *New York Morning Journal*, a Proctor article on the future of vaudeville promised that "our continued policy of cleanliness in all vaudeville offerings always comes first in our line of thinking"; indeed it was seen as its "most valuable asset." A book on vaudeville writing published in 1915 warned would-be sketch writers to avoid that which would "bring a blush to the cheek" of sister, wife, or mother.[10] The view of women as pure and unsullied, notions of what was fit for the ears and eyes of children, and concepts of what was proper for the happiness and entertainment of upright middle-class Americans is exemplified in the concerns of the vaudeville entrepreneurs, and they become high irony when one considers the kind of ethnic fare which was considered suitable in American entertainment from the 1880s until the 1920s.

As if to further emphasize that they were after a solid and respectable trade and stress that they were trying to vitiate an image of vaudeville as vulgar and common, the big entrepreneurs put up lavish theaters to house their offerings. Respectability was what they sought, and they spent lavishly to provide settings which would prove to the middle class that everything was all right, that nothing possibly offensive could take place in such opulent surroundings. Proctor promised "plenty of laughter, pretty women, fine scenery, gorgeous costumes, good music, comfortable chairs, polite attention" and ushers from whom "politeness is exacted." If this were not enough, like Keith, he specified to the public that "entertainments are carefully supervised and censored."[11]

Kevin Brownlow, an historian of silent film, noted that early silent film was an entertainment of the working classes and immigrants, while vaudeville was for the middle class. Even today, the surviving vaudeville houses, now mostly used as movie theaters, give evidence of the plushness, solidity, and affluence which the entrepreneurs sought to convey.[12] In this, American vaudeville contrasts with British music halls and their deep roots in working-class culture. Philip Slater has noted the American middle-class imperative against making a fuss, and, indeed, in vaudeville theaters the audiences usually did not participate in the show. After all, patrons of the medium were solid citizens. Woodrow Wilson, for example, during his term as governor of New Jersey could regularly be seen in a seat at the Palace Theatre in New York.

10.

Organization and Structure

Reflecting cultural differences in the expanse of the American continent, certain vaudeville circuits dominated particular sections of the country; there was a distinction between the big time, with two-a-day performances of an eight or nine act bill, and the small time, which featured fewer acts coupled with a film. With Albee as directing genius, the Keith-Albee circuit attempted to head off all competition and succeeded to a remarkable degree. Some other circuits continued to do business to the end of vaudeville, but to a large degree the Keith-Albee circuit was dominant.

A small time circuit was the starting place for most vaudeville acts. Life on a small time circuit differed from that on major circuits. Often the theaters were located in small towns, and performers played split weeks rather than full week-long engagements. Sometimes the theaters were in the major cities but in less splendid theaters. Since much of the booking was done through the Keith-Albee offices, weekly reports were filed by the small house managers with the central office in Chicago, where the Western Vaudeville Managers Association booked acts in cooperation with Keith-Albee. Often in small time circuits there were fewer acts than the standard big time eight or nine act bills, but the acts themselves were very much alike with dancers, singers, mimics, acrobats, comedians, sketches, and so forth—the standard format. Yet, small time circuits could be shoestring operations too. Fred Astaire recalled one theater he played in his early days where the manager, whom he liked a good deal, was ticket-taker, pianist, stage and property manager, and announcer, all rolled into one. Sometimes, momentous events occurred on the small time; for example, Sophie Tucker was playing a small time house, the Maryland Theater in Baltimore, when she agreed to use a tune by the black song writing team of Sissle and Blake and thus helped launch two important careers for American jazz, ragtime, and musical comedy.[1]

Even small time circuits got to be big business. Percy G. Williams operated a dozen theaters, mostly in New York City. Sylvester Z. Poli centered his holdings in New England, while the Pantages and Sullivan-Considine organizations worked the territories between Chicago and the west coast. Ackerman and Harris held forth in the northwest, Gus Sun and Kohl-Castle in the midwest, and Fred Motzart largely in Pennsylvania. There were even some towns where prominent managers operated relatively independently, booking their own acts. However, in both small time and big time vaudeville the trend was toward consolidation and rationalization. While still building his chain early in his career, F. F. Proctor was porter, ticket-taker, booker, and poster-man in his operation, but by the end of his life, he lived and worked like other big business tycoons. Consolidations were the rule; Keith bought out the Percy G. Williams string for some six million dollars, and Marcus Loew, the king of small-time vaudeville, acquired both the Pantages and Sullivan-Considine circuits for a time.

There was an air of constant wheeling and dealing in the world of the vaudeville tycoons. By early in the twentieth century there were already several vaudeville millionaires.

Proctor began to enlarge by acquiring smaller circuits. He eventually controlled a string from New York to Chicago. To fill in bookings to the west coast, he formed a coalition with the western Orpheum Circuit developed by Martin Beck to book vaudeville from coast to coast, for fifty-two weeks a year, from a central booking agency; the deal ultimately failed to materialize but it gives evidence of the expansionist thinking of the vaudeville oligarchs. Eventually, even Proctor merged; he was absorbed by the Keith-Albee interests when he lost control of his prime New York Theater—Proctor's Fifth Avenue—and entered a merger to avoid open warfare. It lasted for several years but was dissolved on Proctor's suit in 1911. The situation was so desperately competitive that Proctor, for example, held all business conferences at his home in Larchmont for fear of opposition spies.

Other powerful, big time opponents besides Proctor also fought the Keith-Albee power. At various times William Morris, Martin Beck, Oscar Hammerstein, and the Schubert brothers mounted direct attacks on the Keith-Albee combine. They coralled coveted acts, raised salaries, and set up houses in direct competition with them; but in the end the dominant powers remained Keith-Albee, and they eventually forced out most of their opponents. In so doing they employed many weapons, including a blacklist which they used, for example, on any actors who appeared for the Schuberts. Fred Allen felt the thrust of the Keith-Albee monopoly power when he signed with Schubert and found himself banished to the small time.

Perhaps the most powerful instrument of Keith-Albee power was the United Booking Office (UBO) set up in 1906. Eventually located in the fabled Palace Theater office building which had passed into Keith-Albee control, agents vied with one another in peddling their properties to bookers from various circuits. There was a clear hierarchy with small time agents working on the fifth floor allied to the big time agents on the sixth floor. It was a mad house, and the air was rife with talk of percentages, split weeks, and long tours. Ostensibly supervised by the Vaudeville Managers Association, the UBO was actually an oligarchy of the most powerful managers and was influenced heavily by Keith-Albee. It excercised a near monopoly over talent, and it was a power which endured despite the strenuous efforts of talent representative William Morris. The UBO took a lavish percentage of actors' fees at the source, some 10 percent, while exacting another 5 percent for services, and 2.5 percent from agent's fees. It was a kickback system which netted the UBO an enormous amount of money.

Thus, the monopoly tendencies in vaudeville paralleled those in the oil or steel industries. Keith-Albee had a way of absorbing independent bookers and managers and utilizing their talents to further their own power. Nor did they mind buying off potential competiters, for example, the UBO gave the producers Klaw and Erlanger some $150,000 to stay out of vaudeville for ten years during one of their expansion periods. Beyond this, the combine used blacklisting and boycotting, going so far as to employ actors as spies who reported backstage conversations with colleagues to the central office. The Keith-Albee executive manager, J. J. Murdock, tended to behave in standard corporation style; he kept his social distance from both patrons and actors and gave the collection of fees first priority.

While neither powerful individuals nor organized groups had much success in resisting Keith-Albee, the most serious actors' efforts came from the group known as the White Rats. It is no surprise that the idea was an English import, since ideas about labor organizations in England were generally in advance of those in America. Many of the sort of labor trials which Americans were to undergo in the twentieth century had already taken place in England a decade or two earlier. Thus it was that an English music hall performer named Harry Montford came to America and fought to organize a variety actors' protective organization similar to one he had known in Britain called the Water Rats—Rats being "star" spelled backwards. Spearheading the organization was a small group which included some of the leading vaudeville acts of the early part of this century, among them Dave Montgomery and Fred Stone, Weber and Fields, Eddie Foy, and J. C. Nugent. After some internal discussion as to whether they should opt for an exclusive organization or a trade union emphasis, they called a strike in 1916 against what they saw as intolerable working conditions. Actors had to pay for their own props, material, and scenery and resented the lack of commitment on the part of management which could cancel without notice any act which was judged to be unpopular. Control of the performer's route was solely in the hands of the managers, who could blacklist or banish an act to the small time. In addition, actors were plagued by petty graft in the form of pay-offs to various backstage workers who could easily sabotage an act if they wanted, a fate which befell Cole and Johnson, one of the great black two-man acts to play Proctor's theater. The grievances were undoubtedly real, and the actors saw themselves living in a tough world and carrying all of the risks alone. But, the problems were internal as well as external; some of the White Rats, mirroring the resistance to unionism which was occurring in other occupations, resented being classified with labor and resisted being tied to the American Federation of Labor.

Yet, the White Rats did leave a mark, even if only in frightening management and exposing the middle-class self-image of some of the leading vaudeville actors. They published a trade journal called *The Players,* and Fred Allen maintained that it was widely read in New York and that he himself was fascinated by its reviews and trade information, which included a description of routes available, song publishers, boarding houses, hotels, and the like. As if the internal dissensions and opposition of management were not enough, the leading trade journal *Variety,* whose publisher Sime Silverman detested Keith and Albee, was lukewarm over the White Rats. They were particularly skeptical about Harry Montford and some of the White Rats' organizational policies. Lacking supportive federal labor legislation and a unity of purpose, in the end the union was undermined by the Keith-Albee interests, who blacklisted George Fuller Golden, one of the more militant leaders of the Rats, for life. Keith-Albee eventually even took over the Rats' Clubhouse on West Fourty-Sixth Street in New York and conspired to form a company union called the National Vaudeville Artists (NVA).

E. F. Albee dominated the National Vaudeville Artists, and talk of strikes and actors' rights faded away. The NVA contented itself with establishing a hospital in upstate New York for which collections were made in film theaters long after the demise of vaudeville. It also exacted tribute from actors who appeared at NVA benefits. One positive development under the NVA from the performers' point of view was the establishment of a protected material department which was a move in the direction of preventing the kind of open piracy of material which had characterized variety from its inception. The White Rats story was re-enacted many times in American labor history. What began as a fraternal order, uneasily transformed itself into a trade union of sorts, and then faded into company unionism by World War I.

None of the Keith-Albee competition was more colorful than the Hammersteins, and none was more diverting than William Hammerstein, the son of Oscar I and father of Oscar II, whose career as a lyricist in collaboration with Richard Rodgers revolutionized the American musical theater. Oscar I, a German-Jewish immigrant, made serious forays into the world of opera, mounting formidable opposition for a time to the Metropolitan itself.

Through the leadership of his son Willie, Oscar Hammerstein I made an impact on vaudeville with his often bizarre doings at the Victoria Theater. Hammerstein and Keith-Albee had made an agreement which divided New York into spheres of vaudeville influence. Eschewing the puritanism of Keith-Albee, Hammerstein was a daring showman, and his programs at the Victoria Theater and its roof garden were an interesting showcase of the bizarre, freakish, and sensational. The appeal of Hammerstein's offerings may be another example of Philip Slater's contention that we are most bedazzled by that which we deny most fervently. Hammerstein's promotions brought in rich box office receipts; they included Ethel Conrad, who had shot one of the leading social lights of New York, Jim Corbett, the boxing champion; Dr. F. A. Cook, the controversial explorer who claimed to have reached the North Pole before Scott; and Evelyn Nesbit, the central figure in the lurid Thaw-White murder case. In addition to these luminaries, the Victoria regularly offered Python dancers, dour nonsmilers, lead comics, contortionists, fierce uglies, women with tiny waistlines, principals in sensational trials, and assorted committers of mayhem. Other bills included Olympic athletes, newspaper cartoonists, sports figures, and sharpshooters. In 1913 a Scottish Lord appeared as a singer in an effort to pay off a debt on his estate, unfortunately with little success. Had he been involved in a murder case instead of being an indifferent vocalist, he might have made enough to pay his mortgage, since Miss Nesbit lasted for eight weeks at $3,500 per week. Hammerstein followed Proctor in trying to cater to the public's taste for the bizarre. The Keith-Albee empire did not. Not until its dying days in the early 1930s would the Palace feature a sports personality, when Bill Tilden the tennis star took a turn.[2]

In seventeen turbulent years the Victoria grossed some $20 million. Much of the appeal was based on ballyhoo, and one observer noted that a certain convicted killer would have committed murder once a week to gain a regular place on Victoria bills.

Although Hammerstein was beloved in the vaudeville sub-culture in a way Albee never could be, much of his appeal was based on downright skullduggery. For example, announcing that his roof theater was magically cooled, he heated the elevator so that when the delighted patrons emerged at the upper level, they indeed felt immeasurably cooler. This kind of tactic was typical of vaudeville publicity as a whole. It was perhaps symptomatic that even in those inchoate corporation days, gigantic individual personalities could still affect an entire organization by holding the key to effective action. Only one year after the premature death of Willie Hammerstein, the Victoria closed its doors and passed into the folklore and legend of vaudeville.

Martin Beck was a German immigrant who had come to America with a troupe of actors. In the mid-1890s he worked as a waiter in Chicago before joining a vaudeville company in San Francisco; he later dabbled in real estate before becoming manager of a variety theater. Beginning with locally financed theaters, he built a chain to rival Keith-Albee. His Orpheum Circuit had booking offices in Chicago and dominated big time vaudeville between that city and the west coast. In the best cartel fashion the two giants agreed to divide the country and work their territories without poaching on one another. Eventually, there was conflict when Beck chafed at these restrictions and strove to invade the East. Finally there was a merger in which the Keith interests were dominant in a new Keith-Orpheum Circuit.

In invading the East, Beck upset agreements between Hammerstein and Keith-Albee that divided territories and booking rights. Injunctions were threatened and Albee bought back booking rights he had sold to Hammerstein. Even before the Palace opened its doors, Beck's holdings were down to 25 percent, and the Palace had become not just the prime Keith-Albee house, but the prime vaudeville house of the entire medium.

The Palace opened on March 24, 1913, as a high class, high cost house; seats brought the then unheard of price of $2.00, twice the cost of a seat at Hammerstein's Victoria. It was a fast-paced house, repleat with so many notables and headliners that the management made one futile attempt to limit the number of bows and curtain calls an act could take. Few headliners could resist the offer of a Palace engagement; in its run of twenty years, only Al Jolson, who was under exclusive contract to the Schuberts, and Sir Harry Lauder, tied to William Morris, of all the great vaudeville stars did not play this house.

The Palace's opening night revealed how much more sophisticated vaudeville had become since the opening at Tony Pastor's. Ethnicity was played down and rough-and-tumble acts had diminished; the Palace presented a ballet company, a Spanish court violinist, a pantomimist, a skit written by humorist George Ade, a monologist, a wire act, a cartoonist, and comedian Ed Wynn. Almost all the greatest acts played this storied house, but here too the Keith-Albee purity policy was strictly enforced. All women performers wore stockings, the notorious folk who graced the Victoria were banned, and even acts based upon physical deformities were not booked. Sophie Tucker was a headliner at the time, but was fired for singing a suggestive song which asked "Who Paid the Rent When Rip van Winkle Was Away?" A playlet focusing on the hypocrisy of divorce laws yielded the same result for the legitimate actress Nazimova. Even so, many actors found themselves able to negotiate the rules successfully. The fabled Sarah Bernhardt appeared in some scenes with Lou Tellegan, one-time husband of opera star Geraldine Farrar. W. C. Fields, Fanny Brice, Annette Kellerman (her swimming act complete with stockings), Douglas Fairbanks, Anna Held, the Avon Comedy Four, Irene Franklin, Joe Cook, Blanch Ring, Hugh Herbert, Houdini, Eva Tanguay, the Marx Brothers, Irene and Vernon

Castle, and many more appeared at the house for runs of varying length.

Palace audiences tended to be discriminating and commented freely, at times in the manner of the English music hall. Yet business was such in the good years that often three-fourths of the audience was from the subscription list. From the actor's point of view the Monday matinee was the key. Sophie Tucker called it the "auction block."[3] Marian Spitzer was associated with the management of the theater for many years and corroborated Sophie Tucker's assessment of the situation. For it was this performance that the bookers, actors' agents and big time talent buyers like Ziegfeld, Belasco, and the Schuberts attended.[4] After the show the assorted business representatives retired to the booking offices upstairs in the Palace Theater building to argue over which acts would be assigned the most coveted positions on the Keith-Albee routes, decisions which could mean forty weeks of work. More clearly than in most other fields of endeavor, a successful Palace run was the pinnacle.

Proved acts had devoted followings, and the pressure was on beginners who had to appear before tough colleagues and critical audiences. It was a hard-boiled world. Yet, in one sense vaudeville was easier on material than television. An actor could polish the same material and present it on a circuit over many years, since he usually made only a single circuit appearance in any given year.

The Palace presented nine acts during a weekly bill, with an intermission for refreshment. Performers gathered on Monday morning for rehearsal and to become acquainted. It was important not only to know colleagues on the bill, but also to be acquainted with the stage hands, musicians, and lighting crews. The house manager was in charge and timed the acts carefully, running the entire operation with a firm hand. The theater itself was lush, with a marble lobby, comfortable seats, and lovely chandeliers. In the halcyon days a bill of acts might set the management back $20,000 to $30,000 a week, while the box office take was often $500,000.

Films, introduced as novelties or chase acts in the vaudeville houses, were their undoing; by 1933 the Palace went the way of most other vaudeville houses and became a movie theater. Its nineteen-year reign was probably unparalleled in popular theater history. The last two-a-day bill appeared in January of 1933; then the Palace that had seen the talents of Jack Benny, Ray Bolger, Will Rogers, the Astaires, Gallagher and Sheen, Smith and Dale, Frank Fay, and Van and Schenk, to name a few, closed the two-a-day grind forever. To be sure there were subsequent temporary revivals, but vaudeville really died that January of 1933, a victim of depression, of movies, of change itself.

Thousands of acts had traveled the circuits and were the merchandise of business enterprises. They ranged from small time with small pay to the top circuits. Many acts started in amateur nights which were organized by managers who took strings of aspirants to various amateur night performances in hopes of hitting the big time. Fred Allen, for example, began his career in vaudeville as a member of an amateur string playing theaters in his native Boston, as did Sophie Tucker in Hartford.

Attending to the needs of traveling troubadors was the sub-culture of the vaudeville boarding houses and hotels. Fred Allen recalled living among small time actors in New York boarding houses; he gave a picture of charming bedlam with acts using various parts of the house to rehearse during their long at-liberty periods. The sounds must have mystified the uninitiated, as bird acts, sopranos, acrobats, mimics and monologists worked their wares while waiting the call of an agent who might summon them to a split week in the hinter-land.

Unfortunate actors spent many a night sleeping in railway

stations while waiting for connections. The small time circuits which survived best seem to have been conveniently located between places on big time circuits, thus enabling more established acts to pick up extra salary between regular engagements. Split weeks at the management's convenience were a special form of hell, and actors often had to make difficult mid-week connections at a moment's notice. Theater managers held absolute power over acts and could cancel without notice. In addition, they sent reports to the central booking offices and acts could not appeal a bad notice.

The major circuits often sent out acts grouped together as a complete bill for twenty-week tours. There were two such tours a year, with actors often taking off the summer to rest and polish their routines. Sometimes there was bitter fighting among people locked together on these twenty-week sweeps around the circuit. Fred Allen remembered vividly the jealously and carping that erupted during the forced intimacy of these long sojourns.[5] But if there was dissension, there was also considerable camaraderie and generosity, and the claim by some of being born in a theater trunk had real substance in fact.

A theater bill revealed the rating of a given act. The opening act usually consisted of tumblers, jugglers, acrobats, animals, clowns, or kids; it was in a tough position to attract audience attention and received minimal salary. Patrons were still finding their seats, and it was difficult to play to hub-bub. Fred Astaire experienced a dreadful quiet when he and his sister completed a kid act that no one had been able to hear for all the shuffling and mumbling.[6]

The second place act often included a song and dance with patter of the "Who Was That Lady I Saw You With Last Night?" variety. This immortal line was first uttered by Weber and Fields in one of the early roughhouse acts. In number three spot was usually a short comedy sketch. Spots four and five would be star acts, the former usually a single, the latter often a multiperson act featuring dancing or novelties. Position five, just before intermission, was the second most prestigious place on the bill and would, therefore, attract star quality acts. The sixth position was difficult because it was important to maintain the pace and interest built up by acts four and five. Since the audience would be making their way back to their seats, this position would often feature a comedy dumb act (i.e., one which did not depend upon spoken lines) to recapture the attention of the audience. Act number seven was often a full-stage performance featuring a playlet, either comedic or serious, and perhaps starring a well-known actor or actress from the legitimate stage. The eighth position on a nine-act big time vaudeville bill would be the featured act, the star. This was usually the place for the highlight comedy act of the bill for which the audience had been waiting expectantly all through the other performances. The closing act encountered some of the same problems as the opening act, namely, movement among the audience. Often an act was featured that did not depend exclusively on being heard. Thus, an ideal closing act would be an animal act or perhaps a balancing or acrobatic performance.

The headliner always held the next to closing spot on the bill, commanded the highest salary, and had the choice dressing room. Many headliners guarded their prerogatives zealously and sometimes caused resentment in the rest of the company; others inadvertently caused problems for colleagues simply because they were so good they were hard to follow. Bill "Bojangles" Robinson, the great black dancer, for example, was so well received that anything that followed him was anticlimactic. Building a balanced, well-paced bill was a delicate art, and bringing a unity out of its diversity was a challenging task.

Vaudeville process was not whimsical; it was planned to depict widely experienced American values, ideas, and problems. On this subject few writers have yet matched the insights of Gilbert Seldes in his pioneering popular culture study, *The Seven Lively Arts.* Despite his having misunderstood the nature of jazz and ragtime, like most commentators of his time, Seldes' analysis of vaudeville still seems fresh and insightful today. His commentary was undertaken in a serious manner; he did not patronize his subject, nor did he engage in pompous complexities in order to establish the respectability of his enterprise. While admitting that vaudeville dealt with light materials, Seldes insisted that it demanded artistic precision and excellent timing. Vaudeville had to be swift, neat, and true to itself. Seldes wrote, "refined vaudeville was a thing I disliked intensely" and went on to observe that "like other popular arts in America, vaudeville is required by the tradition of gentility to be cultural."[7] To him, the proper music was jazz and ragtime, a real vaudeville dance was a stunt, and a playlet should be pure burlesque with a touch of self-parody. Highbrow tid-bits he thought ruinous to vaudeville spirit. He regretted certain artists having succumbed to the inducements of respectability. He liked one artist because she had "something roughly elemental and something common and pure."[8] There was something of a frontier disdain for the effete in Seldes that vaudeville touched. He asserted that vaudeville "can exist very well without the Theater Guild audience; I wonder whether that audience can exist as well without variety."[9] It is almost as if Seldes had sprung from some Jacksonian myth or as if he were re-creating a Rousseau argument about the natural appeal of spontaneity over calculated high art. Whatever the reason, his analysis of the demands of the medium were echoed by actual participants. Sophie Tucker, for example, years after her halcyon days in vaudeville remembered the importance of timing. She insisted that it was crucial to open with a bright song to get the attention of the audience, to follow with a dramatic one to arouse interest, and to top off with a novelty number for laughs followed by a fast rag to milk applause.

Most acts played against standardized scenery, though

various kinds of stage backdrops were used to offset acts of specific types. One-man and two-man acts played before the drawn curtain, thus allowing time for scenery changes on the stage behind. Standardized sets included a cloth drop woodland scene, a three-dimensional room set, a center-door set simulating the entrance to a pretentious house, and a parlor, office, and kitchen set with variations. Vaudeville was the first mass-produced medium, and while it retained certain individual idiosyncrasies, it also embraced standardized formats.

As we have seen, vaudeville entrepreneurs were beset by the fear that someone in the audience might be offended by certain types of material, although it is important that this did not extend to ethnic material. Yet, during the forty years of vaudeville supremacy, there were enormous changes in the country which were reflected by the medium. Urbanization, the influx of immigrants radically different in culture, the industrialization of the nation's economy, and increased overall complexity characterized the America of vaudeville. One scholar has described the importance of vaudeville in helping American society to accommodate these changes and of its symbolic significance in interpreting ideas of success to the audience.[10] Certainly, one of the driving forces of the medium was its quest for respectability, and this drive is exemplified in its business methods, the design and decoration of theaters, the growth of a star system, the inclusion of longer productions on the bill, and the presentation of performers from the legitimate theater.

The style of humor grew more sophisticated and less explicit as urbanization increased, but vestiges of the earlier style remained. No act exemplified rough-house comedy more than Weber and Fields, whose humor included assorted bits of mayhem. Ethnic comedians who appeared as either Dutch/German or Jewish characters, Weber and Fields existed on a routine of choking, sticking fingers into eyes, stomping on sore feet, and so forth. One contemporary 1915 commentator fell back on human nature arguments in explaining vaudeville humor, insisting that while these antics produced laughter, human nature insisted that the victims of the attack not really be hurt, thus anticipating the Tom and Jerry cartoon of the 1940s.[11]

Violent bodily affrontery was a stable theme in vaudeville humor. George M. Cohan in 1913 shrewdly noted that things that made people laugh in vaudeville routines would make them "probably ashamed of doing so" if "they saw them described in print."[12] He went on to list such sure-fire laugh-getters as whacking a man on the back in the cause of friendship; whacking a woman, thinking she was a man; stepping on a sore foot; taking away the chair a bundle-laden man is about to sit on; imitating the walk of the person ahead; stumbling over a rug; being intoxicated and showing it; leaving an argument and bending inward to avoid the expected kick in the seat; defying a wife thinking mistakenly that she is not there; repeatedly failing to light a cigar; and so forth. His was a litany of frustration and humiliation of the broadest sort which yet fit the definition of good taste and passed the tightest kind of censorship. Perhaps an American morality which found violence acceptable but sexuality censorable pervaded vaudeville as it would later pervade popular entertainment media.

Much of the humor was based on a kind of human debasement which must have been closely attuned to the perceptions of the observers. George M. Cohan went on to judge that the Weber and Fields business of poking the finger in the eye was "worth a large fortune in itself," yet Cohan observed that this sort of humor was based on "inflicting of pain." He felt that pain at a not serious level had elements of the ridiculous and that in presenting this kind of situation "the stage merely mirrors life itself"—noting that a person falling on ice often provokes laughter in the beholder.[13] The pain that was the basis of much humor to Cohan's shrewd eye was manifested in certain dominant themes and settings. He believed that "nothing blatantly suggestive shall be treated," thus censoring not only profane words but clear sexuality itself. Brett Page, in a 1915 book on writing for vaudeville, lists the following themes "of universal interest": politics, love, marriage, woman's dress, woman's suffrage, drink, husbands, and money.[14] He presents these as the surest basis for writing interesting and successful material. Two characters held up as sure-fire vaudeville material are the fool and the sucker; in the former case laughs result from someone being made to seem a fool, in the latter case from an expectant "sure-winner" losing out.

Many acts used music, and the prime source of their music was the Tin Pan Alley publishing houses. Performers would often come to publishers seeking new material. The publishers had special house pianists who played their latest material for the actors, and special arrangements in terms of royalties or putting an actor's picture on the cover of sheet music could often be worked out. Before the coming of radio and to some extent large-scale record distribution, vaudeville was the chief means of merchandising popular songs.

The search for fresh material and the revamping of old routines was a constant problem. Vaudeville was not nearly so ubiquitous a consumer of material as were television and radio later. Many acts used the same material in their acts for years. For example, Gallagher and Shean featured one tune for years that became so famous that hundreds of people sent them verses, including one professor at a Big Ten university, who sent some fifty versions of the rhymes they tossed back and forth in their act. Jack Pearl, who played comic dialect characters, gained his greatest fame as the German Baron Munchausen on radio and resented the fact that audiences anticipated that he would do nothing but German comedy.[15]

Topical material was a staple from the beginning, and more

than one artist testified to his careful perusal of the newspaper for possible items. Even the circumspect Tony Pastor made references to the current issues of working men and to female fashions. The average vaudeville bill was a balanced affair, as noted previously, but the array of specialties was staggering. Kid acts were prominent, particularly those of Gus Edwards, who featured a large company of child actors in large-scale musical productions he had written himself. From his shows came many of the later headliners of vaudeville.

Fred and Adele Astaire began as a kid dance act touring the small time with their mother. Ned Wayburn, perhaps the preeminent dance director of the period, wrote a baseball act for them for $1,000, and they opened it in Proctor's Theater. However, they ran afoul of the upright and respectable Gerry Society, which was formed to guard against cruelty to children. But it was not the Gerry committee which forced Fred Astaire's temporary retirement since he lied about his age, as did many others; it was the coming of that awkward age at which a temporary retirement to school became necessary.

Rough acts with much banging about lasted to the very end, as did magicians and escape artists. None of the latter added more mystery and excitement than the immortal Houdini, who would be immersed headfirst in a tank of water, arms and legs tied, and emerge with dry hair after being placed behind a screen.

There were acrobats, blackface dancers and singers, monologists, drawers of sand pictures, bird imitators, cartoonists, and female impersonators. Fred Allen recalled one female impersonator who, in taking his final bow, removed a wig to reveal a male haircut, then removed that to reveal another female wig, which was in turn removed to reveal a male haircut again.[16]

There were violinists, animal acts, ventriloquists, bicyclists, strong men, and "nut" acts like that of the famed Ed Wynn, who invented eleven-foot poles for people you wouldn't touch with a ten-foot pole. Other bizarre antics included the strong violinist who performed on his instrument while an English bulldog hung from his bowing elbow. Another musical martyr played the piano upside down with the instrument on his stomach while his back was arched. A renowned monologist worked with a singing goat. Another innovator gained fame by dancing on a xylophone by which he rendered the tune danced to. Perhaps the most bizarre of all the animal acts was one in which those natural enemies, cats and rats, performed tricks together.

11.

The Ethnic Immigrant as Object of Humor

Post-Civil War America saw the beginning of the rough-house variety theater and its transformation into polite, big time vaudeville. It also coincided with the reappearance of dandyism in men's clothing styles and a certain behavioral laxness in theater audiences. As late as the first decade of the twentieth century, *Variety* would campaign for an end to rowdyism in the vaudeville theater. Vaudeville comedy was socially sanctioned fun-making. It was often directed at minority populations, and it grew in intensity as new immigrants began to settle in American cities. The urbanization of racial humor was a hallmark of the late nineteenth century. However, even before the big influx of new immigrants, blacks provided a focus for the comedy, as they had since minstrel days. The Irish, who were largely urban and had been coming to America in large numbers since the turbulent potato famine days of the early nineteenth century, provided another. Ironically, many of the actors who promoted the stereotypes were themselves from the group in question. But, from the earliest beginnings of variety, vaudeville acts reflected and re-enforced Irish, Black, Jewish, Dutch-German stereotypes, to name a few.

131

These highly visual images were referred to as "stock characters." An Irishman wore chin whiskers and a plug hat, jigged, and drank whiskey from a hip flask; German-Dutch comedians wore big stomachs, checked pants, chin whiskers, derby hats, and blond hair, and spoke frightfully misconstrued English; the Jews wore hooked noses, walked in a shuffle, rubbed their hands together in anticipation of a good deal, wore battered derbies jammed down on their heads, and made frequent references to the tailoring trade making the pants too long. The blacks depending on whether they were urban or rural, wore super-duds or tattered overalls, walked in a shuffle, spoke malapropisms and moved slowly but with grace. A popular nonracial stereotype was the tramp comic who represented the underside of American life in a comic way; so famous a performer as W. C. Fields broke in using this kind of material. All of these characters wore highly exaggerated makeup to insure audience identification and build expectations. Their clothes, makeup, and manners provided stereotypes which the audience easily recognized.

Of course, with passing time and growing sophistication, most of the stereotypes grew less obvious and heavy-handed. Yet, as late as 1915, Brett Page's guidebook on vaudeville insisted that while stock racial characters had been heavily used, there was still plenty of material left in them for laughs. While obvious and blatant cruelty may not have been the purpose of ethnic humor, and even though at least some of the presentations seem to have approximated good-humored jesting, the humor did accomplish something in the eyes of the middle-class audience. The effect was to dismiss them as less than human and to make it problematic that the real travail of ethnic immigrants and American blacks could be dealt with in any natural or realistic way at this time.[1] Perhaps a parallel can be found in American naturalist writer Jack London. Concerned with the sufferings of the lower classes and eager to depict their plight as realistically as he could, London was nonetheless a racist without parallel, as his writing on the black boxing champion Jack Johnson clearly establishes. These strangers and native blacks were like Chaplin's little tramp at a society party—out of place, out of step, and out of order.

Some ethnic people objected to the portrayals on the vaudeville stage, but Joe Laurie, Jr., an ex-vaudevillian who compiled an encyclopedic record of vaudeville trivia, noted there were no pressure groups and no successful third generations to feel ashamed of immigrant origins at the height of these presentations.[2] Laurie chronicled the progression of ethnic humor in tracing the development of the "two-man" act, which entailed two males performing comic dialogs with added songs and dancing. The originals were blackface comics who actually tried to look and sound authentic, but they were followed by acts made up of a blackface comic and a white straight-man. Then came acts doing Irish, Dutch, German, and Hebrew comedy. The final development of this genre was Italian comedy. The billings were significant: "The Sport and the Jew," "Irish by Name but Coons by Birth," "The Merry Wop," and "Two Funny Sauerkrauts."[3]

Laurie's work is significant since he combed the files of *Variety* and culled from it representative paradigms of typical vaudeville material. The reviews of the famed vaudeville critic Epes W. Sargent, who wrote under the name Chicot, corroborate the authenticity of Laurie's material. Ethnic references and characterizations were everywhere, often in quite unexpected places. Thus, in a typical school sketch, the characters were: "Tony-Italian," "Abey Maloney Goldstein—Jewish Boy," and "Rastus Johnson—Colored Boy."[4]

In addition to being clearly identified by his stereotyped costume, a stock Irishman was robust, combative, and belligerent. Ever ready with his fists, he struck out at his partner, sometimes throwing bricks. Often drunk and making frequent references to Saturday night drinking bouts followed by highly enjoyed fisticuffs, the stage Irishman was almost invariably a manual worker and often as not itinerant. In common with plantation blacks, he was devil-may-care and irresponsibly happy despite his confinement to the hard world of a coal miner, hod carrier, bog-digger, railroad worker, or street apple-seller. He was, in short, representative of the newly urban pro-letarian, and his material often made reference to labor disputes.

One Irish act noted that:

> Oh we are two rollicking roving Irish gentlemen,
> In the Pennsylvania quarries we belong.
> For a month or so we're working out in Idaho,
> For a month or so we're striking rather strong.
>
> Oh we helped to build the elevated railway,
> Oh the steamboats we ran for many a day,
> And it's divvil a hair we care the kind of work we do,
> If every Saturday night we get our pay.[5]

One of the most popular of the Irish variety acts sang this song depicting nomadic, carefree, irresponsible workers happy with their lot at a time when in real life the Molly Maguires were striking the mines. Variety patrons received a message at variance with the deadly conflict over the rights of labor, often largely Irish immigrant labor, being fought out in the coal fields. If this made the image of the conflict more sooth-ing, it was at a considerable price.

Another popular Irish act of the post-Civil War period opened with two stock players selling apples. In their song they referred to themselves as "so happy, light, and airy," boasting that "with the shovel we're dandies" and that "now we have an easy job" even though both were "Irish Knights of Labor."[6] Strikes were frequently mentioned in this kind of material, but they were treated in ways which tended to defuse feelings and mislead people as to their actual potential for ex-plosive violence in this period when Irish workers were find-ing the going very difficult indeed.[7]

Stock Irish situations invariably turned on drinking, brawling, and heavy labor. Laurie recounts a typical storytelling act in which one of the characters shouts inquiringly down a deep hole. A voice in Irish dialect answers that he is building a subway. When asked when it will be finished, the voice responds that it will take five years, whereupon the questioner allows that he will take the elevated train home. The story humor revolves not around concepts of Irishness but around the idea that a working-class situation necessitates an Irish dialect.

A storyteller act involving two Irishmen named "Pat and Mike," was among the most widely repeated formats in vaudeville. In one example, Pat visits his friend Mike who is ill in the hospital, but not before he has "stopped off in a few thirst emporiums." By the time he reaches the hospital, he has a "nice brannigan on," and he tells Mike a story of what happened to him in church on a recent Sunday. Mike keeps asking him to repeat the story, each time asking him to lean in a little closer, until Mike finally admits that it's not the story that interests him but Pat's breath, which is "like a whiff from heaven."[8]

Irish two-man acts involving a straight man and a comic were also usually in Pat and Mike style. They typically included self-deprecations, such as Pat insisting that he is a "Spanyard" and resenting being "taken for a Mick." After complaining about his treatment by a "Nagur" barber, Pat relates how he entered a "friend's salune." He ultimately learns that the grape skins he sees on the floor are really the eyes of patrons, and the owner remarks that "some of the byes had a fight here lasht night." Again, violence and love of fist fighting and mayhem were recurring themes.

Irish comedy dramatically exemplified the irony of interethnic rejection. In a Pat and Mike routine where Pat learns that of forty-one men killed in a gas works explosion, forty were "eyetileians" and only one Irish, he moans "Oh, the poor man." In another act, ethnic conflict is coupled with violence when Pat notes that he has been insulted by some "dagoes". When Mike makes insulting remarks about Pat's tormentors, Mike silences him with the admonition that he not speak ill of the dead.[9]

There were great Irish vaudevillians, among them George M. Cohan and his family who made up a famed foursome. Later he played the musical comedy stage with great success. Pat Rooneys made up three generations of famous vaudeville singers and dancers; the last of them played an old man in the 1950s musical *Guys and Dolls*. Even the first Rooney sang a song which spoke of his being "a day laboring man" and made light of his daughter's debut in a ballet under the outlandish name of "Mamselle Lashorty." He scoffingly declared that her name was really "Bridget McCarthy." Yet the first Rooney would plaintively wish in another song that all policemen were Irish, that St. Patrick's Day could be the Fourth of July, that somehow he could make the laws and help the cause of the working man. In short, in an era when shops put out signs reading "No Irish need apply," the plight was acknowledged, but vaudeville did little to create empathy in its audiences.

With the coming of Pastor's policy of polite vaudeville, Irish acts became less rowdy but no more realistic. Pastor himself revealed certain decent sentiments; he is on record as having protested anti-Semitic statements by a newspaperman, but his policy did little to help the Irish image.

The song "Drill Ye Tarriers Drill" is now often seen as folk material, but was originally sung by Irish vaudeville teams, especially by one named the Four Emeralds. It refers to men working on a railway and in one line adjures "Drill, ye red micks, drill."[10]

In short, if you were a vaudeville theatergoer, you saw Irishmen as violent, drunken, and usually unmarried, caught in a world of physical labor, untrustworthy agitators, and happy irresponsibles. Despite the fact that Irish burlesques were sometimes hissed or egged off the stage and were sometimes even condemned by organizations of priests, the stereotype persisted well into the twentieth century.

There were many Jewish vaudeville actors, including some of the headliners of their times; but they did not all perform as "Jew comics." From the end of the Civil War to the turn of the century only a handful of dialect comics actually appeared, but their small numbers belied the popularity of their image in vaudeville theater. Most actors portraying comic Jews in this period seem themselves to have been Jewish. The arch-stereotype of a second-hand clothing dealer cum hock-shop owner was not widespread until this century. It would have made little sense at a time when the relatively few Jewish Americans were largely of German or much earlier Sephardic origin and were often upper class and highly educated.

Like the Irish, Jews had made noteworthy contributions to the winning of the Civil War, but their rapid acculturation was disrupted by the arrival in America of a radically different kind of Jew. After the late nineteenth century Jewish influx from Russia and the old Austro-Hungarian empire, the vaudeville stage projected a Jewish image at once crafty, cowardly, cringing, and whining. One of the earliest "Jew comics" sang a song about his love-to-be which began:

> Her father keeps a hock shop,
> With three balls on the door,
> Where sheeny politicians can be found.[11]

Unflattering epithets were common when the "Jew comics" had a real vogue in the 1890s, and the characteristic image was a slouching man in ill-fitting clothes with a derby jammed down over his ears and his beard brushed to a point. The typical demeanor was a woebegone expression set off by funereal music. Joe Welch, one of the most famous of these comics, would gaze at the audience and ask, "Maybe you tink

I'm heppy?" In his monologues Welch talked of his family,
of his fear of hoodlums and the courts, and of his business
ventures. Always the themes of business acumen, cheapness,
craftiness, and fear lay near the surface of the sadness.
One of Welch's famous stories gives an illustration. When
he and his son "Jakey" go to a restaurant, they find a fly in
Jakey's "zoop." Papa advises the son, "Eat your zoop and vait
till you com to the fly, den tell de vaiter and he'll bring you
another bowl of zoop for nothing"—thus turning misfortune
into advantage by unwholesome guile.[12]

The cringing gestures of the 1890s slowly gave way to a
stereotype of a hearty good-natured businessman, open-
hearted and less morose, but still crafty. A popular song from
the transitional period proclaimed the performer a "Bully
Sheeny man" who treated his customers "the very best I can"
in his clothing store "way down on Baxter Street" where it
was possible to buy clothes from him "awful cheap."[13] Joe
Laurie Jr. asserts that Jess Dandy was the comic who initiated
the newer Jewish vaudeville character, discarding the traditional make-up and clothing. Others soon followed suit, including the popular actors Sam Bernard, Barney Bernard,
Monroe Silver, Julian Rose, and Andy Rice.

Rice's character was typical, as he wore normal street
dress and affected only a slight accent. In one of his most famous monologues he discoursed about a wedding, a favorite
topic of these actors:

> There were two hundred in the grand march, we invited one
> hundred, expected eighty, so we ordered supper for fifty!
> The supper was a success, very little pushing. The hall was
> decorated with fifty shamrocks from an Irish ball the night
> before. They must have had a great time, because every
> chair in the place was broken! We had three detectives
> watch the presents, and my three brothers watched them!
> We had fine presents. Rosenblum sent his card, the tailor
> his bill, Mrs. Bloom a fruit bowl, cut-glass from a dollar to

ninety-eight cents! Stein, the crockery man, sent six little steins and could they eat! The wedding cake was made like a ship. The little Steins were left alone with it and they sunk the ship.[14]

Another transitional Jewish character comic was Ben Welch, a brother of the Joe Welch mentioned above. Carolyn Caffin, who was widely admired for having written a perceptive analysis of the vaudeville of her time in 1915, described Ben Welch's "shiftless, slouching, casual gait" and insisted that he made the audience feel that he was a real person. With his "bent knees and furtive stride" and his "crafty" smile, Ben Welch would assert that "anyman what's smater than I am I don't want to do no business with." Yet, Caffin found the character genial, smugly self-satisfied, and content, confident that if anything were to go wrong, he would turn it to his advantage.[15]

Ben Welch's monologues stuck to familiar territory. He noted the nice merchandise his suit was made of and then admitted that he acquired it in a restaurant from a patron who was "still eating." In a surprisingly contemporary vein he used to state that his seventeen year old boy "smoked Oakum," and that under that influence he purchased St. Louis. The audience was also told that the boy carried a "little silver pencil he sticks into his wrist," and that the last time that happened, he was elected governor. Topping off the monolog with a reference to stinginess he admitted that when his son stuck the pencil into his wrist, "I paid the rent."[16]

Probably the most prominent of the monologists was Julian Rose, whose most famous routine "Levinsky at the Wedding" was based on the situation of a man who had risen too fast. Levinsky resents a wedding invitation which tells him that his "presence" is requested because he misreads it to mean his "presents." A burlesque of manners has Levinsky comment that the hosts provided napkins which were even clean! He also refers to guests who are afraid to sit down because they

are wearing borrowed pants and ends by noting that Finnegan
was really not such a good fighter after all, since Levinsky,
his two brothers, and a couple of cousins nearly licked him,
thus perpetuating the brawling Irishman and the crafty Jew
at the same time.[17]

Joe Laurie Jr. reconstructed a two-man act called "The
Straight and the Jew" in which the Jewish character wore
traditional make up. The routine opened with a coward theme
in which the antagonist is Irish. When the straight man asks
"Mr. Cohen" why he is running, Cohen says that he is running
to "prevent two fellows from fighting." When asked who the
two are, he replies, "An Irishman and me."[18] An occasion
for evoking and at the same time ridiculing Jewish immigrant
aspirations arises when Cohen states that his boy is an eye
doctor. To the straight's observation that Cohen's son had
been a chiropodist, the immigrant replies with aplomb that his
son "began at the feet and worked his way up." After some
pessimistic wife and mother-in-law jokes, Cohen and the
straight man argue over a recent dinner at which the straight
claims that they had eaten ham while Cohen steadfastly maintains that the dish was salmon. References to Jewish dietary
rules were a staple of Jewish comedy for years; in one act,
Smith and Dale are lost and starving in the arctic when they
stumble on a ham which Smith excitedly and joyously claims
is a smoked salmon.[19]

After Jewish comics and actors had become leading performers, one noted vaudevillian asked his audience apolo-
getically, "What, me Jewish? I'm no more Jewish than Eddie
Cantor." One of Fanny Brice's most famous routines was of
a Jewish mama at the beach, carefully and ubiquitously super-
vising every move her children and husband make. For Fanny
Brice, the dialect was probably as foreign as it would have
been for an Irish Tammany politico, since her family came
from France. She picked up the Eastern European Jewish
accent from her life on the Lower East Side of New York. An

ironic note in the unflattering Jewish character comedy is that many of the managers and entrepreneurs were themselves Jewish.

Jewish character comedy carried with it a note of apology. It had none of the hearty, even aggressive self-proclamation that marked Irish comedy. There was an almost physical shrinking back from true encounter, a kind of subliminal stealth and fundamental dishonesty. The Irish character was not without its own apologies, but it had an outgoing pride and exaltation in sheer physicality that is totally lacking in the Jewish stage character. An Irish character was almost always seen as a horny-handed, hard-drinking, brawl-loving, manual worker who made no apologies for it; Jewish characters lived on the edges of society, in trades like tailoring or in a parasitic business venture like loan-sharking. In both, a vocabulary of derision was seen as fit for middle-class audiences.

12.

Vaudeville Images of Blacks and Women

The vaudeville stereotype of blacks proved to be more blatant and ironic than that of any other ethnic group. Other groups achieved a certain detente at the expense of self-respect, but no other group was more thoroughly excluded or paid a higher price for their partial acceptance. In the period after the Civil War, black performers were rare and generally unwelcome even in the rough-house variety shows of the beer halls and honky-tonks.

In his famous study *An American Dilemma,* Gunnar Myrdal states that opportunity is the most important prerequisite for achievement and that opportunity has simply not been there for black Americans in most fields. As late as 1929–30 only ninety-eight blacks were listed in *Who's Who,* and few of them had made their mark in science, business, or the military. Yet, the public image of entertainment gave the impression that this was not so.[1]

The popular notion that the entertainment media have provided an open channel for black achievement seems dubious in the light of the evidence. A number of outstanding black performers appeared in the vaudeville houses of the early twentieth and even late nineteenth centuries, but most images presented to the audiences were by whites wearing the make-up called "blackface." Blackface comics were very popular in the period after the Civil War, though blacks themselves rarely appeared in variety. Taking their cues from the minstrel stage, the popular image was of sentimental plantation blacks yearning for those secure and happy slavery days of loyally serving the old master. Many actors began in blackface, continuing to use the dialect speech of minstrel shows. As time passed, many dropped the dialect but retained the makeup. Joe Laurie, Jr. reports that there were some blackface acts which even did Jewish character material, or, as he put it, "told Hebe stories."[2]

Apparently, there was something that compelled young actors to use black makeup. Laurie says that it was possible to get away with more things in this makeup, that it signalled to the audience that something humorous was about to happen, and that it required little outlay for elaborate costumes.

Early blackface performers based their parodies of black preachers or black savants on white conceptions. One early blackface actor delivered political and scientific harangues repleat with pretentious delusions and pathetic misuse of common words. The image evoked naivete coupled with ignorance and even stupidity. One such act, billed as "The Watermelon Man," portrayed a shuffling, cringing, slow-moving, irresponsible plantation black man. The chorus of his song asserted "Oh, dat watermelon land of goodness" was where he wanted to go to die, to "jine de contraband chillun."[3]

An emerging stereotype of freed Blacks as contrasted with that of the loyal and simple old plantation hands was of a chicken-stealing, gin-drinking, razor-toting, crap-shooting, not-to-be-trusted irresponsible, who was unable to make any sort of contribution to his own advancement. This theme played primarily before Northern audiences in the variety theater, and it is important to note that even during the Civil War itself,

Northern sympathies for abolition were often either tepid or nonexistent. The draft riots of 1864 involved lynchings of blacks in New York, and the hostile reaction of Northern troops to black comrades-in-arms may have paved the way for acceptance of a Southern view of black people in vaudeville.

In make-up and in general social tone, the variety stage blackface acts were close to tramp acts in spirit and intent. On the other hand, some actors, among them the renowned minstrel Lew Dockstader, appeared in blackface but did not ape the prevailing white concept of black manners and outlook. They merely performed nonethnic material while attired in blackface. Blackface acts continued even after the Pastor revolution; indeed Pastor presented one on the very first bill he put together for polite vaudeville.

Black preacher acts, which featured pseudo-spirituals, appealed to polite vaudeville, and many popular white acts used such material. One member of a team would move and think slowly, while the other would be a lively, banjo-playing sport who provoked incredible misconceptions of reality from his naive partner. In one act, the feature-song lyrics pledged undying loyalty to a certain Protestant denomination which was then readily shifted for a bribe.

The most durable blackface act was that of the Caucasians McIntyre and Heath. They played virtually the same skit for some fifty years, beginning in the late 1870s. Typically, one of the team portrayed a shabby, genteel, loyal black, an update of the loyal plantation "darky," while the other was a newly urban "coon dandy," the assertive loud mouth. The social portraits ranged from servile to uppity and were characterized by comic derision, distortions, and broad caricatures.

The proliferation of blackface was remarkable, and any list of actors who used it would include Al Jolson, Lew Dockstader, Eddie Cantor, Jay C. Flippen, Frank Tinney, the Kaufman brothers, Jack Norworth, Sophie Tucker, and countless others. Norworth, who appeared later with his wife, Nora

Bayes, and wrote several standard popular songs, began as a monologist and singer in an act he called "The Jailhouse Coon."[4]

Caroline Caffin exemplified the sophisticated vaudeville critic's view in analyzing the blackface humor of Frank Tinney. Tinney, she wrote, came as "near to the genuine, native darky humor as any one of the blackface tribe," exemplifying "childish bashfulness and self-satisfaction." She noted his "artless confiding" as he revealed all of his personal affairs to an audience whose laughter baffled him. Tinney's character also used the obligatory shuffling gait and word twisting.[5]

Sophie Tucker avoided the mocking mannerisms that marked other blackface acts, but nonetheless she broke into vaudeville in that guise. Billed often as a "Coon shouter," she sang songs like "Rosie, My Dusky Georgia Rose," but in her finale would withdraw a glove revealing a white hand to the audience. Yet, her relations with black artists transcended those of most other performers of her time. As previously noted, Eubie Blake and Noble Sissle, who remembered her with great affection, sold her their first tune, "All Your Fault," when she appeared at the Maryland Theater in Baltimore. In addition, her greatest hit, "Some of These Days," was written by the black composer Shelton Brooks, who also penned "Darktown Strutter's Ball."

Brooks' work was brought to Sophie Tucker's attention by a black woman who toured with her for years as kind of maid-companion-counselor and who occasionally appeared in her act. Yet, when Sophie included this woman in her act, she noted that she was "toddlin as only colored people with their inborn sense of rhythm can," and her dialog included the line, "Here's yo' chair, honey chile." Tucker had the reputation of being more willing to use the material of black artists than most other whites in vaudeville, yet her remarks exemplify the tendency to see blacks in vaudeville stereotypes.[6]

In the last decade of the nineteenth century, black people

became a visible presence on the vaudeville stage. Although the old sentimentality remained in the form of the "mammy" characters which came to prominence at this time, new materials and new ideas also become popular. The coon song, popularized both by vaudeville actors and by the new record industry, developed certain major themes; according to Gunnar Myrdal, these most often included chicken theft, wife beating, and razor slashing.[7] But changing conditions were symptomized by the first all-black touring show, *The Creole Show*. It was modeled on minstrels and debuted in 1891; it played throughout the country for five years. The playlet *Octeroon*, first presented in 1895, departed from the minstrel image in a significant way by dealing with the previously forbidden topic of sex among black people. Usually, black material excluded sexuality and love songs as subjects for white audiences.

The 1890s were noteworthy for another harbinger of change—the first black vaudeville star. His name was Charlie Case, and he was so light skinned that, like Bert Williams after him, he donned blackface makeup. Born in Lockport, New York, of a black mother and an Irish father, he was widely regarded as a great monologist. Arthur Hopkins, a noted producer of the period, asserted that Case was the "greatest master of unexpected statement in the world."[8] Writing and performing his own material, Case was an exceedingly sensitive man who played most of the great vaudeville circuits of his day, though he received relatively small salaries and was much put upon as a pioneer. Part of the legend that surrounds him is the claim that a lukewarm audience response would throw him into deep depression.

Case concentrated on family affairs, the theme again being self-deprecation; for example: his father was a "peculiar man," a mystery to his children but understood by his wife, who could always tell when he had been "skidding." His father was "a great one for finding things," having picked up and brought home what turned out to be an armload of wood. He explained that his father did not mean to take anyone's property, that in fact the family already had a great deal of wood "just like it."[9]

By 1910, Case was appearing without blackface on the Loew's Circuit, explaining that there were "so many blackface comics around." Although there is no record of the content of this act, the symbolism of it is still intriguing. Case died of an accidental self-inflicted gunshot wound. With little choice and almost no space for action, Case evoked a black image that whites could accept, as did many talented men who followed him.

Between 1890 and 1917, some black entertainers attempted to slough off the prevalent vaudeville caricature by turning to serious theater and musical composition. Scott Joplin, ragtime's greatest creator, thought of himself as a serious composer of significant and lasting music. James P. Johnson, that elegant master of Harlem Stride, likewise saw himself as a serious American composer and worked in longer musical forms, composing contatas and operas, few of which he ever saw performed. It is typical and ironic that Scott Joplin's opera *Treemonisha*, into which he poured much of his personal and financial resources, was never fully performed until some sixty years after it was written. At its first performance in Atlanta in 1972, Harold C. Schoenberg, a reviewer for the *New York Times*, rhapsodized over Joplin's splendid work. However, the world of early twentieth century America presented few possibilities for the recognition of black achievement. To be sure, here and there certain people had a flash of insight and were able to transcend the prevailing white stereotypes. However, such recognition often came from Europeans. For example, Ernest Ansermet had high praise for the clarinet and saxophone playing of Sidney Bechet during his 1919 European tour with the orchestra of Will Marion Cook.[10]

In the early years of this century, several black acts became prominent on the white vaudeville circuits. Trade papers reported that by 1907 there were some 270 black principals of 1,450 performers in vaudeville.[11] Even before the turn of the century, black vaudevillians like Sam Lucas had played Loew's Circuit, Billy Kersands had done his dance routines, and Tom McIntosh and his wife toured in comedy sketches and rough house. In 1897 Ernest Hogan introduced the cakewalk, which quickly became a national craze. Then, as later, vaudeville nourished other theatrical forms; Sam Lucas played the part of "Uncle Tom," touring as the only black in an otherwise all-white company.

The most memorable and in many ways the most gifted black vaudevillian of this period was Bert Williams. With his partner, George Walker, he triumphed in vaudeville tours and musical comedies, some of which the partners wrote themselves. Williams capped his success with starring appearances in the Ziegfeld Follies.

Bert Williams was born in the Bahamas in 1876 and was so light that he had to perform his famous routines in black-face makeup. His family moved to mainland America, first to New York and later to California, where it is said he aspired to enter Stanford University. A bookish, articulate young man, who was interested in philosophy, Williams' vaudeville use of the Southern black dialect was as much an artificial acquisition as was Fanny Brice's use of Eastern European Jewish speech. As a boy he was an expert mimic of both people and animals and began his career as a banjoist in San Francisco honky-tonks, where he met George Walker. Williams had extensive experience in minstrel shows, and Walker had worked in medicine shows. The producer of a Victor Herbert musical discovered them doing a lobby act in an Indiana resort. He brought them East where a major part was written into the show for them.

The titles of the musical comedies the pair helped to shape were significant: *The Sons of Ham, In Dahomey, The Policy*

Players, Bandanna Land, and *Abyssinia.* The black musicians Will Vodery and Will Marion Cook wrote and arranged the music of the latter two.

The characters which Williams and Walker portrayed reinforced established stereotypes. Walker affected fast urban manners and flashy clothes; James Weldon Johnson described his stage character as a "sleek, smiling, prancing dandy."[12] Another writer saw the Walker character as "a sporting Negro, dressed a little too high, spending generously whatever he was able to borrow or filch."[13]

If the Walker character was a stereotype of an urban, restless, and assertive man, that of Bert Williams was, in part, a continuation of the image of unenlightened innocence. One writer remembered him as "mournful and melancholy, quaint and philosophical" with the "discouraged shoulders, shambling gait and stumbling dialect of the ignorant Southern Negro."[14] James Weldon Johnson characterized the Williams image as a "slow-witted, good natured, shuffling darky."[15] And yet there was something in Bert Williams which always lay between laughter and tears even in his stage character. His fate was to be "lazy, careless, unlucky," a man for whom "everything went wrong."[16] In one of their typical routines, the wily Walker tried to beguile the gullible Williams into attempting a bank robbery. After some recondite dialog, Williams showed that he had, after all, caught on since he refused, insisting that "you can't smell no flowers through a stone wall."[17] Williams had a distinguished career apart from Walker; he continued as a single act after his partner's death in 1911 until his own untimely death some ten years later. Williams assumed this naive and innocent theatrical image with great reluctance. The traits he portrayed were foreign to his personality and experience, but he would retain them to the end.

For all his world-wide success, Williams remained saddled with the essential character epitomized by his song from his first musical show, *Sons of Ham.* The song was entitled "I'm a Jonah Man," and Williams could never really escape the confines of that identification. When he joined the Ziegfeld Follies in 1910 at the invitation of Abe Erlanger, the cast threatened to strike; the threat disappeared when they saw how well Williams' comedy went over with the audience. Williams was not the only black actor to feel the lash of a white boycott. The famed dancing team of Irene and Vernon Castle used the dance orchestra of Jim Europe as their accompanists for an engagement at Hammerstein's, but the house musicians refused to have black musicians in the pit, whereupon the Castles performed with their orchestra joining them on the stage.

Traveling with an all-white show in those perilous times was a trying venture for the sensitive Williams, but Ziegfeld supported Williams, as did Will Rogers. However, the consciousness levels were less acute than they are today and there was little to challenge an audience's acceptance of pet prejudices. Resigned to his fate, Williams always used the service entrance in hotels.

In 1904, Williams gave a command performance for King Edward VII of Great Britain. During rehearsals, Williams became flustered because so many visitors from the royal palace were in the way. In untypical anger, he chastised a stout gentleman in a red vest who turned out to be the king himself. Later, the easygoing, accessible monarch joked with the actor about the incident, and Williams said, rather poignantly, "I was grateful that the thing had happened to a monarch with such a sense of humor, that we were not in Georgia or Texas under similar circumstances."[18]

In one of his popular songs he sang a kind of preacher's stump speech, familiar in vaudeville routines. During his sermon, Parson Johnson sniffs the air and detects the aroma of gin. He entreats in his song:

Brother, if you want more preachin', save a little dram
for me. From that smell it is plain to see somebody here's
holdin' out on me.[19]

W. C. Fields said of Bert Williams, "He was the funniest
man I ever saw and the saddest man I ever knew."[20] In private clubs when he would lean in easily and begin to tell his
stories to enthralled circles of acquaintances, he would pause
first to ask, "Are we all Negroes here?"[21] It is reported that
Ring Lardner felt Williams was uncomfortable in the *Follies*
and that writers did not know how to give him the proper
settings or material. Hiram Brown, later an important film
executive, insisted that Williams' "high talents were largely
wasted," and in an unusual insight for the time he observed
that "somehow or other, laughing at Bert Williams came to
be tied up in people's minds with liberation, charity, and the
thirteenth amendment."[22] It was peculiarly fitting that Williams after 1905 opened his act with the song "Nobody." Perhaps more than any of his other material this song, with its
poignant references to loneliness and oppression, revealed the
private man in the public spotlight.

Not all blacks in vaudeville appeared on stage. Some, like
Will Vodery, wrote songs and conducted pit orchestras. According to the famed Harlem stride pianist Willie "The Lion"
Smith, Vodery was Ziegfeld's music director and wielded
dictatorial control over things musical in several Follies productions. Later, Vodery was a staff arranger for Fox movie
studios.

Other Blacks appeared on the vaudeville stage in Bert Williams' time and after. Some appeared in relatively neutral settings, performing as wire walkers, fiddlers, ventriloquists, and
so forth. Ernest Hogan, a comedian and composer, was said
to have changed the comic black image in a more Harlequin
direction. Yet, Hogan featured a song called "All Coons Look

Alike to Me," which James Weldon Johnson called a "byword and epithet of derision."[23]

Probably most renowned after Walker and Williams was the team of Bob Cole and J. Rosamund Johnson. They toured large cities with their own company and wrote musical plays; their bookings included Proctors' leading New York theater. Here, too, there were elements of self-derision. Cole wrote a musical which broke with the minstrel tradition and thereby extended the development of American musical theater, but it was nonetheless entitled *A Trip to Coontown*. Together these touring vaudevillians pioneered in writing the first black operettas, *The Shoofly Regiment* and *Red Moon*.

Florence Mills, who died young, started as a "pickaninny" in a black act; later she starred with her sister on the Pantages Circuit and shortly before her death was the featured performer in *Shuffle Along*, the all-black musical success written by Eubie Blake and Noble Sissle. Miller and Lyles, another well-known vaudeville act, wrote and starred in *Shuffle Along*.

A few black artists made big salaries. Buck Washington and John Bubbles, the famous Buck and Bubbles of vaudeville, toured the circuits at $1,750 per week in the late 1920s. Bubbles would gain immortality in the theater as the first Sportin' Life in Gershwin's *Porgy and Bess*.

Many black vaudeville actors had connections with jazz and ragtime and developed and popularized new dances. Some great blues singers, for example, Bessie Smith, Ma Rainey, and Ethel Waters, toured in vaudeville. By the 1920s with vaudeville in full swing, Harlem innovations became popular. New actors broke in; among them was the popular dancer Bill "Bojangles" Robinson, whose funeral parade would wind down Broadway in the late 1940s past the Palace Theater, then a movie house, lighted up in his honor.

On the subject of black ethnicity, Joe Laurie, Jr.'s distillate of typical vaudeville acts is highly instructive. In the typical monolog act a story is included about a "colored girl" who announces that she is getting married. When she admits that she has no beau, she explains that she is going to marry someone she met at a funeral, in fact the "corpse's husband," who claimed that she was "the life of the funeral."[24]

A standard black act was that of a stump speaker (whom Laurie describes as an "old colored preacher"), who carries a large book under his arm which he slams each time he makes a point. He opens his sermon singing the following lyrics to the tune of "St. Louis Blues."

> Ashes to Ashes
> Dust to Dust
> If the black gals don't get you
> The high yallers must.[25]

Laurie discusses a typical ventriloquist who worked with two dummies, one Irish, one black. The ventriloquist and the Irish dummy toss insults back and forth until a "Negro voice" is heard coming from a small box. The Irish dummy says, "The Naigur wants to get out." The ventriloquist exclaims, "Why I'm surprised at you calling him a Naigur. His name is Sambo. He is the same kind of little man that you are; only he is of the colored race and you are of the white race." The Irish dummy then called the black one "Eight-ball" and is in turn called "Irish," whereupon they fight and are separated by the ventriloquist. When the black dummy starts to tell of an incident at his house, the Irish dummy says, "You don't live in a house, you live in a tree." Sambo goes on unperturbed: "We were going to have company in our house and Pappy started scratching his head and I said, 'Guess the company has arrived' so we had to kill the company."[26]

Like the ventriloquist, double blackface acts were typical vaudeville presentations. The stage directions describe one actor as the "tall, lanky, nigger type," his mate as the "small, dumpy, nigger type." The tall is the straight, his partner the comedian. They make their entrances to Bert Williams' "Nobody." In the course of the dialog, supposedly comic stuff, they talk about being "sick from eatin' too much watermelon." The straight comments that "There ain't no such thing as too much watermelon. Nigger, you ain't got enough stomach, that's all." Later the comic talks about the straight's "gal" as being black. The straight replies that "when she stands beside you, you look like a bottle of milk," and goes on to say that "she calls me chocolate" to which the straight replies that if the comic is "chocolate," he must be "licorice." After this dialog the comic misreads numbers for letters, which leads the straight to remark, "You just plain ignorant; you kaint spell nor nothin." When the straight asks the comic where he spends most of his time, the reply is "jail." When the comic and the straight dispute the truth of one another's assertions, during the course of the argument they call each other "nigger," "black cloud," "baboon," "midnight," "boy," and "big mouth."[27]

Most of these routines played before white middle-class audiences in the lead houses of the big time, but there was an all-black vaudeville circuit called the Theater Owners Bookings Association, or TOBA. A suggestion of what life was like on the TOBA may be gleaned from the wry inside claim of what the letters really stood for—"Tough on Black Actors."

TOBA existed for some twenty years between the world wars. Most of the houses were in the South, but a few existed in larger Northern cities like New York, Philadelphia, and Chicago. Hundreds of black actors found work on this circuit, and some thought it a proving ground for talent and a temporary meal-ticket. Its material ranged from the ubiquitous blackface comedy to one-act plays. Like the big time, there were tumblers, ventriloquists, magicians, comics, singers, dancers, and so on. Bessie Smith played the circuit, as did Ma Rainey and Ethel Waters. If the problems faced by blacks in the United States were mentioned at all on the

TOBA, it was in terms which a white audience might not have understood.

If the Irish, Jews, and other immigrant types were an alien presence in the dominant culture, blacks were the domestic strangers—pariahs and outcasts from white society. For each immigrant vaudeville character it was necessary to signal a presence to the audience by means of an absurdly stylized costume. In blackface comedy, the image was simple and direct. Yet, it is important to note that many black actors did comedy in blackface, and not always because of lightness of skin. It was as if the intention was not to risk lack of recognition on the part of the audience.

Recognition was not a major problem for black actors or for white acts in blackface. The black image was both in accord with a historic tradition and a comfort to a white middle-class society reluctant to face the moral realities of race prejudice in America. Most vaudeville humor about black life tended to dismiss blacks as being less than human beings and to deny them mutuality of feeling and experience with the audience. It discounted the possibilities of black leadership, as for example in the case of the "colored preacher" stump speech. W.E B. duBois, as long ago as 1903, wrote of the importance of the black churches to ethnic survival,[28] but the figure of the black preacher in vaudeville was a caricature of ineptitude, pretense, and personal corruption.

Bert Williams' life exemplified the notion that black vaudeville actors lived at two levels; but the schizophrenic nature of such existence was acknowledged only under the most secure circumstances. When Bert Williams asked if all those present were "Negroes" before continuing with his stories, he was expressing something he never could to whites, even those who had been the most solicitous of his well-being.

Employment at the expense of self-esteem was the price of a job in vaudeville just as surely as it was of a job as a pliant servant in a white home. But there was an essential difference. Richard Wright and James Baldwin wrote of secret ways of getting even that were open to recalcitrant restaurant workers or servants,[29] but such revenge was not possible in the vaudeville theater except by the use of secret language or the most subtle of comments. Williams' moments of honesty voiced the inner strains of his double life and the wrenches that his dual existence must have caused.

The institutional doors were closed to blacks in employment, education, and labor unions. For example, it was not possible for them to mount the kinds of protest the Irish did, nor were they able to acquire the economic base and what that came to mean in terms of personal security and community acceptance that was open to Jewish immigrants. The portrayal of black people in vaudeville, the roles they played, the materials used, and the bargaining position they were in, all tend to affirm their experience in the society at large.

It is difficult to make a definitive assessment of the impact of vaudeville on American attitudes toward ethnicity. Certainly, it would not be too much to assert that ethnic material was the most common type of vaudeville comedy. It was everywhere. Yet, more needs to be known about the actual materials themselves and about thematic frequency. Perhaps the chief problem is the difficulty of recreating the views held by millions of people three to ten decades ago. The problems of historical generalization seem especially formidable in the special case of a mass audience.

It seems true that the new and the strange were grist for the vaudeville mill. Simply to be different was to open up the possibilities of being demeaningly funny. To depart from middle-class speech, food habits, or work patterns was to become a possible subject for comic derision. Thus, in addition to the black, Jewish, Irish, German, or Dutch characters, the tramp and the rube figures were favorite targets.

Rube comic characters performed in rural clothes complete

with farm hat, overalls tucked into boots, and a straw in the mouth—naive victim of the city slicker. However, in time these characters became more sophisticated, and the updated Rube upholding rural integrity became a Palm Beach suit wearing, wise-cracking farmer who turned the tables on city slickers.

By contrast, the tramp figure remained pretty much unchanged over the years. Perhaps the most renowned tramp actor was Nat Wills. Carolyn Caffin saw this character as "happy, tattered, slovenly, red-nosed," a "rogue, glorifying in his detestation of work and water and gaily oblivious of the rights of property."[30] Could anti-middle-class values have been put more succinctly? Wills' tramp lied because he loved to. Yet, even in his happy disregard for middle-class standards, the tramp also told darky stories. Wills' material included some of the most blatant and vicious material in all of vaudeville, including one story of a Southern colonel visiting a Canadian hotel. Upon asking for the "head nigger," he is informed that he is in the Queen's country now and that he should say "colored gentleman." Upon announcing that all he wants to do is give the "head nigger" a large tip, he easily wins agreement, and all objections melt.[31]

Vaudeville material seems to have reaffirmed the ideas and concerns of those who came first to America. Vaudeville seems to have made the goal of acculturating ethnic peoples more difficult, stressing ethnic inferiority as it did.

The situation evokes a dilemma faced by Richard Wright in his youth. Asked to settle a disputed statement by two white bosses, he realizes that anything he says will cost him his job. There simply was no place to go.[32] Bert Williams' fate is another perfect example. He was beloved by Will Rogers, empathized with by the irascible W. C. Fields, and employed and protected by Florenz Ziegfeld, but he still felt the mark. Never was he to be a member of vaudeville's inner-circle social clubs.

The case of women in vaudeville has yet to be researched, but certainly the material about women underscored standard sexist attitudes. Women were either objects of sexual curiosity or wifely ogres. Most awful of all was the image of mothers-in-law, and women's suffrage was a sure-fire topic for comedy. The fact that the material was funny to middle-class mass audiences might constitute a parallel to ethnic comedy in the extent of the deprecation. What is not clear is the extent to which women collaborated in the presentation of the image.

Vaudeville offered genuine opportunity to many women. From the start women were headliners, and the earliest English music hall companies touring here included women. By the turn of the century, women singles were much sought after. Vesta Victoria, who came from the English music halls, was an early star, and within two decades many women head-lined; one of them, Kate Smith, set two records for long runs at the Palace Theater.

By no means were the leading female acts merely cowed pawns in the hands of male managers; often they were tempestuous, arrogant, and jealous of their rights. Some acted as their own managers. None exemplified female power more than Nora Bayes, who fought for every stage right and courtesy, argued for salaries and billing, and generally won. Married for a time to her stage partner, Jack Norworth, Nora Bayes wrote material with him including the popular tune "Shine on Harvest Moon." Her billing at this time featured her name in large letters under which would be the phrase, "Assisted and admired by Jack Norworth" in much smaller print.

Lilly Langtry, Elsie Janis, Eva Tanguay, Irene Franklin, Marilyn Miller, Marie Dressler, Fanny Brice, and Sophie Tucker occupied important places on the vaudeville stage, and in that rough-and-tumble world of fighting for prerogatives, they often out-maneuvered the management. Their popularity gave them economic and political leverage. It is hard to think of another area in which women were able to wield this kind of power or where they attained comparable opportunities for their talents.

By 1927, Sophie Tucker, for example, played the Pantages Circuit at $5,000 a week. Sophie Tucker exemplified the grit and determination of vaudeville women. As a star, she exhibited a powerful ego that could compete in a world of tough business values. After her appearance in the *Ziegfeld Follies of 1909,* she said that "those hard-boiled first-nighters liked Sophie Tucker and wanted more of her." Sophie said it all when she vowed that "it's up to you to protect yourself."[33] In the transitional free-enterprise-cum-monopoly economy of vaudeville, women often did as well as the men. Tucker herself said that the biggest star of her vaudeville days was Eva Tanguay, who received $5,000 per week.[34]

Despite clear antecedents in France and England, vaudeville as a popular form of entertainment flourishing from the 1880s until the depression of the 1930s was distinctly, even hopelessly American. In its form, content, and processes it both reflected and reinforced basic tendencies of American thought and action, concomitantly reflecting transformations in American life. Beginning as a frontier and itinerant form of entertainment, inchoate in form and largely whimsical in structure, it followed the centralizing tendencies of America and emerged by the turn of the century as a highly organized, differentiated, standardized, and centrally controlled form of mass entertainment. Vaudeville would have been unthinkable without urbanization, big business monopoly, mass transportation, the American ideal of getting ahead, big-scale immigration, the appearance of identifiable ethnic minorities in urban centers, the emancipation of women, the freeing of slaves, and the urbanward trek of rural immigrants.

It became a highly organized form of mass entertainment, yet, unlike film and radio-television, it was not removed from its audience. It was immediate and personal, particularly in the early days. Once the big business interests developed and the size of the theaters grew apace, a certain intimacy was lost, and performers who depended on subtle gestures were lost. Still, vaudeville was always live. Carolyn Caffin said, "It is this feeling of good-fellowship that makes the audience love to be on confidential terms with the performers, to be treated as an intimate."[35] Victor Moore once observed, "Vaudeville can never come back, as it was essentially an intimate theater, and in the big picture theaters of today, the vaudeville bills as we knew them would be lost."[36]

Vaudeville fell victim to several ills, and critics offer all kinds of opinions. Some say that the material finally grew thin and the humor seemed stale and finally vulgar. Others insist that an unending process of refinement finally undermined its spirit and vitality. Several long-time observers say that it faded because monopoly control and unwise management stifled originality. Yet, of all the villains perhaps the most deadly were technological inventions, particularly movies and radio.

Since early nickelodeon days, Marcus Loew and other small time vaudeville entrepreneurs had combined live acts with films. Later, the small time format of vaudeville acts plus a feature film turned around. By the 1920s many vaudeville houses were converting to film theatres, and the vaudeville circuits shrank in number. Two-a-day performances, the stock of big time vaudeville, changed to continuous performance, and even in the eastern part of the country, the one-time stronghold of the art, only about half a dozen big time theaters remained.

During this decline, Marcus Loew became dominant as he expanded his empire of film presentation houses. Keith-Albee joined with the Orpheum Circuit and Pathe Pictures. It eventually merged and finally disappeared in a deal engineered by Joseph P. Kennedy with Radio Corporation of America which led to the formation of the R.K.O. film studios. Even the National Vaudeville Artists, the company union formed in the ashes of the White Rats, became Hollywood oriented.

In many ways organized vaudeville was an outlet for repressed feeling. If suggestive material was censored after Pastors' time, still vaudeville institutionalized anomic insanity in its comedy and in the bizarre nature of its other offerings. In its institutionalization of the highly unusual and its dissemination of a vision of ethnic immigrant minorities and blacks, vaudeville mirrored American cultural anxieties. It was the first and only mass entertainment medium until the coming of radio. Vaudeville acts carried with them key messages about ethnic behavior, labor disputes, scandal, the draft, love, marriage, fidelity, promiscuity, war, and work.

Like their counterparts elsewhere in the world of entrepreneurship, the robber barons of vaudeville expressed the general business ethics of the community at large and viewed talent as an object to be manipulated for profit. Some critics, nostalgic for the earlier days before the coming of big business, noted the growing coldness which accompanied large scale organization.

Vaudeville was an opulent source of talent that nourished later mass media. A formidable list of vaudeville graduates performed in radio, television, the movies, musical comedy, and the legitimate stage. Pat Rooney, appearing in a brief vaudeville revival in the 1940s, called it the great "college" where artists learned their craft. This is not to say that live performances in theaters ended abruptly. On the contrary, throughout the 1930s and well into the 1940s, New York theaters like the Paramount and the Capitol, and even some in the smaller cities, featured name performers or big bands, though often in connection with a film. But the days of nine-act, two-a-day big time vaudeville were dead. The American mass media moved inexorably from the live to the canned, from the spontaneous to the planned.

Part Five

Baseball
and Urbanism

Frank Baker, "Home Run" Baker to the fans and managers, is feared by every pitcher who has the misfortune to face him on the diamond. One of the Athletics' best, he is known off the field as a gentleman.

—Baseball Card, 1910

13.

Urban Growth: The Brooklyn Case

Arsenic and Old Lace was a 1944 film derived from an earlier stage success. The plot depicted the doings of a group of people whose personalities exhibited various stages of dottiness. Two elderly sisters cured the problems of lonely old men by serving them poisoned elderberry wine, and the victims were subsequently buried in their basement by a nephew, who was convinced that he was Theodore Roosevelt laying aside Panama Canal yellow fever victims.

Another nephew viewed reality through the persistent means of a baffled double-take, while a third was a homicidal killer who had been remodeled by a dissolute plastic surgeon to look like Boris Karloff in one of his monster roles. The ambience, in short, was of old, settled ways that were eccentric, accepted, and cozy. The setting, however, was not a village, but pre-World War II Brooklyn, New York. The film's action takes place in a big, comfortable Victorian house with fumed oak panels and wide staircases. Even the dress of the aunts is village America.

The film opens with a prelude set in Ebbets Field. A game is in progress, and when the umpire calls a Dodger batter out, the stands dissolve into mayhem, people race onto the field, and unmitigated yet unfulfilled violence follows as even the hotdog vendor throws aside his portable stand and joins the melee. Suddenly there is a close-up shot of the umpire lying on his side, patiently drumming his fingers on the ground as the action takes place all about him. Clearly, this is old stuff to him as he quietly yet exasperatedly waits out yet another wild scene in Ebbets Field. As the scene dissolves to the emerging Manhattan skyline, a narrator says something like "meanwhile, in the United States proper, just across the river. . . ."

To be sure there were moments of high drama and mayhem in the real Ebbets Field; the legends about Brooklyn and its baseball team were folk-like, fanciful, and, above all, persistent. No other professional athletic enterprise approached the Dodgers as a source of material for sports writers, radio comics, vaudeville actors, and film writers. In a commercial-industrial urban society, the myth of the Dodgers persisted and was even reinvented and re-created when there may have been little basis for it in reality. Somehow the legend bespoke things that the American people yearned for or missed. Even the great teams of the late 1940s and early 1950s, which were assemblages of athletic talent often rated among the greatest in history, were referred to in the newspapers as the "Daffiness Boys" or "Dem Bums," references originating with the wacky teams of the 1920s and the dismal clubs of the 1930s.

The reception accorded Roger Kahn's book *The Boys of Summer* revealed that the aura of Brooklyn baseball still radiated warmly. The book was near the top of the best-seller lists for months; its author made appearances on television talk shows, and the players depicted were fetched from the obscurity of their civilian pursuits. It is doubtful that a book about the St. Louis Browns, the Boston Braves, or even the Philadelphia Athletics or the New York Giants would have provoked such a response. There was something about the

Brooklyn Dodgers that was different, something about the way the legend reflected cultural and social change that persisted in the American consciousness.

It is often claimed that Americans have been confounded by their cities, that dominant attitudes have been a mixture of awe and contempt. Urban history frequently tends to highlight knotty problems that defy resolutions. When Ernest Burgess reviewed some thirty years of sociology doctoral dissertations executed under his direction at the University of Chicago, he found major themes to be anomie and loss of community.[1] Sociologist Robert Park saw urbanity as a mask replacing personal relations and found that detached individuals found themselves enmeshed in problems foreign to village society.[2] For Lewis Mumford, the organizational design of the urban community kills spontaneity. He found a lost individuality in the city which suited the crowd while containing an uninhabitable inner core. Technological innovations swept human judgment aside to form a modern nightmare, and Mumford indicts the capitalist law of urban growth which obliterates all natural features and tends to despoil nature; he found that megalopolis gives rise to violence, to communication by advertising, to the bureaucratization of life decisions, to the inflation of land values, and to a physical congestion which catalyzes antisocial expression.[3]

Within this context, Louis Wirth, over a generation ago, wrote of the nervous tension of the city, of its racial segregation, of demographic separations by income and status, and of the decline in personal relations in cities. With the weakening of the sense of neighborhood, recreational services had to adjust to mass society.[4] If, as Wirth then suggested, urban life weakens the folk tradition, produces segmented roles, and replaces primary contacts with secondary ones, then perhaps it is in the popular culture phenomena, among them sports, that a whole people clings to a common experience. It is through sports, and more particularly, through the development, flowering, and demise of the Dodgers of Brooklyn, that we can glean some clues as to changes in the urban society of the period.

Baseball, or a sport very much like baseball, seems to have existed long before the alleged Abner Doubleday-Cooperstown invention, and its development as the "national game" paralleled the industrial and urban growth of the United States. It is in interplay with the developing features of mass society that baseball takes on its meaning as both a participatory and a passive experience for Americans. Lewis Mumford blames capitalism for the urban breakdown of local autonomy and for the dissolution of primary relationships; yet it seems clear that even in Federal America, competition and commercial values abounded in towns.⁵ New York and Charleston, for example, had chambers of commerce even before the Revolution. The Federal towns were similar in size to English provincial cities before industrialization and were already experiencing what would later be called the urban problems of crime, sewage disposal, and fire control. Nonetheless, merchants, financiers, and landlords spurred urban growth during the Colonial and Federal periods, and it was their successors who controlled and guided the development of baseball as a prime urban sport.

Throughout the nineteenth century, as the British game of rounders evolved into American baseball, the nation itself was transformed by a series of social, technological, economic, and political events. Contradictory attitudes about the city as a locus of negative values have a long history in America, exemplified by the agrarian preferences of Thomas Jefferson. Yet, by the 1820s, the city was quite visible and accepted as a part of the idea of progress in a nation politically reconciled to Jacksonian ideals. The fortunes of the city were inexorably bound up with the fortunes of agriculture. As agriculture prospered or waned, anti-urbanism thrived or vitiated. However, anti-urbanism has always been endemic among American thinkers and politicians, even with the twentieth century recognition of our overwhelmingly urban nature. Jefferson, Bellamy, Bryan, and Emerson exemplified the anti-urban bias of American reforming impulses. In the late nineteenth century Bryan would assert that the prosperity of the cities rested on rural welfare; he said that if the cities were destroyed and farms saved, cities would rise again, but that the opposite case would produce ruin.[6]

Technological and demographic change exerted great influence on the developing structure of baseball. Towns and cities grew up and expanded along canals and railroad lines. Horse cars, large-scale bridge construction, and electric trolley systems facilitated movement of city dwellers. The electric light bulb, the telephone, and the subways opened new vistas to city people. Cheap magazines and newspapers in the period after the Civil War allowed a form of communication which replaced village conversation patterns and affected baseball's popularity by featuring sports news as city rivalries developed.[7]

The influx of new immigrants from southern and eastern Europe, the onset of big city political machines, the construction of the first tenements, and the instituting of city social services also characterized the urban scene after 1865. The take-off period of American industrialization and the location of factories in cities drew people away from rural areas. Accompanying these dynamic events was the rise of slums, urban crime, and civic corruption. It was a period of enormous boom and vitality, and even a dissenting intellectual like Frank Norris could acknowledge the excitement.

It was in an environment of men on the make—a world of politicians and contractors and civic tumult—that baseball became established as a professional activity which could reflect glory on a community. There had been earlier suggestions of civic pride in the nineteenth-century tendency to adorn cities with trees and parks, thus expressing an optimistic naturalist expectation about the city as a dwelling place.

Yet, there were also ominous tendencies in the menace of youth gangs and the rising need for public aid for the poor in New York during the 1830s and 1840s. The rise of the robber barons after 1865 would find a counterpart in the entreprenuerial world of early professional baseball. Many critics and historians have correctly noted that it was a time when things were in the making.

The sharp increase in the size of urban populations was a salient fact of the take-off period of American industrial capitalism. In 1860 only one in five Americans was a city dweller; by 1900 the figure was one in three and by 1930 one in two.[8] Moreover, the patterns of urban growth tended to exacerbate divisiveness as city neighborhoods became separated by class and ethnic identity. Formerly middle-class single-residence areas became subdivided into smaller multiple-rental units in a downward status spiral. New developments in transportation and communication produced the so-called street-car suburbs of the later nineteenth century, while the tendency of cities to incorporate independent villages contributed to metropolitan complexity. This growth stimulated the provision of such services as sanitary engineering and gas and electric power.[9]

By 1882 there were some four hundred streetcar companies in the world hauling over a billion passengers a year, and even nineteenth century suburbs exhibited familiar twentieth century characteristics: affluence, uniformity, centerlessness. fragmentation, segregation, and consumption. Meanwhile, William Dean Howells noted the rise of two new important urban types: the immigrant and the millionaire.[10] Within cities, ethnicity often shaped neighborhood structures, with black neighborhoods tending to be more permanent and homogeneous than those of other ethnic groups. Ethnic peoples found varying rates of accommodation within the American fabric, with Jews and Italians finding their way more slowly than, for example, the Irish.[11]

Thus, decentralization and concentration appear to have proceeded at the same time that more affluent Americans were escaping the increasingly congested cities. The coming of the automobile—the numbers of which increased dramatically from some eight thousand in 1900 to over 26 million by 1930—further facilitated these processes. The auto had been largely a toy for the rich, but it revolutionized city life with the coming of Ford's Model T and foreshadowed the decline of the trolley as an important means of urban and interurban transportation.

Even during the declining birthrate years of the 1920s, urban populations increased by 23.1 percent.[12] Zoning, shopping centers, highway construction, urban planning, rising land values, and housing shortages all became familiar in the American urban scene of the twentieth century. Meanwhile, older institutions like the family and the neighborhood seemed unable to cope with complex new, city-based problems. These developments helped shape the structure of professional baseball as it became the prime urban spectator sport of the new America.

Probably no other American urban place has received the mythological treatment accorded Brooklyn. In a nation growing more urbanized and more conformist, the persistent Brooklyn legends gained wide acceptance and the borough's baseball team became an integral part of the aura. To explain the popularity of Brooklyn as a humorous topic is to understand that somehow life in the "boisterous borough," as one famed sports journalist once described it,[13] appealed to many Americans. In a drab era, Brooklynites represented vitality, color, eccentricity, and charm, at least to distant observers.

Yet, there is a note of wistfulness, too, the poignancy of identification with the loser. In 1951, Dr. Max Theiler, winner of a Nobel Prize, for example, announced that he was buying a season's pass to Ebbets Field with part of his prize

money because he was for the underdog.[14] This note of inferiority seems to have been crucial to the Brooklyn mystique,
and scoffing outlanders stimulated a sense of solidarity among
the oppressed.

Brooklyn seems always to have been a mere suburb, a
place where people came to sleep or to escape from the roar-
ing vitalities and important events of Manhattan. Early nineteenth century newspaper advertisements designed to attract
immigrants to the still-independent city extrolled its rural
qualities. Yet, as early as 1844, Edgar Allan Poe wrote of
Brooklyn, "I know few towns which inspire with so great dis-
gust and contempt." He scoffed at the "silvered gingerbread"
of its "preposterous" houses, which were "places of painted
white pine, fifteen by twenty."[15]

By the twentieth century, Brooklyn came to be popularly
viewed as the ultimate in bizarre urbanism, but it also seems
to have represented something typically American, judging by
mass media representations. To emphasize the Americanness
of movie characters, Hollywood films of the 1930s and 1940s
often injected Brooklyn citizens who made frequent reference
to their legendary baseball team. When Bob Hope and Bing
Crosby encounter fellow American Dorothy Lamour on a
South Sea island in *The Road to Zanzibar,* she immediately
asks them how the Dodgers are doing, and in *Guadalcanal
Diary,* brave World War II soldier-patriot William Bendix
dies with the happy thought of a Dodger victory. Countless
war films presented the archetype infantry company with a
stock Brooklynite and a typical Texan shoulder to shoulder.
The famed vaudevillian Willie Howard laced his monologs
with Brooklyn references and Dodger commentary. In doing
a one-man impression of the Moscow art theater complete
with pidgin Russian, he slipped in the words "the Brooklyn
Dodgers" every second line or so while acting out the cold
Siberian musings of a dark Russian soul in a searing domestic
tragedy. In later times, a standup comic made his reputation

by retelling Brooklyn dialect stories of trips to Coney Island, betting pools in high school, life in the local pool room, and dying with the Dodgers. While much of his audience may not have recognized it, the basis of Jackie Gleason's "Ralph Kramden" episodes is life in the tenements of Irish Brooklyn.

Nothing so identified Brooklyn as Brooklynese, that piquant and rich caressing of the language by Brooklyn tongues. Typical was the episode in the film *The Fighting 69th* in which a cocky and troublesome young recruit played by Jimmy Cagney spoke of eating "ersters" (oysters) to an indulgent Father Duffy, played by Pat O'Brien. The dialect is disappearing now with the media-induced homogenization of speech patterns and the movement of many older Brooklyn residents to the middle-class confines of Long Island.

Brooklynese was an exotic lingo, in some ways an analog of London cockney in that it was strikingly individual and identifiable and perhaps provocative of as much antagonism and indulgence. In addition to interchanging the "oil" and "earl" sounds, there was the invention of words such as "irregardless." Comments such as "If you don't stop, I'll left you have one" provoked humor from imaginative sportswriters of the 1920s and 1930s, who did much to enhance the Brooklyn legends. Stories about Brooklyn syntax proliferated, nourished by occasions like the time the announcer at Ebbets Field reported, "A little boy has been found, lost." The Broadway popularizer Damon Runyun, whose stories formed the basis for the musical play *Guys and Dolls,* created Ethel and Joe, two denizens of the borough of Brooklyn, and depicted their innocent and quixotic ways in a cozy but eccentrically antic world. The virus even captivated Thomas Wolfe, who portrayed Brooklyn speech in his piece "Only the Dead Know Brooklyn," when he wrote "troo" for "true," "dere's" for "there's," "you'se," for "you," and "Bensenhoist," for "Bensenhurst." These quirks were noticed, at least in passing, by much of the rest of America.

But the humor was also deprecating and patronizing. Typical was the one-line joke, "So you come from Brooklyn; got your passport?" Like the opening scene of *Arsenic and Old Lace*, much humor about Brooklyn stressed deviations from middle-class norms of speech and manners. Here was a curious subspecies of American, accorded differential esteem by New Englanders and Westerners, but in most ways not to be taken seriously. An example was the famous 1940s assertion that Brooklyn was the most loyal ally of the United States in time of war.

There was a cultural strangeness to Brooklyn. It was the shambling town of "dems" and "dese," and the home of Murder, Incorporated. It was resplendent with delicately quixotic names like Flatbush, Bensonhurst, and Bushwick, but there seems to have been an attraction about the place. Perhaps the appeal has something to do with an enduring sense of neighborhood. Branch Rickey, who was for some years president and chief stockholder in the Brooklyn baseball team, lived in the borough from 1942 to 1950 and stated that "it doesn't take that long to fall in love with the place . . . our whole family did."[16] A survey taken in 1916 by the *Literary Digest* concluded that most of the citizens of Brooklyn had lived in the same house in the same neighborhood for their entire lives.[17] As late as March 1941, the transplanted Georgia author Carson McCullers wrote a piece called "Brooklyn Is My Neighborhood" for *Vogue,* in which she revealed, "It is strange in New York to find yourself living in a real neighborhood."[18] She wrote about her neighbors, the corner drugstore, and people who retold tales of the traditions attached to local houses. It was an essay filled with feelings of love and pleasure in one's surroundings.

Brooklyn began as a series of separate settlements and gradually amalgamated into a city which became a borough of New York. The first European settlers came to the Gowanus area and the Flatlands in 1636. Even in those days of

Dutch control, there was a note of cultural diversity furnished by the presence of French Walloons. Such diversity grew enormously in the next three centuries as Scandinavians, blacks, Italians, Irish, Germans, Hungarians, and countless others flocked to the city.

Early nineteenth century advertising stressed the bucolic nature of the area, emphasizing its easy access and village charms. Many immigrants came to Brooklyn out of a desire to establish themselves in a small town. In 1834, population growth and consolidation had advanced to the point where the first Brooklyn city charter was promulgated, but farms still surrounded the amalgamated city, and not until the 1890s would all of King's County be included in the charter area.

The Irish were the first immigrant group to make a significant mark. They eventually settled throughout the area, scattering from what was called Irishtown. German settlers were present in notable numbers by the 1840s, but it was the Irish who dominated politics. Ethnicity was to prove an important source of political differentiation from the middle of the nineteenth century onward. The first Roman Catholic diocese was established in 1853; at that time, Irish political leaders like McLaughlin, McCooey, and Murphy dominated the Brooklyn Democratic party and had established a patronage machine which lasted for many generations. J. F. Hylan and W. J. Gaynor served as mayors of Brooklyn before moving on to govern greater New York City. By the 1800s, an Irish immigrant descendant named Tom Kinsella was editor of the renowned *Brooklyn Eagle,* the newspaper of Walt Whitman.

In time, other immigrant groups grew large enough to challenge the Irish dominance. By 1854, enough Jews had gathered to found the first Brooklyn synogogue. Prominent in the tailoring trades, Jewish influence would grow steadily until the turn of the century, when the first Jewish Democratic leader, Hymie Schorenstein, from Brownsville, would become the political power of that neighborhood. Kosher eating places and a flourishing Yiddish theater symbolized a strong Jewish presence.

Many areas came to be ethnically identified, for example, the Italians dominated in Red Hook, the Scandinavians in the dock areas, and the Jews in Brownsville. Ethnicity sometimes even influenced baseball loyalties, and it may have been the ethnic quality of Brooklyn that fed the strangeness, the sub-species aspects of much of the humor about the borough.

Foreign immigrants were not the only marginal people in Brooklyn. Blacks had been in residence there since the colonial era. Once a hot-bed of abolitionist sentiment, Brooklyn gave refuge to former slaves and by the 1890s included a black upper class, black churches, and, later on, African societies and separatist groups. In 1898, a black was appointed to the board of education, but not until 1948 would Brooklyn send a black representative to the New York State Assembly.

Population mobility depended on technological innovations in transport, and Brooklyn was peculiarly affected by succeeding stages of invention. Even before the Civil War, Brooklyn was regarded as a dormitory suburb. By 1860, with a population of some 100,000, it was the ninth largest city in the country. By the 1880s, a fully developed system of elevated railways served much of the city, and residential expansion followed the rails. The electric trolley followed in due course, further dispersing the population as the city became known as the city of trolleys. The Brooklyn baseball team would draw its most famous nickname, the Dodgers, from the proliferation of trolley lines which served the city long before the coming of the subway.

The Brooklyn Bridge, one of the most famous of all the city's structures, opened in May of 1883 after thirteen years of construction. It was hoped that it would end traffic congestion, but instead it hastened the tide of immigration from the

Lower East Side of Manhattan and did much to increase Jewish and Italian populations.

Other developments flowed as population and transport grew. Frederick Law Olmsted, who designed Central Park in Manhattan, completed a similar project in Brooklyn, the famed Prospect Park. The Luna Amusement Park, constructed at Coney Island, attracted some 4 million visitors in 1904, while the Navy Yard added a sea-going orientation to the borough's activities.

In 1896 the remaining independent towns amalgamated into King's County, and in 1898, in spite of strong local opposition, Brooklyn became a borough of greater New York City. Besides the largest concentration of foreign people in the country, New York gained in its new borough an area in which over 80 percent of the residents were renters. Throughout the period of growth and consolidation, typical municipal provisions appeared. In addition to the transportation systems and parks, Brooklyn in this period added its first system of organized charities, the first museum of arts, and branch libraries. The proliferation of tenements—a new style of architecture—produced regulatory legislation in the 1880s.

Unlike other areas undergoing amalgamation, Brooklyn once had a civic identity of its own, and even in a city of such striking divergencies, one commonality would be devotion to the local professional baseball team. Long after its amalgamation to greater New York, a well-known Brooklyn banker would assert, "We still exist as Brooklyn, when the Dodgers take the field."[19]

14.

Baseball in American Culture: The Dodgers

As a mass spectator sport, baseball differs from others in that passive-spectatorness and active play participation intermingle. Some years ago *Sports Illustrated* assigned Robert Frost to cover the all-star baseball game in Washington, D.C. In a charming and shrewdly written piece, Frost evoked the charms of the national game suggesting that indeed every boy has come to bat with the bases loaded and two out.[1] In that sense, a dramatic empathy becomes possible between player and spectator that may be more direct than in other sports. In the sand lot baseball games, children unsullied by adult participation make up the rules and play by them. If play is the doing of a thing for its own sake, then baseball became the first mass spectator sport in America to psychically capitalize on youthful play experiences.

Ralph Barton Perry observed that American sport is marked by "the large place which it fills in the public consciousness throughout all classes of society."[2] Lewis Mumford saw mass sport as providing the elements of spectacle, competition, and arresting personalities. The spectacle supplied an esthetic element lacking in urban industrialized society, providing the viewer the opportunity to act as a Greek chorus whose outcries can affect the course of events. Thus, in Mumford's analysis, there is a participatory element in spectator status, a sense of being useful.[3] According to popular legends, no baseball fans were more enthusiastic than those who frequented Ebbets Field. Contemporary sociologists and psychologists of mass sport echo the intuitions of Mumford, asserting that in mass sport the spectator becomes more important than the player in that the game is no longer played solely for the benefit of the participants. Thus, mass sport becomes a means of social control in a new sense, a weapon against boredom, a way of supplying vicarious exhibitions of manliness. Excitement is also a key element in Mumford's analysis, with sport supplying an element of chance which industrial society by its very nature reduces.[4]

Other social scientists have found mass sport an analog of American consumerism, providing continuity in an era of rapid change through the existence of team loyalty over time. At the same time the stadium setting sanctions behavior which in other circumstances might be taboo. Scholars have also noted the large part which sport plays in mass society, evidence being the disproportionate space alloted to sports by newspapers and television. Thus, mass sport is viewed as a means of social control, a kind of safety value for the emotions which at the same time provides stability in its repeated psychic rituals.[5]

Striking personalities have always been an important feature of baseball lore. As Mumford has pointed out, a sports hero is, above all, masculine and possesses skills an amateur strives for. Prominent among the heroes of the twentieth century have been movie stars and sports figures, who have been accorded the kind of adulation elsewhere reserved for royalty. American sports heroes are presented as an elite, suffused with the values of the Boy Scout Oath. Only an occasional writer like Ring Lardner would capture the truth about the lives and values of sports heroes. Gaudy, brawling types like Babe Ruth or mean-spirited competitors like Ty Cobb take on the trappings of Sunday school virtue in journalistic writings and folklore.

Baseball rapidly became the possession of hard-headed business types, but it seems always to have been portrayed as the kid's game and its heroes as fervent child lovers. At the Cooperstown Hall of Fame there is a painting of Ty Cobb in uniform umpiring as a boy slides into a base. Anyone familiar with the life-style of this baseball immortal knows how far from real life this picture is. The famed "Black Sox" scandals of 1919 in which the Chicago White Sox threw the series to the Cincinnati Reds is typically capped by a story in which a little boy rushes up to the fallen Chicago hero, "Shoeless Joe" Jackson, and pathetically begs, "Say it ain't so, Joe."

Beyond the exemplification of the puritan and the puerile in American culture, baseball culture displayed a kind of ritual, a slowness, a movement which often achieved balletic beauty: an outfielder leaping for a ball, a shortstop whirling to fire a retrieved ball to first, or a pitcher coming down from his windup. These are rituals that one can see repeated on amateur diamonds throughout the country, and a ball field in South Carolina is immediately recognizable to one who has played on the fields of New York or Montana.

Baseball became highly legalistic too, and the commissioner —in the person of Judge Kensaw Mountain Landis, who was installed directly after the Black Sox scandal—ruled by fiat. On the field, too, litigation is common, as the umpire enforces the rules against transgressors, some of whom are ostracized or exiled. Yet, cheating is also built into the rules of the game, as in the hidden ball, the kicking of a ball out of a fielder's hand during slides, and the act of "stealing" a base or "stealing" coaching signals.

In regard to what he called the "litigousness" of Americans, Perry insisted that Americans were more concerned for insisting on their rights than on respecting them. Above all, baseball like other professional sports emphasizes winning. The bacchanalia of the winners and their supporters approaches orgiastic proportions with tooting of horns, the flowing of wine and beer, dancing in the streets, and tearing up the field after the event. Perry again is accurate when he says that American sports extoll winning and that to win is "esteemed above grace, or form, or adherence to a code."[6] If there has been a tendency to extoll the puritanical and to emphasize and enforce the law in baseball, there has also been open admiration of players who gain their ends in a roughhouse way by bending or even breaking the rules. Fans tend to see them as colorful and applaud Leo Durocher's famous observation, "Nice guys finish last."

Professional baseball developed in concert with the course of urban history in America. Franchises became established in large cities, and team loyalty became part of the pattern of civic pride. For many years teams tended to remain in place, no matter how dismal or poverty-striken the franchise. With the urban take-off after World War II and the increase in mobility, owners began to move franchises to new cities in search of more profit.

In baseball, many options are possible at any moment, depending on the responses of the players. Even winning the World Series is fleeting. There is little time for resting as renewed efforts enter into the inevitable plans for the next season, and next season may very well find last year's winner deeply mired in the second division. In this sense baseball competition epitomizes the American notion of success, that one is only as good as his last outing, that the game will be played again for the loser too, that there is never an ultimate resting place or identity from which one can serenely view the world and partake of it. The contest renews for the losers too, and the losing Dodger fan's hopeful cry of "Wait 'til next year" has real meaning in the life of the game.

We have already seen that Ralph Barton Perry's analysis of American characteristics seems to apply to baseball as it reflects the culture of America. His ideas are intuitive, philosophical generalizations based on the observations of a lifetime. Moreover, there is an ironic flavor to his musings as he points out that each nation is made up not only of a "compound of many characteristics, but of opposite characteristics."[7] In American sport, fighting and arguing about winning are expected even to the point of nastiness, but with the final verdict the loser is expected to exude gracefulness and to come to the winner's quarters to extend warm congratulations. Thus, baseball's World Series ritual bears out Perry's notion that we are "both harshly competitive and humanely idealistic."

Advancing capitalism in America was closely connected with the enculturation of immigrants. Boys' baseball fiction exemplified the idea of rising through effort and cleanliness in good Horatio Alger fashion. No big-league player exemplified the Alger virtues more than Christy Mathewson, the legendary pitcher who neither smoked nor drank nor played games on Sundays. Widely admired for his uprightness, Mathewson was a genuine Protestant hero. However, for immigrants who made their way into the game, qualifying for hero status involved some uneasiness. For example, Hank Greenberg, an awesome Jewish slugger for the Detroit Tigers, found himself confronted with a World Series game, the ultimate moment of his professional career, on the most holy day of the Jewish year.

Perhaps Perry comes closest to another crucial aspect of baseball culture when he writes about the American suspicion of those who are not joiners or who do not "play the game." For him American individualism is "collective individualism, originating from the sense of collective power,, manifested in the Westward Movement. Thus, the American individualism which he sees as dominant is nonetheless imbedded in an imperative of gregariousness.[8] Perry's notion that we are motivated most by attainable rewards typifies baseball as it does the Horatio Alger idea that anyone who observes certain moral precepts can attain worldly success. Winning becomes a kind of holy venture and failure a sin in which only the individual's flaws are to blame. Perry further asserts that "American success must be recognized success—not by the God of things as they are but by one's neighbors." As if he had baseball with its passion for statistics in mind, Perry asserts that public success must be "not only measurable but observed, recorded, applauded, and envied."[9] The description seems to fit not only players but spectators as well. Fan participation in a victory certainly includes the events being retold, flaunted, and argued over, and, perhaps above all, recorded in the record books to be retrieved in the future as a small piece of personal immortality. Perry's notions extend to the media which he saw as enlarging the scale of the victory process, making for a close relationship between "success and publicity." But success and fame are tied to urbanism, and he noted that "American pride of achievement is local as well as national," each state, city and region being "out to make records."[10] Baseball rivalries at the spectator level are acted out as conflicts between localities. In Major League cities, for example, loyalties tended to be regional as well as local, and people identify with teams representing other area cities. A contemporary recognition of that situation has been the renaming of city teams for entire states, perhaps as a box office inducement.

Baseball's rise to dominance came after the Civil War, paralleling rapid industrialization and urbanization. The claim that baseball was invented by Abner Doubleday in 1839 in the charming upstate New York community of Cooperstown has little, if any, truth. Branch Rickey attests that baseball executives seeking a gate receipt stimulus during the depression of the 1930s conceived the idea of establishing a Hall of Fame and pronounced the year 1939 the centennial of the game.[11] They based their plans on a dubious claim A. G. Spaulding had made earlier in the century. The Cooperstown-Doubleday myth had been discredited many times, but journalists cooperated with the centennial planners, and the Cooperstown idea became established.

Perhaps Spaulding's original intention was to discredit the idea that the all-American game could have been of British origin. However, the origins of baseball, while somewhat obscure, can be found in the English games of rounders and cricket. Early baseball used cricket terms and cricket equipment, the game having been introduced into the American colonies sometime in the mid-1750s at a time when there was scant impulse toward recreation in America. As early as the 1760s, a children's book of games printed in London carried a description of a game similar to baseball.[12] There is some evidence that Washington's men played a variation of baseball, and the description of a game like baseball also survives in the diary of a Princeton student of the 1780s.[13] However, in a society with almost no urban culture and a subsistence economy, there was no role for commercialized sport.

In the 1820s the only relatively organized sport was horse racing, although cricket was widely played. Between 1840 and 1860 baseball supplanted cricket as the favorite game of Americans.[14] However, as late as 1858 a prominent sports manual devoted eighteen pages to cricket and only four and a half pages to baseball.[15]

The game of Rounders with its four bases and its putting out of a runner by hitting him with a thrown ball is the model for the development of baseball. Baseball evolved from a five-base to a four-base game and switched from the oblong to the diamond square after a period of using a triangular field. Two competing variations were called "Town Ball" and the "New York Game." Sometimes wickets were used and sometimes stakes until bases finally became dominant.[16]

The 1840s, a period of considerable activity in private associations, saw the founding of the first organized baseball club, the New York Knickerbockers. These were amateurs, gentlemen of the middle class, who banned profanity and played the game for reasons of health and morality. It was a period in which moral activism invaded associated life in the form of temperance and antislave societies, women's rights groups, and peace organizations. The game reached such a level of popularity that by the middle 1850s one urban newspaper, *The Brooklyn Eagle,* complained over the scarcity of vacant lots because of the proliferation of baseball fields. The first efforts to organize a permanent league of teams occurred late in the 1850s.

The 1860s seem to have been the period in which baseball underwent some of its most crucial changes. While some clergymen claimed that the playing of the game would lead to social peace and a tempering of the violence attending other games, professionalism began when the Brooklyn Excelsiors first paid a player on a surreptitious basis. The Cincinnati Reds became the first openly professional team, and by the end of the 1860s some fifteen thousand patrons would pay to see a game between all-star teams in New York City. Thus the transition from a gentleman's game played by amateurs to a professional spectator sport was well under way in the decade after the Civil War. With these developments, interest in cricket rapidly faded.

It was a time when other sports such as bicycle racing, tennis, boxing, and golf also gained public favor, but baseball was uniquely suited to an urban society. It was played on a self-contained bucolic field, and spectators could see the entire panorama at once. In addition, it rose to dominance at a time when urban land values allowed for relatively simple business arrangements in terms of land acquisition. Public surface transport also proved to be adequate in an age when large parking lots near baseball stadia were still unnecessary.

Blake McKelvey, the urban historian, is convinced that the

increased pace of commercial and industrial life acted as a catalyst for baseball's rise to dominance as a mass spectator sport. In his view it provided release and relaxation from middle class tensions in this formative period.[17] Civic pride spurred urban groups to promote baseball as a matter of local patriotism. At the same time, the rules of the game became standardized and gambling was forbidden in the name of professional ethics.

The proliferation of city teams necessitated codifying the rules of the game, and in 1865 the players of some one hundred teams banded together in the National Association of Baseball Players. Intercity rivalries grew, and the touring Cincinnati Reds encouraged other cities to organize similar ventures. Towns tended to consolidate their teams into one club to represent their city, and in 1876 the ancestor of the present National League was founded. In 1882 Chicago opened the first wooden grandstand baseball park; concrete and steel stadia were first constructed in 1909. The founding of the American League in 1890 led eventually to a World Series between the champions of the two leagues in the year 1903.

Competition between cities was the basic form of baseball rivalries; it was an enactment of the capitalist ritual in a Darwinian sense of the fittest surviving. The game became sanctified during the Progressive era which saw regulation of its practices increased and the establishment of the tradition that the president of the United States threw out the first ball on opening day in the nation's capital. The organizational development of professional baseball paralleled the growth of big corporations and in time included similar practices and structures. Nor were players exempt from these values; sports writers complained as early as 1910 that the players' sole interest seemed to be the size of their salaries.

Thus, economic and technological innovations influenced

the world of baseball. By 1927, for example, multiple ownership was banned in the name of free competition and the re-
serve clause was adopted. Similarly, the trolley, the subway,
the automobile, the taxi, and the bus would all influence the
location and design of baseball parks. Even the invention of
motion pictures had an impact when John McGraw of the
New York Giants first used them for training purposes in the
1914 season. The growing popularity of movies eventually
made big leauge baseball more available to the mass public
through newsreels and world series films.

The aura of Brooklyn was intimately connected with the
myths of Dodger baseball and the antics of their fans. Its
persistence is evidenced by the fact that as late as the 1950s
when the Brooklyn Dodgers included some of the greatest
players in the history of the game, their newspaper cartoon
symbol was still a fearfully decrepit Bum. Philip Roth, himself
prone to strong partisanship for the Brooklyn Dodgers, noted
that Brooklyn was "a region then the very symbol of urban
wackiness and tumult."[18] The stories about the team, about
the antics of the fans, and about the stadium itself reinforced
the concept of "urban wackiness"; in a sense, they are an out-
post of American eccentricity, the final locus of harmless,
genuine, urban expressiveness.

During the 1950s, the Dodger management gave further
sanction to bizarre behavior by promoting music night, during
which anyone bringing a musical instrument to Ebbets Field
was admitted free. An assortment of amateur saxophonists,
tubaists, trumpeters, drummers, and guitarists showed up, but
the "wackiness" prize must surely have gone to two energetic
souls who pushed a piano through the gates of the ball park
one cacophonous evening. As James Thurber is supposed to
have said about some of his Ohio relatives, "We had quite a
time quieting them down." Only the playing of the "Star
Spangled Banner" silenced the uproar, allowing the game to

begin.[19] This kind of urban tumult was front page feature
news and added new dimensions to the Brooklyn image of
being virulent and eccentric.

The persistence of the myth of Brooklyn madness and its
analog of fervent loyalty to the Dodgers constitutes a kind of
nostalgia for a stability that seems to be passing quickly in the
bewildering changes of the twentieth century. Brooklyn behavior, at least as reported to the culture at large, seemed
dependably consistent. A sports writer who covered the Dodgers for the *New York Daily News* clearly evoked the myth
when he asserted that Brooklyn was more a state of mind
than a place. Of particular significance is the state of mind
of sophisticated journalists who perpetrated the image and
then clung to it gleefully.[20]

Brooklyn was rich in baseball lore and history, and the city
claimed many firsts. A Brooklyn team, of which there were
many, challenged and met the gentlemanly New York Knickerbockers in the 1850s in match play. An all-star game between Brooklyn and New York players was the first at which
admission was charged by supposedly amateur teams. Most
famous of the early Brooklyn teams was the Excelsiors, who
pioneered the so-called New York version of the game. Civic
pride, perhaps rallying from a sense of inferiority induced by
being called New York's bedroom, produced additional firsts
for Brooklyn baseball of the 1860s. It is claimed that Brooklyn
saw the first stolen base, the first road trip, the first bunt, the
first spit-ball, the first curve ball, and the first enclosed ball
park (built at the Capitoline Grounds). It was from a Brooklyn team that the Philadelphia Athletics first lured a player by
promising a higher salary. While the sport evolved from ama-
teurism through covert professionalism to outright professionalism, numerous teams flourished in Brooklyn; the Excelsiors defeated the famed Cincinnati Reds in 1870 before
twenty thousand patrons in an exciting match at the Capitoline
Grounds. It was during the 1870s that some of the best Brook-

lyn teams turned professional, and entries competed in various relatively short-lived, semi-organized leagues during the next two decades.

The owners reflected capitalist business styles of the period. They were local people who depended on local financing while acting in a paternalistic manner towards their employees. Personally acquainted with the fans of Brooklyn, these early entrepreneurs were oftener than not the descendants of Irish immigrants who had themselves only recently arrived at a state of affluence.

The American Association team, owned by Charles H. Byrne, Joseph J. Doyle, and Ferdinand A. Abell, struggled manfully to show a profit and remain in business. This triumvirate incorporated and sold stock to other businessmen who appear to have been motivated by the desire for profits, civic pride, and (perhaps) the quest for recognition in the community.

In 1884 Brooklyn's team won the American Association championship and played the New York Giants of the National League in a kind of incipient World Series. In 1889, the Brooklyn Superbas won the championship under the leadership of an Irish manager, William H. McGunnigle, whose team also included many Irish players. In 1890 the Brooklyn franchise moved to the National League; it won the pennant in its first year and again in 1899 and 1900, managed by yet another Irishman, Ned Hanlon. By this time the Capitoline Grounds of the Civil War days had been abandoned for Washington Park, so named because George Washington had taken an evening's respite on his way to a Long Island battle during the Revolution in the very area of downtown Brooklyn in which it was located.

The year 1890 was an important one for Brooklyn baseball because Mr. Charles Ebbets, a decendant of one of the early Dutch families of old Bruecklen, joined the firm as bookkeeper and public relations man. A sincere, hard-working man who had worked previously as an architect, Ebbets eventually acquired majority control of the stock, became president of the club, and helped put Brooklyn on the baseball map and into the national consciousness.

The nicknames of the Brooklyn team as it shifted around in various leagues in the late nineteenth and early twentieth century were based on meaningful experiences in the life of the community. The Superbas, for example, took their name from a vaudeville act well known to the local citizenry, while the 1890 National League champions acquired the name "The Bridegrooms" because six of the players had recently assumed that status. The nickname Dodgers ultimately stuck and resulted from the fact that the city was laced with a network of electric trolleys which clanged through its neighborhoods, particularly in the ball park area.

Not only did the names of the ball parks—for example, Ebbets Field—have a certain immediate life reference, their locations followed developments in urban transportation. For example, in 1890 when new owners moved Washington Park to the wilds of Eastern Parkway, locals referred to it as going "half-way to Europe." Shortly after, in 1898, Charles Ebbets moved the park back to downtown Brooklyn, where it was readily accessible by trolley.

Place names are socially suggestive; for example, the new Washington Park location was near an area known as "Guinea Flats," after the large Italian immigrant population settled there by the late 1890s. Abuse and even refuse flowed from Guinea Flats in the direction of enemy outfielders, particularly if they were members of the New York Giants. The New York Giants—Brooklyn Trolley Dodgers-cum-Superbas-cum-Bridegrooms rivalry was one of the urban myths that seemed to come alive in the sanctioned confines of baseball stadia. The situation was unique; for some fifty-six years, New York was the only baseball city with two teams in the same league, enabling partisans of both teams to be present at each encounter. In addition, the New York Giants established themselves in the first decades of the twentieth century as a formidable team, winning numerous pennants, appearing in World Series, and assembling outstanding players, many of who are now in the Baseball Hall of Fame. This contrasted sharply with the dismal showing of Brooklyn teams which were stuck in the second division in the first two decades of the century.

Another reason for the rivalry lay in the intensely personal nature of baseball ownership and management partisanship in the days before the flowering of the corporate spirit. Before the days of bureaucrats and offices standing between teams and their publics, it was not uncommon for owners, stockholders, and club officials to be familiar sights to the stadium crowds. Ball parks were cozy structures, lineups were announced from home plate, and players traveled to the games in open carriages in the early days of this century.

While some of the ill-feeling between the Giants and Dodgers stemmed from the fact that the more successful Giants drew larger crowds, the catalytic event was an incident in which the Giants' manager, John McGraw, insulted Charles Ebbets, the Brooklyn owner, as he sat in his accustomed seat at new Washington Park. It was a painful public insult for Ebbets who could not match the expletives available to McGraw, and the episode took place before thousands of fans who were accustomed to look expectantly in Ebbets' direction during key moments in games. Also feeding the rivalry were the inferiority feelings of Brooklynites (beginning to be fanned by the public media), the wide acquaintanceship of players on both teams, and the fierce personal bitterness between the two managers who had been teammates on the Old Baltimore Orioles.

It was, as a matter of fact, the Old Baltimore Oriole owners who purchased a controlling interest in the Brooklyn team at the turn of the present century . nd installed Charles Ebbets as president. The nucleus of the Dodger teams which won

pennants in 1899 and 1900 was made up of Old Oriole players like Ned Hanlon, Wee Willie Keeler, and Hughie Jennings.
Some of these players were of a heroic mold; the pitcher
"Iron Man" Joe McGinnity, for example, pitched and won a
double header and once won five games in six days. Wee
Willie Keeler, only five feet, four inches tall and weighing 140
pounds, was a fearsome place hitter, batting for an average
of .359 during four seasons with Brooklyn. This slight athlete
coined the phrase, "I hit 'em where they ain't," to describe his
tactics.

These early players, whose exploits and sayings are still
repeated in sport histories and in occasional newspaper
columns, are a kind of lost tribe of sport, victims of the extensions of communications technology. They played at a time
when World Series results were announced inning by inning
on signs hoisted in the town square of every small town in
America. To be remembered as a baseball hero is to have
achieved some kind of statistical distinction, or to have perfected a tactic still used in the game, or to have coined a saying or perpetrated a particularly egregious piece of incompe-
tence. This last characteristic distinguished Brooklyn baseball
in the halcyon days of the 1920s.

Throughout the history of Brooklyn baseball, many team
players came from small towns. There is a strong rural flavor
to the stories and antics of players from the golden age of the
1920s. The evocative tales of Ring Lardner, based on his
newspaper days covering Brooklyn baseball, depict antic rural
innocence let loose in the big city. In his memorable story
"Alabi Ike," for example, even Ike's teammates—themselves
only slightly more sophisticated—are astonished at his nit-
witted innocence and elaborate excuses.

Outstanding Brooklyn players of the first two decades of
the twentieth century came from towns like Alpharetta,
Georgia; Montville, Connecticut; Rock Island, Illinois; Pitts-
ton, Pennsylvania; Llewellan, Pennsylvania; and Hamilton,

Missouri. Typical was George Rucker, nicknamed "Napoleon," or more simply "Nap." Rucker was a paradigm baseball star of the period before World War I. A Southerner and a farm boy, he was recommended to the Dodgers by young Grantland Rice, later one of the most literate of American sports writers. Rice had seen him playing in the South and recommended him to Dodger scout Larry Sutton, who discovered many Brooklyn players before World War I. Scouting was at that time much more informal than it is today.

Rucker toiled from 1907 to 1915 with very poor teams to support him; the Dodgers were mired in sixth or seventh place during his tenure, only once rising to third. Yet, Rucker stuck with the lowly Dodgers and managed twice to win seventeen games in a season, won eighteen once, and twenty-two once, with teams that finished well back in the standings. For example, his seventeen wins in 1908 made up a large portion of the total team victories; they won only fifty-three for the entire season. Other talented performers would find themselves in a similar position in other lackluster periods of Dodger history.

During this period, Ebbets consolidated his control of the team in an era in which its roster included, in addition to Rucker, such early stars as Jake Daubert, Otto Miller, and Hall of Famer Zack Wheat. Typical of the approach of that more personal era, Ebbets attained control over the team by gaining the backing of local businessmen. In what would now be unimaginable, given the complexity of baseball organizations, Ebbets once met his payroll by borrowing money from his star, Zack Wheat. In the days before player unionization and absentee corporation ownership, such simple and direct arrangements were possible.

Like American industry, the management-ownership side of baseball went through levels of personal ownership before reaching the corporate stage. Early in his career, Ebbets combined the club presidency with field managerial duties, but growing specialization eventually put an end to this dual role. However, from the turn of the century to the 1930s, baseball was controlled by the personal preferences of individual moguls.

Motivated by his background in architecture and ever responsive to new trends in transportation, Ebbets began buying up lots in an Italian ghetto area called "Pigtown," which lay between Bedford and Flatbush. Even though the new site was farther from the center of town than Washington Park, it was accessible by subway and trolley to some 90 percent of the borough. Here he hoped to build a two-tiered stadium designed to seat twenty-two thousand patrons.

The project was originally estimated to cost $200,000, but cost over-runs sent the final price to over $400,000. Hard pressed for funds, as he always would be, Ebbets sought financial support from local people. Retaining 50 percent of the stock himself, he sold half-interest in the club to the McKeever brothers, Steve and Ed. The McKeevers had known Ebbets for thirty years before becoming his partners. They were descendants of Irish immigrants and came from the old Second Ward of Brooklyn.

Originally a plumber, Steve McKeever diversified into wide-ranging contracting interests in steam-fitting and sidewalk construction; his firm had held contracts on the elevated railway and the Brooklyn Bridge. In supplying the capital needed to complete the construction of the new stadium, the brothers became vice presidents of the club and, like Ebbets, familiar sights to the patrons of Ebbets Field.

The opening of Ebbets Field on April 5, 1913, was festive; bands played, ceremonies abounded, and pitcher Nap Rucker led the Dodgers to victory over the New York Yankees in an exhibition game. The field itself was cozy, fans shouted to players, bull pens were open, and bantering antics became the rule from the start. Roger Kahn grew up literally within yelling distance of Ebbets Field in the 1930s and recalls how he could hear the shouts of the players and even see their expressions during games. It was a place to see a baseball game and experience keen participation in the drama of onfield events. In the late 1960s Leo Durocher recalled his 1939–1947 managerial stint with the Dodgers and remembered how fans would line either side of a narrow passageway shouting advice or abuse depending on the events of the previous day as he and his players walked to the playing field. Also promoting the myth and extending the coziness were practices going back to the days of Washington Park, when the players rode to the park in open carriages in full uniform. Later on, ads appeared on both the trolleys and elevated trains promoting game attendance, and in 1914 the local newspapers helped as the *Brooklyn Eagle* established an honor roll of free ticket winners. On specified days, the management distributed tickets to children in schools and orphanages.

The atmosphere of intimacy made the top management people readily available. For example, in the 1920s, Vice President Steve McKeever personally signed bleacher passes for boys who helped clean up the park prior to games. A familiar figure to patrons, he would sit in his accustomed seat behind home plate sipping milk and bantering with fans. Player accessibility was facilitated by the fact that many of them lived within walking distance of the park, a tradition that lasted until the Dodgers moved to the West Coast. Steve McKeever's daughter would drive to Ebbets Field, where boys vied with one another to open her door in exchange for a pass to the game. Ebbets himself traveled to sign each of his players to their contracts in the off season. Typical of the Brooklyn managerial style was the personal nature of the exercise of power. Ebbets reigned in an era of dominant personalities. Moguls like Clark Griffiths in Washington, Connie Mack in Philadelphia, Barney Dreyfuss in Pittsburgh, and Colonel Rupert and the Stonehams in New York were examples of the breed. In Brooklyn the emphasis was on local community ownership and control of the team.

In the days of Ebbets-McKeever ownership, the Dodger board of directors was composed completely of citizens of Brooklyn. Ebbets forbade alcoholic drinks in the stands, but developed promotional gimmicks to encourage attendance which, it was originally calculated, required a daily average of four thousand customers to keep out of the red. Only in the dismal and lackluster mid-1930s would Brooklyn attendance fall off; it remained high even for some outlandishly inept teams.

15.

Wacky Failure: The Daffiness Boys

Players who made good newspaper copy were crucial in the evolution of the Dodger legends. Four Brooklyn newspapers and the leading New York dailies assigned imaginative reporters to cover the team. In the pre-World War I era, several characters set the tone at Ebbets Field, and the image of comic farce baseball reached gargantuan proportions by the 1920s when newsmen dubbed the Dodgers the "Daffiness Boys." Most notable in the early days were outfielder Casey Stengel, manager Uncle Wilbert Robinson, and pitcher Leo Dickerman; after a particularly galling loss due to a teammate's egregious error Dickerman announced—or so a reporter claimed—"From now on it's a case of everyone for their self."[1] Manager Robinson, an ex-butcher and former Baltimore Oriole, was round, innocent, unlettered, and gorgeously profane, a kind of unspoiled nature-child of sport. Easygoing and apparently often confused, he became familiar to and beloved by the citizens of Brooklyn, who would refer to his wife as "Ma" and shout advice after the rotund figure as he made his bumbling way along the streets.

Wilbert Robinson reigned as manager from 1914 to 1931

and established a tradition of buffoonery and spontaneity that
has seldom been matched in baseball's annals. Perhaps it was
fortuitous, or perhaps it was just that the Brooklyn team
tended to attract oddities; whatever the case there certainly
was a basis in fact for Philip Roth's designation of Brooklyn
as the ultimate in "urban wackiness" as far as baseball was
concerned. Certainly, Uncle Robby was a delight to newspapermen in search of colorful copy. His appearance—he was
once described as shaped like Santa Claus—gave evidence of
affability and jocular awkwardness. Stories about him exemplify a kind of whimsical irresponsibiilty and easygoing-
ness which would be hard to imagine in the current day of
well-groomed, serious managers. Although he seemed to have
had a good eye for bringing along new pitchers and reviving
fading ones, Robby was new to the managerial ranks when
appointed in 1914. His personality would seem to have signalled the growing urban sport madness in the years from
1914 to 1931. Here was a man who once signed a pitcher to
his team because he played piano well during spring training.
Once, in a fit of pique at reporters, who rather adored him for
his newsworthiness, he let them pick the lineup for a game.
In 1916 spring training at Daytona, the ex-catcher vowed that
he could catch a ball thrown from an airplane by the re-
knowned aviatrix, Ruth Law. The fine hand of Casey Stengel
intervened, and it was a grapefruit which splashed over the
chest of a hysterical Uncle Robby who screamed that he had
been "kilt," as Stengel and his cohorts roared with laughter.
It was typical of the man that he subsequently claimed that
had it been a baseball he would have caught it. Endearing
tales of his naivete proliferated. It is claimed that he once put
a player named Cox in the lineup because he couldn't pro-
nounce the name of the player he really wanted.

   Absentminded and vague, he often forgot the names of
long time members of his team and would sometimes refer to
a player as "whosus." Yet, in the initial period of his reign he

managed to win two pennants—in 1916 and 1920—and some excellent players worked under his leadership, including Jake Daubert, Otto Miller, Rube Marquand, Nap Rucker, Casey Stengel, and Zack Wheat, the Flatbush hero of his day. Yet, the Dodgers established no victory dynasty and their fortunes fluctuated wildly. For example, after the pennant victory of 1916, 1917 saw them in seventh place; after the 1920 pennant, 1921 followed with fifth place. In the years from 1914 to 1920 the team finished third once, fifth three times, and seventh once—a generally dismal performance.

Meanwhile, the legend of oddness continued as bizarre events characterized Dodger efforts in the field. Moreover, Brooklyn fans were coming into their own as vocal critics not only of the opposition but of the failures of their own heroes. One Brooklyn player of this period played with cotton in his ears in order to dull the jeers of hometown rooters. A shortstop was supposed to have been so wild in his throws that he endangered the well-being of fans on the first base side of the infield. In the 1916 World Series which the Dodgers lost to the Boston Red Sox, Babe Ruth, then a Boston pitcher, won an overtime game in which he pitched thirteen consecutive scoreless innings. In the 1920 Series which the Dodgers lost to the Cleveland Indians, the Indians made the first grand-slam home run in World Series history and Cleveland fielder Bill Wambsganns executed an *unassisted* triple play. This Series also included the first home run ever hit by a pitcher.

During the 1920 season alone, the Dodgers played three successive games of twenty-six innings, thirteen innings, and nineteen innings, all of which were lost. During that same season, the fining of a Brooklyn pitcher for speculating in tickets recalled the ominous 1919 Black Sox scandal. All of this, however, was mere prelude to what was to come in the so-called Golden Age of Sport in the 1920s.

There seems to have been enough truth to foster the myth. Superstitious and stubbornly intuitive, Uncle Robby selected his pitchers on hunches, always preferring that they be physically large. During exhibition seasons in the Florida league of the 1920s, he would show up on the wrong day or at the wrong field for games. More than once he scheduled the same pitcher two days in a row. These are typical of the tales that survive about his eccentricity and ineptitude. Once he even had his men bat in the wrong order. On another occasion he restrained Chick Fester from banging his bat on the dugout step during a rally lest he wake up the dozing pitcher, Jess Petty.

While Manager Robinson seems to have expressed little vindictiveness or anger toward his players, he did have a senseless feud with the *New York Sun,* which withdrew its coverage of the Brooklyn team, thereby exacerbating the destructive feud between Uncle Robby and Steve McKeever. The split, which resisted all healing efforts, had a deleterious effect on Brooklyn prospects as the two men, one the president of the club, the other a senior stockholder and treasurer, rarely spoke to one another. When Mayor Walker of New York evinced interest in buying the club, marveling that it still drew good crowds with dismal teams, he remarked at how difficult it was to do business with the club, that they were impossibly slow in responding to even the most urgent business.

It was true that Robby let the team go about its business with only the lightest of controls. Training rules were flaunted with impunity. Robby was the kind of man who could establish a "Boner Club" to fine transgressors and then promptly become the charter member himself when he sent the wrong lineup to the umpire, a fact gleefully pointed out the next day by the *New York Sun.*

Yet, Dodger ineptitude was a kind of safety valve. Even today, long after the silence has descended on Brooklyn baseball, the term "Dodger skull" conveys a sense of flagrant public error in the baseball arena. The Dodgers came to symbolize glorious but earnest losing, losing with gusto and innocent effort. There was something funny about Dodger failures that caught on in a nation where failure in other fields was regarded with anxiety.

The Dodgers' record from 1920 until Uncle Robby's retirement in 1931 reveals two fourth-place, one first-place, one fifth-place, one second-place, and seven sixth-place finishes. Actually, on at least two occasions, the Dodgers contended for the pennant until near the end of the season. Despite the dismal showings, some good players cavorted at Ebbets Field, among them Babe Herman, Al Lopez, Dazzy Vance, Fresco Thomson, and Jake Fournier.

Charles Ebbets, who had been ailing for some time, died in April of 1925. A game with the Giants was in progress at Ebbets Field when the news reached the teams, but the game was completed on Uncle Robby's insistence that Mr. Ebbets would have wanted it that way. The crowd stood for a moment of silence and the Brooklyn players affixed mourning bands to their uniforms as the usual Giant-Brooklyn tumult ensued. President Heydler of the National League, in the formation of which Ebbets had played so crucial a role, ordered the postponement of all league games on the day of the Ebbets funeral. Moreover, many leading figures in the game gathered for the funeral at Trinity Church in Brooklyn. Ebbets willed his estate, which consisted entirely of Brooklyn baseball interests, to surviving members of his family. These observances must seem extraordinary to baseball enthusiasts of the 1970s who could hardly imagine similar expressions for the passing of a present-day club president. The corporate style has tended to downgrade the personal visibility of baseball executives as it has other big business executives.

The dominance of key figures during the formative period of baseball did continue in the period of mature expansion of professional sport. People like Ebbets, Connie Mack, Barney Dreyfuss, Colonel Jake Rupert, Ed Barrow, and Branch

Rickey seem not cut out for work in faceless bureaucracies.
The size of organizations alone obviates a more personal
style; for example, it would be unimaginable for a club
president in these days of large staffs and increased division
of labor to personally sign each of his players to a contract in
the manner of Charles Ebbets.

The intimacy of Brooklyn baseball's top leadership can be
seen from the realignment of power which took place after
the death of Mr. Ebbets. Ed McKeever, who had originally
helped him to gain control of the club and build Ebbets Field,
took a chill at the Ebbets funeral and died a few days later.
The death of two men who exerted both ownership and
management control was a blow to the small, tightly knit
group who made policy. The newly designated president was
none other than Uncle Wilbert Robinson himself, the trusted,
time-honored field manager of the club. Although he seemed
to have no particular aptitude for front-office leadership he
was nonetheless selected because of his popularity with the
followers of the team. Robby moved into the front office and
Zack Wheat, an outfielder who later was inducted into the
Hall of Fame, became acting field manager. The team faltered, and, after some attempts at consultation, Robby re-
sumed the field managership, acting for some time in the dual
capacity of team manager and club president. However, at the
executive level the Brooklyn organization was seriously divided. Steve McKeever and Wilbert Robinson feuded bitterly,
resisting all well-intentioned efforts to patch up their
differences.

The most striking legend-provoking antics occurred in the
years immediately after the death of Charles Ebbets, when
many talented newspapermen covered the Dodgers, among
them Roscoe McGowen, then with a Brooklyn paper and later
with the *New York Times*. Other splendid journalists including Tommy Holmes and Quentin Reynolds also provided accounts of Dodger doings. Then, as later, newsmen were an
integral part of the Brooklyn baseball scene, acting almost as

members of the organization, giving advice, carousing with players, and embellishing their material. Thus, the main source of the lore was newspaper accounts of the 1920s. Some of the stories and the images spread quickly and were picked up and embellished in vaudeville routines, radio programs, and movies. Ineptitude approaching silent movie comedy routines made up the substance of this kind of material.

Many stories illustrate how close and casual the relations were among members of the baseball team in those days. The outstanding Dodgers of the 1920s came from towns like Orient, Iowa; Ausable, Michigan; Buffalo, New York; Alameda, California; and Winthrop, Maine. For the most part they had limited education and were rural in outlook, and some of the antics of the players may have been the result of rural people finding themselves in the country's most cosmopolitan city.

It was the newspapers who coined the term "Daffiness Boys" and wrote of the "light-hearted flock" representing Brooklyn in the National League. They were something special, a legend really distinct from all others. There were other losing teams, but their comedic potential, as revealed in the public media, never approached that of the Dodgers.

The chief knights of madness in the 1920s were Jake Fournier, the erstwhile first baseman; Dazzy Vance, a pitching immortal now in the Hall of Fame; and the unique Floyd "Babe" Herman. In a sense there was irony in their being remembered as ringleaders in mayhem because all three were excellent players, Herman's fielding and base-running excepted. One of the charming legends about Herman concerns his scorn for locker-mate Fresco Thomson's hitting. The Babe is reported to have complained about the indignity of dressing next to a .230 hitter; whereupon Thomson announced his chagrin at having to dress next to a .230 fielder.

The Babe was the instigator of horrendous public misplays which are solemnly attested to by observers. Purchased for some $10,000 from Memphis, where he was discovered, he

was only twenty-three when he made his debut at Ebbets
Field. A warm, open-faced, stubborn young man whose feelings could easily be hurt by aggressive instruction, he had
amassed impressive batting averages in the minor leagues.
Singularly rural in appearance, with his cheeks bulging with
tobacco, Herman could easily have played a rube comic in
vaudeville. On August 15, 1926, the Babe perpetrated one of
the most flagrant boners in the history of baseball, one which
was picked up by all the wire services and forever marked the
mid-1920s Dodgers as the "Daffiness Boys." With three of his
mates on the bases, Herman made a hit to right field. Once he
embarked upon the bases, the Babe seemed to sever all contact with the rest of humanity. The man on third scored, but
Dazzy Vance held up on second, thinking that the ball would
be caught. When it wasn't, he ran to third and started for
home, but, thinking that he might be thrown out at the plate,
headed back for third base. The man on first, all confidence,
rounded second and headed for third, while the isolated and
independent Herman, hoping to stretch what he regarded as a
sure double into a triple ran headlong around the bases. In the
end all three came to rest on third base. In the ensuing uproar,
two of the players were called out while the fans roared and
Manager Robinson approached apoplexy. The *New York
Times* reporter wrote, "Being tagged out was much too good
for Herman."[2] Yet, fans forgave much in their outfielder because he could hit. In his career at Ebbets Field he had season averages of .340, .381, .393, and .326. Some writers wrote
of him as an intelligent and charming man who was a warm
father and loving husband, but to Dodger fans of the 1920s he
was the master of the big skull. A popular vaudeville routine
of the period involved a taxi driver leaving a patron at Ebbets
Field, who when told the Dodgers have three men on base
asked, "Which base?"

The Babe's antics off the field also filled sports columns.
He was supposed to have left his son sleeping in a box seat

after the conclusion of a game, so that he had to return to the park to fetch him. Another time he told Joe Gordon of the *World Telegram and American* that he resented the clown image fastened on him, explaining that his feelings had been deeply hurt. Contrite for once, the reporter promised to refrain in the future. However, when the newsmen offered to light the stub of a cigar the Babe pulled from his pocket, he was waved off with the assurance that it was already lighted.

Years later, when Herman's son became assistant manager of the Metropolitan Opera Company, the good natured Babe remarked that his boy derived his talent from his father.

However, the basepaths were Herman's greatest nemesis. Coming to bat with a man on first base, the Babe slashed a hit to the outfield. The runner on first, thinking the ball might be caught retreated from his dash toward second, while the Babe was stretching his hit into a double, and the players passed each other on the basepaths. On another occasion, it is alleged that teammates passed the Babe on the basepaths, going in the same direction, while the raw youngster pondered the scoreboard or, perhaps, a bird overhead.

The Babe provided striking copy, but he was not alone in his zaniness. For example, Jake Fournier was a really solid player and hated to play at Ebbets Field because of the incessant booing of the fans. He relented, however, when it was explained to him that there was nothing personal in it, that being on first base merely rendered him the most convenient target. Fournier was the team's resident bookmaker, and he also distinguished himself as a disregarder of training rules, an attitude which became endemic with the "Daffiness Boys." While leading some teammates on a postseason western tour, he provoked a minor riot which saw four of them jailed. Once he advised a rookie Brooklyn pitcher on how to pitch to the formidable Rogers Hornsby, Hornsby got his usual hit but not at Fournier's position, which was what he had in mind all along.

Dazzy Vance was second only to Herman in promoting hi-jinks. A high-living rule breaker, Vance was a splendid pitcher in his best days, most of which took place on a team deeply mired in sixth place. The Dazzler was truly magnificent; in 1924 he won twenty-eight games, struck out 262 batsmen, and had an earned run average of only 2.16. To confuse batters already struggling with his powerful pitches, Vance slit the sleeve of his blouse into tatters, so that when he wound up, batsmen beheld a windmill of arms flailing the air. To all complaints, Dazzy is supposed to have retorted that he would not wear a different shirt since the slits gave him luck and that he hadn't washed it since his days in the minor leagues.

Whatever his talents may have been—and they were considerable enough to land him in the Hall of Fame from a team which never once won a pennant during his long tenure—Vance was the ringleader of a hell-raising subgroup within the team called the "0 for 4" club—i.e., getting no hits for four chances at bat. To become members and retain good standing team members had to break training rules without being apprehended. When a pitcher named Jess Petty was detected by manager Robinson coming in after hours and fined, he protested his ejection from "0 for 4." During the reinstatement hearings, which Vance and two colleagues conducted while wrapped in sheets and wearing towels for turbans, Petty presented a letter ghost written for him by a friendly newsman. His application for reinstatement was rejected, when the ruling commission detected a word which Petty could not spell or define.

Reporters claimed that an atmosphere of easy-going madness permeated the luckless, unwinning club and that perfectly serious types became entangled in the prevailing mood of lackadaisical ineffectiveness. Yet, in 1931 the Dodgers made a fine run for the pennant, ending in fourth place, after heading the league for some seventy-five days. Attendance mounted to 1.1 million at home and the Dodgers also drew very well on the road. Wearied by still another failure to win a pennant and depressed over the continuing battle within the front office, Robby left at the end of the 1931 season and a charming era in baseball history ended. Ahead lay the dismal 1930s, a bleak time for the Brooklyn team which from 1932 to 1939 finished third once, fifth once, sixth three times, and seventh twice.

16.

Wacky Success: Depression and Revival

If much of the ineptitude remained, most of the fun was gone; the daffiness era, perhaps totally unsuited to a depression country, was gone. Many of the old carousers were traded or retired. Three managers took the battering during the 1930s —Max Carey, Casey Stengel and Burleigh Grimes—all of whom had played in Brooklyn uniform. Ring Lardner caught the torpor of the period when he wrote that Stengel advised one of his song writing players not to write a tune about the Dodgers unless it was a torch song. It was the period when Bill Terry, the manager of the (rival) New York Giants, once asked, "Is Brooklyn still in the league?"[1]

Rather than the wild aggressiveness of the "Daffiness Boys," this period saw things happening to the Dodgers. For example, the Cincinnati pitcher Johnny Van Der Meer threw the second of two consecutive no-hit games against the Dodgers. To be sure, some colorful players still found Ebbets Field congenial. For example, Tony Cuccinello once refused to slide lest he crush some cigars in his pocket. The imbibing tradition also carried over; it raised havoc with two of the most promising of the younger players, one of whom went berserk in an airplane during a road trip. Then, too, there were outright reversions. Once while running for a fly ball, outfielder Frenchy Bordagaray stopped momentarily to retrieve the cap which had blown from his head. And there were some good players, of whom probably the most promising and the least fulfilled was pitcher Van Lingle Mungo. Winner of sixteen games with the 1933 sixth-place team, Mungo was an unaccountable and untamable type who soon tired of losing close games. After one particularly galling loss because of an outfielder's error, he wired his wife that she should immediately come to Ebbets Field, that if the player in question could play center field, so could she. However, Mungo did have his day in the sun when, because of his magnificent pitching, the Dodgers knocked the Giants out of the pennant race at the very end of the 1938 season.

Still, the mid-1930s were a nightmare for the Dodgers, and manager Stengel could often be seen with his head in his hands during his tenure. Aimlessness continued to be the rule at the front office. Two fired managers were paid off for unfulfilled contracts at higher salaries than their immediate successors received for actively managing the club. Front office policy disasters were matched on the field by a declining attendance. Freddy Lindstrom, who had once been a darling of the New York Giants, ended up at Ebbets Field in 1937 at the very end of a fading career. He was typical of several players who were at that time in Dodger uniform. While running for a fly ball he bumped into a fellow outfielder and the ball fell between them. Laughing uproariously as he came into the dugout between innings, he remarked that he had seen Dodger shenanigans all of his career and now he was part of them.

Most reactions to the Dodgers' ineptitude during the 1930s were not so good natured. Fans and sports writers chided the directors for failing to provide their managers with talent, a fact particularly resented in the case of the popular Casey

Stengel. Changes in the front office and the turnover in general managers added to the confusion. In fact, the soddenness became so rooted that some doleful sports writers asserted that when Burleigh Grimes became manager in 1937, he had proved his suitability by bringing Louisville into last place in the Southern Association the previous season.

Another throwback who might have fit better into the previous period was a portly catcher named Babe Phelps; he was slow of foot, ungainly of manner, but strong of bat. Babe, so it is insisted, succumbed to the old fever by stealing a base with a teammate already on it. More portly even than Phelps was former New York Giant pitcher, Fred Fitzsimmons, known as "Fat Freddy." Something happened to him at Ebbets Field and he put together some extremely successful seasons after being traded at the age of thirty-six. Otherwise the cast was distinguished by relative nonentities like Joe Stripp, Goody Rosen, and Luke "Hot Potato" Hamlin, the latter so-called for his ability to serve home-run balls. It was a team composed of those who had seen better days and those who would never see any days at all. Managers tended to be serious, even the puckish Stengel, and there was little comic relief.

In the face of growing indebtedness, the directors of the club turned in desperation to the president of the National League, Ford Frick, for advice. Frick's recommendation that they bring in Larry McPhail proved to be fateful. McPhail had built the Cincinnati franchise into a winner by expanding the farm system, instituting night baseball, and hiring the gifted Red Barber to broadcast games; he proved to be a perfect fit for the Brooklyn tradition of "urban wackiness." He had left baseball shortly before, announcing that he was about to lose his mind and apparently coming off an emotional crisis. Mercurial, egotistical, experimental, and innovative, he had the fiery temperament needed to rekindle the national imagination about Brooklyn baseball. His coming was a turn-

ing point in baseball enterprise in Brooklyn. Old Steve Mc-
Keever, the last of the old guard, died shortly after McPhail
was installed as vice president, and the new leader enjoyed
practically carte blanche prerogatives.

McPhail ran a personal show at Ebbets Field. His route
was a daring one based largely on borrowing money and taking chances with an enterprise that already owed a considerable amount of money to its chief creditor, a local community
bank. It was the kind of daring that characterized American
business enterprise in the formative period. He flew his team
on road trips, installed lighting for night baseball, and brought
in Red Barber to broadcast games, thereby establishing his
faith that radio, which frightened the more conservative New
York Baseball executives, would stimulate gate receipts. He
bought players, renovated Ebbets Field, hired a group of carefully trained ushers, and offered all sorts of blandishments to
fans. Jesse Owens raced between games, and Babe Ruth acted
as a baserunning coach for a brief time.

As a result, excitement returned to Ebbets Field. McPhail's
energy blew conservative business practices clean out of the
Brooklyn organization. With his borrowed money he put together by purchase and trade a team which reversed Brooklyn's baseball fortunes. To the Dodgers came fine players like
Dolph Camilli, Cookie Lavagetto, Whitlow Wyatt, Kirby
Higby, Dixie Walker, Pete Rieser, Pee Wee Reese, Ducky
Medwick, Curt Davis, Mickey Owen, and Billy Herman.
Some were established stars from other teams, some were on
their way up, a few were minor league finds, and others were
castoffs. To head the team that reporters were beginning to
call the "Hustling Brooks," McPhail chose Leo Durocher, a
former St. Louis Cardinal Gas House Gang partisan with a
reputation for brawling on the field and disputing with umpires.

It turned out that Durocher was a good copy on the field
of McPhail in the front office. It was likely that two such
vibrant egoes as those of Durocher and McPhail would clash,

and in his idiosyncratic style the front office leader fired and rehired Durocher many times.

A revised Dodger image was in the making as Brooklyn took third place in 1939 and second place in 1940. Mayor Walker's observation of years before proved accurate as the 1939 Dodgers attracted over a million fans to Ebbets Field and provided box office appeal on road trips as well.

During the 1930s, newsmen took a cue from the bleacher partisans and referred to the Dodgers as "Dem Bums." It was a nickname which somehow stuck, and the cartoon bum figure often graced sports-page articles about the team. Perhaps the image remained because of the traditional underdog position of the Dodgers and the plaintive Dodger fan cry of, "Wait 'til next year." The Dodgers attracted a national following in most of their years because they seemed more human, more fallible, and more flawed than their counterparts. Perhaps the bum cartoon epitomized a sympathy for the underdog which people, particularly those in the so-called bedroom borough of New York, experienced vividly.

McPhail's uncanny ability to generate excitement seemed in keeping with Dodger traditions, and during his tenure Ebbets Field came to be portrayed as a kind of benign madhouse. It was during this period that movie references to the Dodgers, still depicted as losers, began to crop up. McPhail's era also saw a bar-room murder perpetrated by a Dodger fan angered by the slanderous opinions of a visiting New York Giant enthusiast. The national press services also featured a photo story about an irrepressible Dodger fan who ran on to the field and pummelled George Magerkurth, a burly umpire, because he disagreed with a decision.

The brawling, successful image of the team had a basis in fact. When Dodger Ducky Medwick, Durocher's former Gas House Gang teammate, was beaned on his first appearance in Dodger uniform in June 1940, there ensued one of those not-so-minor riots which saw players pouring onto the field and an exchange of fisticuffs involving manager Durocher. Owner McPhail raged up and down the sidelines encouraging the mayhem.

Thereafter, the promise of riot spurred attendance at Dodger games both at home and on the road. On one occasion an opposing pitcher who was winding up to throw to a Dodger batter experienced a change of heart, turned, and fired the ball at Manager Leo Durocher in the Brooklyn dugout. This was retribution for Durocher who is alleged to have advised his pitchers to "stick it in his ear."

The Brooklyn manager was a living, breathing exemplar of get-up-and-go, embodying values similar to those which built American industry. He was daring, imaginative, abrasive, and aggressive, and sometimes cavalier about rules. Moreover, he became a popular culture figure of such national prominence he was even cultivated by movie stars. His annual appearance on the Fred Allen radio show was the occasion for a take-off on *H. M. S. Pinafore,* based on Dodger themes. Newsreels gloried in Durocher's conflicts with umpires. In them he could be seen kicking dirt back onto the home plate that the umpire had patiently brushed clear moments before.

The son of a New England Railway worker and a pool hustler in his teens, Durocher's popularity in Brooklyn was unquestioned. At one point, Dodger fans collected twenty-five hundred pennies in order to pay one of his frequent fines.

In addition to the charismatic manager, McPhail's players were a colorful lot who prospered in the salubrious Brooklyn surroundings. A new myth was growing. Billy Herman, star second baseman, once remarked that in Brooklyn every game was like the World Series, while another observer remarked that a game at Ebbets Field was like the day the Bastille fell.

Certain players inexplicably gained special public affection. None outdistanced Fred "Dixie" Walker, whose previous career with major league teams had been cut short by injuries

and illnesses. He was twenty-eight years old and nearly
washed up when he was pulled into Ebbets Field in the net
that McPhail cast out to gather talent. Somehow, the southerner became enormously popular with what the press called
"The Flatbush Faithful"—those fans whose loyalty never
wavered. Walker became a formidable hitter in Brooklyn,
especially against the Giants. Articles appeared about him in
popular magazines attempting to explain polyglot Brooklyn's
reverence for a straight southern rural boy. The newsmen
dubbed him, in good Brooklynese, "The Peepul's Cherce."[2]

For some reason McPhail was not keen on the "peepul's
cherce" and had the bad habit of benching him in favor of his
latest new find. When McPhail replaced him with veteran
Paul Waner in 1941, 5,000 fans sent telegrams threatening
to boycott games unless Walker returned. Ultimately he did,
when the aging Waner faded, but the boycott never ma-
terialized and the general tumult in the packed stands continued unabated as the Dodgers contended for the pennant.

Another star was youthful "Pistol" Pete Rieser, so-called
for his affection for cowboy movies. In 1941, at the age of
twenty-two, Rieser hit .343, but sad to say, his great promise
was never realized. His inability to judge the approach to the
fence while chasing flyballs resulted in frequent crashes which
finally caused him serious injury.

The pitching staff was outstanding and very Southern, including starters Whitlow Wyatt, Kirby Higby, and ace reliefer
Hugh Casey. Higby was perversely referred to as "Koiby
Higelby" by the errant fans, at least according to the sports
columns. Many years later in the late 1960s, Higby remi-
nisced for a sports magazine about his days in Brooklyn. With
unabashed nostalgia he asked where else a South Carolina
redneck could learn to love cheese blintzes and baked lasagna.
Two members of this pitching staff—Freddy Fitzsimmons and
Hugh Casey—continued the Brooklyn baseball tradition of

player visibility by operating businesses in close proximity to Ebbets Field.

The 1941 season saw the Dodgers win the National League pennant for the first time since 1920. However, the outcome of the World Series with the formidable New York Yankees was disappointing—the Dodgers losing four games to one. The Series did not lack the drama associated in the public mind with the special flair for disaster attached to Brooklyn baseball. Behind two games to one, the Dodgers were leading the fourth, with two men out in the ninth inning. Then catcher Mickey Owen dropped the third strike which reliever Hugh Casey had just thrown by Tommy Henrich, a Yankee slugger. In true "murderers' row" style, the Yankees exploded a rally, going on to win the game. Even so, 1941 had been a memorable year for Brooklyn baseball. Some 1.2 million people had attended home games, thus helping to pay off much of the team's indebtedness and vindicating the policies of Larry McPhail.

If it had been a colorful and productive season, at least part of the reason lay outside the team itself as bizarre fan behavior took on new forms. For example, the Reverend B. C. S. Benson led fans in public prayer during the pennant drive. In the stands, certain patrons exhibited antics that eventually made them almost as well known as the players themselves. One Shorty Lurice, for example, put together a tramp-clad, off-key brass band dubbed the Dodger "Symphony"—with emphasis on the "phony." They played the Laurel and Hardy song to enemy pitchers and batsmen as they trudged to their positions, and rang out lustily when the Dodgers excelled. An unknown but creative fan gained a measure of fame by blowing up a large rubber duck whenever his favorite, Ducky Medwick, came to bat.

Most famous of all was Hilda Chester, who appeared on national radio programs and was mentioned in the comic writ-

ings of Damon Runyon. She sat in the bleachers ringing cow-
bells to urge on her heroes. When the management offered her
a reserved grandstand seat back of the dugout, she stoutly refused, announcing that she could not relax in "them fancy
seats." Opposing Hilda was "Abie the Milkman." Unencum-
bered by artificial instruments, he relied on a booming voice
and comic propensities to annoy Dodger fans with his deri-
sions. His grandstand debates with "Apple Mary," a loyal
Dodgerite, were epic encounters recalled by a number of writers long after the stillness had set in. Thus, the fans were very
much a part of the charm. One veteran newsman asserted that
Dodger fans were "the noisiest, the most loyal and the screw-
iest . . . unlike the rooters of the other fifteen big league
teams."[3] A psychoanalyst, perhaps in jest, suggested that the
behavior of fans resulted from a love born of suffering.[4]

Expressions of Dodger loyalty sometimes went pretty far,
as in the case of a condemned man whose final question before execution concerned the outcome of a Dodger game with
the Giants, or the Brooklyn signalman whose last message
from Corregidor asked after the prospects of his favorite
team.

It is fascinating to analyze the myth of frantic loyalty
erected before the American public. Whatever the reality may
have been, enough people wanted to believe the lore about the
Dodgers and their fans to make the impressions lasting. There
was something quaint, off-beat, and ruggedly individualistic
about the antics of fans in Ebbets Field, and the legend was
national in scope. For example, one literary scholar recalled
that from the perspective of a Jew growing up in Flatbush
there was something "vaguely goyish" about being a Yankee
fan.[5] Perhaps, too, the charm was a symbolic exemplification
of continuity, community, and comradeship in an increasingly
anomic urban world. Ushers and attendants at the ball park
tended to be of long service, as did the staff of the club, the
baggage man, the clubhouse man, the road secretary, and the

grounds keepers; physical landmarks were unchanging in the intimate setting of Ebbets Field.

Some of the fame of the Dodgers and their fans was certainly due to the clever and charming announcing of Walter "Red" Barber, the radio sportscaster who accompanied McPhail to Ebbets Field. Barber too was a case of cultural accommodation, as he and his quaint Southern country sayings fit snugly into the tumultuous world of Brooklyn baseball. He coined the term "rhubarb" to depict an argument on the field, and when things were going well for the Dodgers, a player might be "sitting in the catbird seat," or "eating high on the hog," or "tearing up the pea patch." These ruralisms caught on in the urban setting, and Barber became a national figure, his sayings immortalized in a story by James Thurber.

By contrast with the mixed glories of 1941, the 1942 season revived the anguish of a scarred past as the Dodgers frittered away a long lead to the St. Louis Cardinals in the last month of the season. The war was on and McPhail was planning to get into uniform. Once more the head of the National League was consulted, and a fateful decision resulted. At a critical point, the control of the Dodgers passed into the hands of Branch Rickey, and baseball and America would never be the same again.

17.

The Robinson – Rickey Experiment

During the 1949 World Series, the Brooklyn Dodgers—by now nearly the group Roger Kahn would immortalize as the "Boys of Summer"—played out a futile World Series with the New York Yankees, winning only one game. Television sets graced the windows of shops in the university section of a medium sized eastern city, and clusters of interested students gathered for hours. A professor of medieval history bemoaned Duke Snider's collapse at the plate; a German-Jewish refuge seeking his Ph.D. in German literature boomed excitement as Pee Wee Reese came to bat; members of Students for Democratic Action exclaimed "come on!" But, to the dismay of these advocates, the Dodgers once again faltered.

These fan enthusiasms illustrate the fact that following the Brooklyn Dodgers had assumed political significance, becoming, in fact, a sign of liberal or even radical inclinations. The underdog myths about the Dodgers at last had a tangible referent: it was the first baseball team to include a black player, and, according to Roger Kahn, it became the most integrated of all teams in the history of the game.[1] Breaking the race barrier in the game which was after all known as the "national pastime" was the work of two remarkable men. Their collaboration succeeded because of their courage and faith in one another and because, despite all the opposition, the time was right. The integration of baseball was a dramatic realization of the promise of the American dream, partly catalyzed by war-time idealism and the conviction that the suffering undergone ought to make this country a better, more democratic place. Branch Rickey's tactics worked, and the doors opened for black players who eventually found positions on all of the major league teams. It is possible that the high visibility of baseball's integration made a significant impact on American society at large.

By any measure, Wesley Branch Rickey was an oddity in big time baseball. A man with a moral conscience who eschewed profanity, he refused beer and cigarette advertising, quoted the Bible, relaxed by reading Greek classics, helped establish the Fellowship of Christian Athletes, and had once been considered for the Republican candidacy for the United States Senate from Missouri. More important, he cherished a dream about breaking the race barrier.

Midwestern by birth and a lawyer, Rickey had coached baseball at the University of Michigan while studying for his law degree. Following a brief, none-too-effective career as a big league catcher at the turn of the century, Rickey opened a law practice in Idaho. However, an offer from the St. Louis Browns won him away from law practice. After working as assistant president of the Browns, he shifted over to the St. Louis Cardinals, becoming president of that club in 1917. At that time the Cardinals were one of the weakest franchises in the National League, having finished in last place in 1916.

Rickey was always a keen judge of baseball talent, and his being outbid for a promising player by John McGraw of the New York Giants led him to create the first farm system. As Rickey devised it, this was a network of minor-league teams either owned by the major-league club or bound to it by working arrangements. It was an inexpensive way to develop players and feed them to the parent club. Employing an extensive group of scouts to comb the hills for baseball talent, Rickey built an empire at St. Louis which yielded outstanding teams from the early 1920s until his departure for Brooklyn in 1942. The most memorable of his teams was undoubtedly the Gas House Gang of the early 1930s, which included the Dean Brothers, Pepper Martin, Sunny Jim Bottomley, Leo Durocher, and other stars.

The often reprinted story about how an Ohio Wesleyan University baseball team coached by Mr. Rickey included a black player who was refused an evening's hotel lodging during a road trip is corroborated by members of his family. His daughter recalls that as a young girl she heard her father's dramatic account of how he persuaded the hotel management to allow the player to stay in his coach's room and how upon arriving there the young man wept and rubbed his hands together repeating over and over, "But for these black hands."[2] This incident ignited a lifelong resolve in Mr. Rickey, for he became a student of the sociology and history of racial affairs in this country. His daughter remembers his library of Lincolniana and black sociology and history, particularly a copy of Gunnar Myrdal's *An American Dilemma,* interlined by her father. Mr. Rickey in a book written towards the end of his life himself mentioned his reading of black sociology and history.[3]

Branch Rickey had a well-developed flair for the dramatic, and it would stand him in good stead during the moving events attendant to the breaking of the racial bar. Black participation in baseball before the signing of Jackie Robinson in 1945 mirrored the trends in opportunites in American life for blacks. From the immediate post-Civil War period until the separate but equal court decisions of the 1890s, there was some latitude for blacks in American life. C. Vann Woodward, for example, carefully depicts black participation in economic, social, and political life in the South during this period.[4] It is an account surprising for its evidence of the relative relaxation of official racial bars even in Mississippi.

While the National Association of Baseball Players opposed admitting blacks in 1867, the ban was not totally realized. According to Robert Peterson, blacks played in the minor leagues throughout the 1880s,[5] and at one point an all-black league was officially recognized as a minor league by the parent organization. Blacks played in the Western League, the Northwest League, and the International League in that decade. The first official ban occurred in the International League as the result of the reluctance of white players on the Syracuse team to sit with black teammates. There were instances in which teams refused to take the field if the opposition included blacks, and by the late 1880s few blacks were still competing. Peterson found only three still active in the higher minor leagues, and they faced considerable prejudice from teams in the North.[6] Hotels barred black players, and fans protested their presence as North followed South in enforcing the Jim Crow laws of the 1890s. Yet, such was the attractiveness of black talents that major baseball leaders periodically made unsuccessful attempts to break the color lines, often by subterfuge. In 1901 John McGraw of the old Baltimore Orioles undertook to sign a black player whom he tried to pass off as a Cherokee Indian, but Charles Comiskey of the Chicago White Sox successfully blocked this attempt.[7]

That there was abundant black talent is evidenced by the 1910 Cuban Winter League results which saw the great Ty Cobb out-hit by three black players. Those athletes who toured the so-called Negro Leagues in the first half of this century included excellent players who are just now rising to national consciousness by their inclusion in the Hall of Fame. Players like John Henry Lloyd, Rube Foster, Josh Gibson, and countless others played too soon to take advantage of the post-1945 opportunities.

On the eve of World War II and during the war itself, there were tentative moves toward breaking down segregation in the major leagues. As early as 1929 Connie Mack, owner-manager of the then powerful Philadelphia Athletics had flirted with the idea, but nothing came of it.[8] The depression made black chances even less promising, and the presence of a large number of Southerners among players and field managers presented special difficulties. But there were pressures to open up baseball. A few major sports journalists—among them Westbrook Peglar and Shirley Povich—criticized segregation in baseball, as had the *Sporting News* as early as the 1920s. Yet, the road would be a hard one, and Clarke Griffith, the veteran owner of the Washington Senators, observed in the late 1930s that the first black player in baseball would be a martyr. The travail of Jackie Robinson proved him an accurate predictor.

War-time ideals, including the promise of greater equality, paved the way for the coming of the Fair Employment Practices Act and the intensification of civil rights campaigns in the mid-1940s. The New York State legislature enacted the Ives-Quinn Act along these lines, and Mayor LaGuardia of New York commissioned a study of black baseball talent; Larry McPhail brought in a negative report in regard to there being black players good enough to qualify for major league teams. He urged that blacks remain in their own leagues and blamed professional agitators for the pressure to include blacks in the established major leagues.[9]

Bill Veeck, known as baseball's bad boy, moved in the direction of integration. Veeck's abortive scheme was simply to purchase a controlling interest in the hapless Philadelphia Phillies and hire only black players.[10] It was a plan to which commissioner of baseball Kenisaw Mountain Landis was rather cool, as he would be to integration efforts in general.

In a sense Branch Rickey and Jackie Robinson were the right men at the right time. The story of a black man's breaking into baseball is pre-eminently the story of the interaction of these two strong and determined men. In the process, Rickey also built a remarkable baseball team, laying the foundation for the "Boys of Summer" team. As Roger Kahn insists, it was the first integrated team and the most integrated team. It had a national following, and being a Dodger fan came to have social and political meaning.[11] If Kahn is an accurate reporter and interpretor, the men he interviewed reflect their having been involved in something deeply moving and compelling when they were teammates of Jackie Robinson on the Brooklyn Dodgers.

Mr. Rickey's point of view was that of a hard-headed, tough-minded realist who, nonetheless, was a man of unshakable ideals. That the strategy he chose was wise, even though personally costly to Jackie Robinson and himself, can be seen by the relatively rapid integration of other teams who followed in the Dodgers' wake. Rickey was not a young man during this travail; he was sixty-one at the time he took over the Brooklyn club and sixty-four when he signed Robinson.

The Brooklyn organization beat the bushes for young talent during the war years, and the yield was plentiful. High school baseball coaches had been contacted, and scouts crossed and recrossed the country in an effort which put together some of the most memorable teams in the history of the game. Rickey-built teams won pennants in 1947, 1949, 1953, 1955 and 1956, and tied for first place in 1946.

With a scheme for bringing blacks into major-league baseball already in mind in 1942, Mr. Rickey let it be known that he was thinking about forming a black league and that he might create an all-black team in Brooklyn, to be called the Brown Dodgers. It was with this cover that he sent scouts Clyde Sukeforth, George Sisler, and Wid Mathews with Wendell Smith of the black newspaper, *The Pittsburgh Courier,* combing the country for the ideal black man to break the racial bar in baseball. In seeking the right man, Rickey felt that he had to be concerned with the whole man, "his habits, his associates, his character, his education, his intelligence."[12] Nor did he let sentiment blind him to the reception his move would receive at the hands of the public. He was particularly concerned about black reaction, worrying about the possible negative impact of exuberant black adulation of the player selected.

In talking with new recruits to his clubs, Rickey would question fledglings about their families and their aspirations. In his early conversations with Jackie Robinson he encouraged the latter to go ahead immediately with his plans to marry. It was a family tradition to bring rookie players home for dinner, and Rickey's daughter asserts that her mother never knew how many guests would be at the table at any one time, nor how long they would be staying.[13]

In moving to Brooklyn, the Rickey family continued the tradition of cozy community that typified Brooklyn baseball. They lived within walking distance of Ebbets Field and became very fond of life in the borough. Rickey's son-in-law, a former executive in the Dodger chain, still claims that there were no fans like those in Brooklyn, that they were the most loyal and supportive of any in the major leagues.[14] Rickey needed that loyalty as he embarked upon his quest.

Rickey's force of character and convictions carried him forward in the face of near total opposition by other major league owners. His wife is reported to have been worried about the terrible ordeal that ensued. Many in the sports writing and baseball establishment, musing over the enforced social closeness characteristic of a baseball team on the road, thought the grand experiment would not work. W. G. Braham, the commissioner of minor-league baseball on August 29, 1945, asserted that, "Father Divine will have to look to his laurels, for we can expect Rickey Temple to be in the course of construction in Harlem soon."[15]

He was alone, beset by insulting letters and anonymous

phone calls. Rickey was convinced that if Robinson did not make the grade, it would be years before a similar attempt could be made. Jettisoning personal sentimentality, Rickey approached the problems Robinson would face with cool logic, often sacrificing personal preferences in the interests of success. Rickey asserted that "this shocking move required, of course, some Booker T. Washington compromises with surface inequality for the sake of expediency." It was the necessity for what he called the "silent reaction to abuse" that Rickey saw as the chief price that Robinson would have to pay. Yet, Rickey recognized the tragic dimensions of that policy, noting that it was "almost too much to ask for." He attempted to understand the personal anguish in store for Robinson, but he said that "no one knows the trials and tribulations of Robinson during these years."[16] Complicating matters was a budding revolt within the Brooklyn Dodgers themselves. Several players including the much-loved "Peepul's Cherce," Dixie Walker, threatened to refuse to appear on the field with Robinson, and Walker even asked to be traded. Somehow, Rickey stood firm, the revolt was squelched, and the integrated Dodgers came into being.

There were dramatic scenes of heroic athletic exploits as Robinson became entrenched both at Ebbets Field and in the national consciousness, particularly after the period of silence ended and he was able to speak out without restraint and act out his own aggressive, flaming spirit on the baseball diamond.

There were many important human factors: Pee Wee Reese becoming the over-all field leader and Robinson's supportive friend and colleague; the sympathetic managership of Burt Shotton; the warm friendship of Spider Jorgenson, the first Dodger to really befriend Robinson; and, ultimately, the growing number of black players in the Brooklyn organization including such stars as Roy Campanella, Don Newcombe, Jim Gilliam, and Joe Black. The Dodgers of the 1947–1956 period provided inspiration for the nation. For once, America was publicly at its best for all the world to see. Black visibility became endemic with the coming of television to households in all sections of the country. The caste system had been openly breached and millions of Americans saw blacks in nonstereotypical roles for the first time. They were participants in the national game, performing their tasks in precisely the same manner as whites and being judged by the same competitive criteria, and many were succeeding. In the early 1950s during a night game at Ebbets Field, for the first time in the history of American sport, five blacks wore Brooklyn livery in a game, thus outnumbering their white teammates.

Rickey was recognized by the National Association for the Advancement of Colored People years later for his signal contribution to the expansion of black American opportunities. Here was a prime instance when a member of the establishment, a Republican, a conservative, a man who believed in the standard American virtues, moved to breach a most notable gap in the democratic promise. His purpose, he always maintained, was to bring more talent to his team; in pursuing that goal, he changed the course of American social development. When Robinson joined the Hall of Fame in Cooperstown, it was fitting that Rickey was on the platform; and when Rickey himself was posthumously inducted, Robinson flew back from a South American business trip to be present. Robinson would write that Rickey was the father he had never known and that he was the son Rickey had lost.[17] In 1950, outmaneuvered by Walter O'Malley, Rickey sold his interest in Brooklyn's baseball team and the man who had wought moral triumph moved from the scene of his great moment.

Under O'Malley's stewardship, the Dodgers reaped the harvest Rickey had fashioned. Pennants flowed and eventually, in 1955, the Dodgers won a World Series triumph over the New York Yankees, a team of different hue and measure.

Finally, after the 1957 season, the team moved to southern California and the Brooklyn Dodgers became the Los Angeles Dodgers. The American penchant for the ultimate profit triumphed over meaningful tradition and reassuring continuity, and the bitter taste lasted. Rickey wrote of the citizens of Brooklyn bereft of their team, and Robinson's dislike for O'Malley was public knowledge. But profit won out and the wondrous fantasy of the Dodgers, from the "Daffiness Boys" to the "Bums" to the "Boys of Summer" passed into history.

Perhaps a mass society reveals something of itself in the spectator sports it pursues. Baseball has given way to football, a sport better suited to television. Baseball is bucolic in nature, played in a lovely fenced-in green field. Watching it on television is like watching through a knot-hole; the beholder misses the panaroma that is an integral part of the activity.

Football seems ultimately more suited to the temper of the 1960s and 1970s, although its impact seems to be waning. However, its uniforms, its pageantry, its violent physical contact, its formations and military terminology, and its use of colleges as a sorting and filtering device are more in line with current American experience than baseball, which still smacks of Iowa cornfields and Carolina cotton patches.

Examining the Dodgers evokes a plethora of considerations, social, economic, and political. Urban change, demographic shift, ethnic development, economic opportunity, psychological awareness have all been a part of the discourse. Then, too, there is the puzzle of the success of *The Boys of Summer*. It's hard to envision another book about another vanished baseball team similarly capturing the public imagination. There was something compelling about the Dodgers, something that set them apart from all other sports enterprises. Perhaps the Brooklyn myth provided a sense of relief from the incessant demands of a success-oriented culture. Perhaps the integration days made them a kind of liberal/radical cause. Maybe the antics and fierce loyalties of the Dodger fans created a sense of life and variety in an increasingly managed culture. Whatever it was, the Dodger myth is still very much alive. Perhaps, in the end we are moved because no other sports environment was nearly as much fun.

Notes

Chapter 1: Recordings and Motion Pictures

1. "Mr. Edison's New Wonder," *Harper's Weekly,* March 30, 1878, p. 31.
2. Thomas Alva Edison, "The Phonograph and Its Future," *North American Review,* May-June 1878, p. 46. Also quoted in Frank L. Dyer and Thomas C. Martin, *Edison, His Life and Inventions* (New York: Harper and Bros., 1919), p. 208.

Chapter 2: Radio and Television

1. A detailed account of Fessenden's importance to the development of commercial radio may be found in Oliver Read and Walter L. Welch, *From Tin Foil to Stereo* (Indianapolis, Ind.: Howard W. Sams and Co., 1959), pp. 224–35.
2. Comment attributed to Sir W. H. Preece, appearing in Frederick Johnson Garbit, *The Phonograph and Its Inventor, Thomas Alva Edison* (Boston: Gunn, Bliss and Company, 1878), pp. 66–67.

Chapter 3: The Red Seal Era

1. Thomas A. Edison, "The Phonograph and Its Future," *North American Review,* May-June 1978, p. 51.
2. Roland Gelatt, *The Fabulous Phonograph* (Philadelphia: J. B. Lippincott Company, 1955), p. 158.

3. "Coon Songs," *Victor Records* (Camden, N.J.: Victor Talking Machine Company, November 1914).
4. Edison Cylinder 9502: "The Merry Whistling Darky," S. H. Dudley, vocalist; unidentified orchestra. (Lyrics quoted are in public domain.)
5. Edison Cylinder D-8: "The Ghost of the Banjo Coon," Arthur Collins, vocalist; unidentified orchestra. (Lyrics quoted are in public domain.)
6. Indestructible Cylinder 885: "A Coon Wedding in Southern Georgia," MacIntyre, Heath & Company, performers; no orchestral accompaniment. (Lyrics quoted are in public domain.)
7. Edison Cylinder 9836: "Stuttering Dick (or, 'The Whistling Coon')," Edward Meeker, performer; unidentified orchestra. (Lyrics quoted are in public domain.)
8. Edison Cylinder 8975: "Parson Spencer's Discourse on Adam and Eve." Len Spencer, performer; unidentified orchestra and sound effects. (Lyrics quoted are in public domain.)
9. "Fisk University Jubilee Quartet," *Victor Records* (Camden, N.J.; Victor Talking Machine Company, Inc., November 1918.)
10. Gelatt, *Phonograph,* pp. 193–94.
11. Ibid., p. 164.
12. Edison Cylinder 4112: "Alexander's Ragtime Band," Billy Murray, performer; unidentified orchestra. Of the late Sophie Tucker, the Edison's Company's 1916 catalog supplements declared that she was "a 'coon shouter' who is considered to be the foremost exponent of that type of song before the public."
13. Quoted in Gelatt, *Phonograph,* p. 149, *n.*
14. Ibid., p. 148.
15. Stanley Jackson, *Caruso* (New York: Stein and Day, 1972), p. 208.

Chapter 4: The Big Band Era

1. Gustave Haenschen to M. W. Laforse and J. A. Drake, personal interview, February 1972; Ithaca, N.Y.

2. Ibid., February 1972; Ithaca, N.Y.
3. Eddie Condon to M. W. Laforse and J. A. Drake, personal interview, November 1971; Ithaca, N.Y.
4. Rudy Vallée (with Gil McKean), *My Time Is Your Time* (New York: Ivan Obolensky, Inc., 1962), p. 123.

Chapter 5: The Postwar Years

1. Quoted in Read and Welch, *From Tin Foil to Stereo,* p. 358.
2. "Mitch Miller—The Country's 'Sing-Along' Master Is Also the Toughest A & R Man in the Business," *New York Times Magazine,* April 19, 1961, p. 46. In this interview, the quoted sales numbers, 75,000 copies, are attributed to Miller, then a senior executive with Columbia Records.
3. Charles Gillett, "Just Let Me Hear Some of That Rock and Roll Music," *Urban Review,* December 1966, pp. 11–12.
4. Spiro T. Agnew, in a speech to a gathering of Republican party supporters (Las Vegas, Nevada, dated September 15, 1970), reprinted in R. Serge Denisoff and Richard A. Peterson, *The Sounds of Social Change* (Chicago: Rand McNally, 1972), p. 308.
5. Gary Allen, "That Music, There's More to It Than Meets the Ear," in *American Opinion,* February 1969, pp. 60–61. Reprinted in Denisoff and Peterson, *Sounds,* pp. 163–64.

Chapter 6: Myths and Beginnings

1. Marshall W. Stearns, *The Story of Jazz* (New York: Oxford University Press, 1956), p. 11.
2. LeRoi Jones, *Blues People* (New York: William Morrow, 1963), pp. 153–55.
3. Ibid., pp. 153–55; also see Leonard Feather, *The Book of Jazz: From Then to Now* (New York: Dell, 1976), pp. 34–42.
4. Gunther Schuller, *Early Jazz: Its Roots and Musical Development* (New York: Oxford University Press, 1968), pp. 3–62; Stearns, *The Story of Jazz,* pp. 11–24.
5. Stearns, *The Story of Jazz,* pp. 104–10.
6. Sidney Finkelstein, *Jazz: A People's Music* (New York: Da Capo Press, 1975), p. 36.

7. Library of Congress Recordings, *Jelly Roll Morton,* Volume 1: *The Saga of Mr. Jelly Lord,* Circle L 14001, side 1, seq. 1, 2: Dave Dexter, *The Jazz Story* (Englewood Cliffs, N.J.: Prentice-Hall, 1964), p. 32.
8. Edwin Newman interview with Lotte Lenja, Public Broadcasting System, 1975.
9. Alan Lomax, *Mister Jelly Roll: The Fortunes of Jelly Roll Morton, New Orleans Creole and "Inventor of Jazz"* (New York: Grove Press, 1956), pp. 58–60.
10. See footnote number 4.
11. Rudi Blesh, *Shining Trumpets: A History of Jazz* (New York: Da Capo Press, 1975), opp. p. 210.

Chapter 7: Louis Armstrong

1. Max Jones and John Chilton, *Louis: The Louis Armstrong Story 1900–1971* (Boston: Little, Brown, 1971), p. 55.
2. Ibid., p. 52; also see Louis Armstrong, *Satchmo: My Life in New Orleans* (New York: Signet Books, 1954), pp. 21–27, 127.
3. Charles Edward Smith, "The Austin High Gang," in Frederick Ramsey, Jr. and Charles Edward Smith, eds., *Jazzmen* (New York: Harcourt, Brace and Company, 1939), pp. 161–82; also see Orrin Keepnews and Bill Grauer, Jr., *A Pictorial History of Jazz* (New York: Crown Publishers, 1971), p. 87.
4. Albert J. McCarthy, *Louis Armstrong* (New York: A. S. Barnes and Company, 1970), pp. 11–33; also see Schuller, *Early Jazz,* pp. 89–133.
5. *New York Times,* July 18, 1971, section II, p. 13.
6. Eddie Condon and Hank O'Neal, *The Eddie Condon Scrapbook of Jazz* (New York: St. Martin's Press, 1973), n.p.
7. Keepnews and Grauer, *A Pictorial History of Jazz,* p. 51.
8. Jack Bradley, "Here and There," *Hot Notes,* volume 4, number 3 (1972), 2, New York Hot Jazz Society.
9. Richard Hadlock, *Jazz Masters of the Twenties* (New York: Macmillan, 1965), p. 31.
10. Ibid., pp. 34, 38–39; also see Schuller, *Early Jazz,* pp. 109, 115–21.

11. Interview with Joe Glaser as cited in Nat Shapiro and Nat Hentoff, eds., *Hear Me Talkin' to Ya* (New York: Dover Books, 1955), pp. 107–8.

Chapter 8: Bix Beiderbecke

1. Richard M. Sudhalter, Philip R. Evans, and William Dean Myatt, *Bix: Man and Legend* (New York: Schirmer Books, 1974), p. 27.
2. Le Roi Jones, *Blues People,* pp. 153–54.
3. Sudhalter et al., p. 75.
4. Hadlock, *Jazz Masters of the Twenties,* pp. 85, 97.
5. Hoagy Carmichael and his orchestra, *Rockin' Chair,* Victor Record, BVE 59800.
6. Sudhalter et al., p. 334.

Chapter 9: Origins of Vaudeville

1. Fred Astaire, *Steps in Time* (New York: Harper and Row, 1959), p. 32.
2. Gunnar Myrdal, *An American Dilemma* (New York: Harper and Row, 1962), pp. 984, 989.
3. Robert C. Toll, *Blacking Up: The Minstrel Show in Nineteenth Century America* (New York: Oxford University Press, 1974), pp. 195–96.
4. As cited in Douglas Gilbert, *American Vaudeville: Its Life and Death* (New York: Dover, 1968), p. 444.
5. Twentieth-Century-Fox film, *Swanee River,* 1939.
6. William Moulton Marston and John H. Feller, *F. F. Proctor, Vaudeville Pioneer* (New York: Richard R. Smith, 1943), p. 49.
7. Ibid., between pp. 96–97.
8. Fred Allen, *Much Ado about Me* (Boston: Little, Brown, 1956), p. 246.
9. Ibid., p. 133.
10. Brett Page, *Writing for Vaudeville* (Springfield: Home Correspondence School, 1915), p. 170.
11. Marston and Feller, *F. F. Proctor,* pp. 78–79.
12. Joe Laurie, Jr., *Vaudeville: From the Honky-Tonks to the Palace* (New York: Henry Holt, 1953), pp. 339, 343, 346.

Chapter 10: Organization and Structure

1. *The Eighty-Six Years of Eubie Blake,* Columbia Record C2S 847 CS 9902, seg. 2.
2. Laurie, *Vaudeville,* pp. 387–94; also see, Gilbert, *American Vaudeville,* pp. 245–50.
3. Sophie Tucker, *Some of These Days* (Garden City: Doubleday and Doran, 1945), p. 151.
4. Marian Spitzer, *The Palace* (New York: Atheneum, 1969), p. 19.
5. Allen, *Much Ado about Me.,* p. 197.
6. Astaire, *Steps in Time,* p. 35.
7. Gilbert Seldes, *The Seven Lively Arts* (New York: Harper and Bros., 1924), pp. 252–53.
8. Ibid., p. 254.
9. Ibid., p. 263.
10. Albert F. McLean, *American Vaudeville as Ritual* (Lexington: University of Kentucky Press, 1965), pp. 3–10.
11. Page, *Writing for Vaudeville,* p. 103.
12. As quoted in Ibid., p. 103.
13. Ibid., p. 106.
14. Ibid., p. 82.
15. Jack Pearl, personal interview with M. W. Laforse and J. A. Drake, New York City: April 8, 1973.
16. Allen, *Much Ado about Me,* pp. 249–50.

Chapter 11: The Ethnic Immigrants as Objects of Humor

1. McLean, *American Vaudeville as Ritual,* p. 120.
2. Laurie, *Vaudeville,* p. 81.
3. Ibid.
4. Ibid., p. 427.
5. Gilbert, *American Vaudeville,* p. 62.
6. Ibid., p. 64.
7. Ibid., p. 65.
8. Laurie, *Vaudeville.*
9. Ibid., pp. 452–54.
10. Gilbert, *American Vaudeville,* p. 72.
11. Ibid., p. 73.

12. Laurie, *Vaudeville.*
13. Gilbert, *American Vaudeville,* p. 228.
14. Laurie, *Vaudeville,* p. 178.
15. Caroline S. Caffin, *Vaudeville* (New York: Mitchell and Kennerley, 1914), pp. 209–10.
16. Laurie, *Vaudeville,* pp. 179–80.
17. Julian Rose, *Levinsky at the Wedding,* Columbia Record, A2310.
18. Laurie, *Vaudeville,* pp. 454–55.
19. During one of their many appearances on the "Ed Sullivan Show," Columbia Broadcasting System, 1950s and 1960s, they used this routine.

Chapter 12: Vaudeville Images

1. Myrdal, *An American Dilemma,* p. 986.
2. Laurie, *Vaudeville,* p. 139.
3. Gilbert, *American Vaudeville,* pp. 79–80.
4. Laurie, *Vaudeville,* p. 141.
5. Ibid., p. 201.
6. Tucker, *Some of These Days,* p. 84.
7. Myrdal, *An American Dilemma,* p. 990.
8. Laurie, *Vaudeville,* p. 174.
9. Gilbert, *American Vaudeville,* p. 176.
10. Quote from an article in *Review Romande* (October 1919) as quoted on album cover of *Superb Sidney,* CBS Record–62636.
11. Abel Green and Joe Laurie, Jr., *Show Biz: From Vaudeville to Video.* (New York: Henry Holt, 1951), p. 96.
12. James Weldon Johnson, *Black Manhattan* (New York: Arno Press, 1930), p. 108.
13. Edith J. R. Isaacs, *The Negro in the American Stage* (New York: Theater Arts Books, 1947), p. 35.
14. Ibid.
15. Johnson, *Black Manhattan,* p. 108.
16. Ann Charters, *Nobody: The Story of Bert Williams* (New York: Macmillan, 1970), pp. 19–20.
17. Gilbert, *American Vaudeville,* p. 286.

18. Isaacs, *The Negro in the American Stage,* p. 32.
19. Bert Williams, *Save a Little Dram for Me,* Columbia Record A2979.
20. Charters, *Nobody,* p. 11.
21. Isaacs, *The Negro in the American Stage,* p. 34.
22. Ibid., pp. 40–41.
23. Johnson, *Black Manhattan,* p. 114.
24. Laurie, *Vaudeville,* p. 431.
25. Ibid., p. 438.
26. Ibid.
27. Ibid., pp. 462–64.
28. W. E. B. DuBois, *The Souls of Black Folk* (Greenwich, Conn.: Fawcett Publications, 1961), pp. 14–151.
29. Michel Fabre, *The Unfinished Quest of Richard Wright* (New York: William Morrow, 1973), pp. 26–27, 454–55.
30. Laurie, *Vaudeville,* p. 205.
31. Nat M. Wills, *Darky Stories,* Victor Record 17768-A.
32. Richard Wright, *Uncle Tom's Children* (New York: Harper and Row, 1965), pp. 6–8.
33. Tucker, *Some of These Days,* p. 76.
34. Ibid., p. 80.
35. Laurie, *Vaudeville,* p. 21.
36. As quoted in Marston and Feller, *F. F. Proctor,* p. 70.

Chapter 13: Urban Growth

1. Ernest Burgess and Donald J. Bogue, *Urban Sociology* (Chicago: University of Chicago Press, 1967).
2. Cited in Morton White and Lucia White, *The Intellectual Versus the City.* (New York: New American Library Mentor Books, 1964), pp. 164–70.
3. Lewis Mumford, *The City in History* (New York: Harcourt, Brace and World, 1961), p. 426.
4. Louis Wirth, "Urbanism as a Way of Life," *American Journal of Sociology,* 44, (July, 1938), pp. 11–13.
5. Charles N. Glaab and A. Theodore White, *A History of Urban American* (New York: Macmillan, 1967), pp. 27–36.

6. Richard Hofstadter, *The Age of Reform: From Bryan to F. D. R.* (New York: Knopf, 1955), p. 55.

7. Harold Seymour, *Baseball: The Early Years* (New York: Oxford University Press, 1960), pp. 42–45.

8. Blake McKelvey, *The Urbanization of America* (New Brunswick: Rutgers University Press, 1963), p. 4; also see R. D. McKenzie, *The Metropolitan Community* (New York: Russell and Russell, 1967), p. 20.

9. McKelvey, *The Urbanization of America*, pp. 76 ff.

10. White and White, *The Intellectual Versus the City*, p. 102.

11. McKelvey, *The Urbanization of America*, pp. 66, 70.

12. R. D. McKenzie, *The Metropolitan Community*, p. 29.

13. Dan Parker, "The Brooklyn Dodgers," *Sport,* October, 1950, p. 34.

14. *Newsweek,* October 29, 1951, p. 89.

15. As quoted in White and White, *The Intellectual Versus the City,* p. 59.

16. Branch Rickey with Robert Riger, *The American Diamond* (New York: Simon and Schuster, 1965), p. 164.

17. Carson McCullers, "Brooklyn Is My Neighborhood," in Mary Ellen Murphy, Mark Murphy, and Ralph Foster Weld, *A Treasury of Brooklyn* (New York: William Sloan, 1949), p. 362.

18. Ibid., pp. 48–49.

19. Ricky, *The American Diamond,* p. 166.

Chapter 14: Baseball

1. As cited in Donald J. Greiner, *Robert Frost and His Critics* (Chicago: American Library Association, 1974), p. 263.

2. Ralph Barton Perry, *Characteristically American* (Freeport: Books for Libraries Press, 1971), p. 21.

3. Lewis Mumford, "Sports and the Bitch-Goddess," in John T. Talamini and Charles Page, *Sport and Society* (Boston: Little, Brown, 1973), pp. 52–63.

4. Ibid., p. 61.

5. Talamini, et al., *Sport and Society,* p. 45.

6. Perry, *Characteristically American,* p. 20.
7. Ibid.
8. Ibid., p. 9.
9. Ibid., p. 10.
10. Ibid., p. 11.
11. Frank Menke, *The Encyclopedia of Sports* (New York: A. S. Barnes, 1963), p. 63.
12. Seymour, *Baseball: The Early Years,* p. 5
13. Ibid.
14. Menke, *Encyclopedia of Sports,* p. 312.
15. Seymour, *Baseball: The Early Years,* p. 14.
16. Ibid., p. 7.
17. McKelvey, *The Urbanization of America,* p. 184.
18. "My Baseball Years," *New York Times,* April 2, 1973, op. ed. page.
19. The author himself was present at one of these evenings in the early 1950s, bringing along an old C-Melody sax.
20. See, for example, John Durant, *The Dodgers* (New York: Hastings House, n.d.), p. 139; Frank Graham, *The Booklyn Dodgers* (New York: G. P. Putnam's Son, 1945), pp. 113, 203, 132, 233, 248.

Chapter 15: Wacky Failure

1. Frank Graham, *The Brooklyn Dodgers,* p. 92.
2. Ibid., p. 106.

Chapter 16: Wacky Success

1. Graham, *The Brooklyn Dodgers,* p. 132.
2. Ibid., p. 183.
3. Durant, *The Dodgers,* pp. 139–40.
4. Ibid.
5. Ronald Sanders, *Reflections on a Teapot* (New York: Harper and Row, 1972), p. 97.

Chapter 17: The Robinson-Rickey Experiment

1. Roger Kahn, *The Boys of Summer* (New York: Harper and Row, 1971), chap. 16.

2. Personal interview with Mrs. Robert Jones, Elmira, New York, October 15, 1974.
3. Rickey, *The American Diamond,* p. 46.
4. *The Strange Career of Jim Crow* (New York: Oxford University Press, 1966).
5. Robert Peterson, *Only the Ball Was White* (Englewood Cliffs, N.J.: Prentice-Hall, 1970), pp. 16, 20–33.
6. Ibid., pp. 40–51.
7. Ibid., pp. 55–56.
8. Ibid., pp. 173–74.
9. Ibid., pp. 179, 185.
10. Ibid., p. 180.
11. Kahn, Chaps. 12, 17.
12. Rickey, *The American Diamond,* p. 45.
13. Personal interview with Mrs. Robert Jones.
14. Ibid.
15. Leonard Broom and Philip Selznick, "The Jackie Robinson Case," in Talamini, et al., *Sport and Society,* p. 237.
16. Rickey, *The American Diamond,* p. 46.
17. Jackie Robinson with Alfred Duckett, *I Never Had It Made,* (New York: G. P. Putnam's Sons, 1972), pp. 68–69; Leo Durocher with Ed Linn, *Nice Guys Finish Last* (New York: Pocket Books, 1976), pp. 177–78.

Bibliography

Agee, James. *Agee On Film*. New York: Ivan Obolensky, 1958.

Allen, Fred. *Much Ado about Me*. Boston: Little, Brown, 1956.

Armstrong, Louis. *Satchmo: My Life in New Orleans*. New York: Signet Books, 1954.

ASCAP. *ASCAP 50th Anniversary Hit Tunes*. New York: American Society of Composers, Authors, and Publishers, 1964.

Astaire, Fred. *Steps in Time*. New York: Harper and Row, 1959.

Barnouw, Erik. *A History of Broadcasting in the United States*. New York: Oxford University Press, 1966.

Belz, Carl. *The Study of Rock*. New York: Oxford University Press, 1969.

Bernstein, Leonard. *The Infinite Variety of Music*. New York: Simon and Schuster, 1962.

Blesh, Rudi. *Shining Trumpets: A History of Jazz*. New York: Da Capo Press, 1975.

Blesh, Rudi and Harriet Janis. *They All Played Ragtime*. New York: Alfred Knopf, 1950.

BMI. *BMI, 1940–1960: Twenty Years of Service to the Industry*. New York: Broadcast Music, Incorporated, 1960.

Bogart, Leo. *The Age of Television*. New York: Friedrich Unger, 1958.

241

Brand, Oscar. *The Ballad Mongers*. New York: Funk and Wagnalls, 1962.

Burgess, Ernest and Donald J. Bogue. *Urban Sociology*. Chicago: University of Chicago Press, 1967.

Charters, Ann. *Nobody: The Story of Bert Williams*. New York: Macmillan, 1970.

Chasins, Abram. *Music at the Crossroads*. New York: Macmillan, 1972.

Chilton, John. *Who's Who of Jazz: From Storyville to Swing Street*. Philadelphia: Chilton Book Company, 1972.

Condon, Eddie and Hank O'Neal. *The Eddie Condon Scrapbook of Jazz*. New York: St. Martin's Press, 1973.

Crowther, Bosley. *The Great Films: Fifty Golden Years of Motion Pictures*. New York: Putnam, 1967.

Denisoff, R. Serge, and Richard A. Peterson. *The Sounds of Social Change*. Chicago: Rand McNally, 1972.

Dexter, Dave. *The Jazz Story*. Englewood Cliffs, N.J.: Prentice-Hall, 1964.

Du Bois, W. E. B. *The Souls of Black Folks*. Greenwich, Conn.: Fawcett Publications, 1961.

Durant, John. *The Dodgers*. New York: Hastings House Publishers, 1948.

Durocher, Leo with Ed Linn. *Nice Guys Finish Last*. New York: Pocket Books, 1976.

Dyer, Frank L., and Thomas C. Martin. *Edison, His Life and Inventions*. New York: Harper and Brothers, 1919.

Ewen, David. *The History of Popular Music*. New York: Barnes and Noble, 1961.

Ewen, David. *The Rise and Fall of Tin Pan Alley*. New York: Funk and Wagnalls, 1964.

Fabre, Michel. *The Unfinished Quest of Richard Wright*. New York: William Morrow, 1973.

Feather, Leonard. *The Book of Jazz: From Then to Now*. New York: Dell Publishing Company, 1976.

Finkelstein, Sidney. *Jazz: A People's Music*. New York: Da Capo Press, 1975.

Friendly, Fred W. *Due to Circumstances Beyond Our Control*. New York: Random House, 1967.

Gabree, John. *The World of Rock*. Greenwich, Conn.: Gold Metal Press, 1968.

Gahr, David, and Robert Shelton. *The Face Of Folk*. New York: Citadel Press, 1968.

Gaisberg, Fred. *The Music Goes Round*. New York: Macmillan, 1942.

Gans, Herbert J. *Popular Culture and High Culture*. New York: Basic Books, 1974.

Garlick, George and Charles Wareing. *Bugles for Beiderbecke*. London: Sidgwick and Jackson, Limited, 1958.

Gelatt, Roland. *The Fabulous Phonograph*. New York: J. B. Lippincott, 1954; revised edition, Appleton-Century, 1966, 1977.

Gilbert, Douglas. *American Vaudeville*. New York: Dover, 1968.

Glaab, Charles N. and A. Theodore White. *A History of Urban America*. New York: Macmillan, 1967.

Graham, Frank. *The Brooklyn Dodgers*. New York: G. P. Putnam's Sons, 1945.

Green, Abel and Joe Laurie, Jr. *Show Biz: From Vaude to Video*. New York: Henry Holt and Company, 1951.

Green, Benny. *The Reluctant Art*. New York: Horizon Press, 1963.

Greiner, Donald J. *Robert Frost and His Critics*. Chicago: American Library Association, 1974.

Hadlock, Richard. *Jazz Masters of the Twenties*. New York: Macmillan, 1965.

Hofstadter, Richard. *The Age of Reform: From Bryan to F. D. R.* New York: Alfred A. Knopf, 1955.

Holmes, Tommy. *Dodger Daze and Knights*. New York: David McKay Co., 1953.

Hopkins, Jerry. *The Rock Story*. New York: New American Library, 1970.

Isaacs, Edith J. R. *The Negro in the American Stage*. New York: Theater Arts Books, 1947.

Jackson, Stanley. *Caruso*. New York: Stein and Day, 1971.

Johnson, James Weldon. *Black Manhattan*. New York: Arno Press, 1930.

Jones, LeRoi. *Blues People*. New York: William Morrow, 1963.

Jones, Max and John Chilton. *Louis: The Louis Armstrong Story 1900–1971*. Boston: Little, Brown, 1971.

Kahn, Roger. *The Boys of Summer*. New York: Harper and Row, 1971.

Keepnews, Orrin and Bill Grauer, Jr. *A Pictorial History of Jazz.* New York: Crown Publishers, 1971.

Keil, Charles. *Urban Blues*. Chicago: University of Chicago Press, 1966.

Larkin, Rochelle. *Soul Music*. New York: Lancer Publications, 1970.

Laurie, Joe, Jr. *Vaudeville: From the Honky-Tonks to the Palace*. New York: Henry Holt, 1953.

Lomax, Alan. *Mister Jelly Roll: The Fortunes of Jelly Roll Morton, New Orleans Creole and "Inventor of Jazz."* New York: Grove Press, 1956.

Macgowan, Kenneth. *Behind the Screen: The History and Techniques of the Motion Picture*. New York: Delacorte Press, 1965.

Malone, Bill C. *Country Music, U.S.A*. Austin, Tex.: University of Texas Press, 1968.

Marston, William Moulton and John H. Feller. *F. F. Proctor: Vaudeville Pioneer*. New York: Richard R. Smith, 1943.

McCarthy, Albert J. *Louis Armstrong*. New York: A. S. Barnes, 1970.

McKelvey, Blake, *The Urbanization of America*. New Brunswick, N.J.: Rutgers University Press, 1963.

McKenzie, R. D. *The Metropolitan Community*. New York: Russell and Russell, 1967.

McLean, Albert F. *American Vaudeville as Ritual*. Lexington: University of Kentucky Press, 1965.

Menke, Frank. *The Encyclopedia of Sports*. New York: A. S. Barnes, 1963.

Mumford, Lewis. *The City in History*. New York: Harcourt, Brace and World, 1961.

Murphy, Ellen, Mark Murphy and Ralph Foster Weld. *A Treasury of Brooklyn*. New York: William Sloan, 1949.

Myrdal, Gunnar. *An American Dilemma*. New York: Harper and Row, 1962.

Oliver, Paul. *The Meaning of the Blues*. New York: Collier Publications, 1960.

Page, Brett. *Writing for Vaudeville*. Springfield: Home Correspondence School, 1915.

Perry, Ralph Barton. *Characteristically American.* Freeport: Books for Libraries Press, 1971.

Peterson, Robert. *Only the Ball Was White.* Englewood Cliffs, N.J.: Prentice-Hall, 1970.

Ramsey, Frederick, Jr., and Charles Edward Smith. *Jazzmen.* New York: Harcourt, Brace, 1939.

Read, Oliver, and Walter L. Welch. *From Tin Foil to Stereo.* Indianapolis, Ind.: Howard W. Sams, 1959.

Rickey, Branch with Robert Riger. *The American Diamond.* New York: Simon and Schuster, 1965.

Rissover, Fredric, and David C. Birch. *Mass Media and the Popular Arts.* New York: McGraw-Hill, 1971.

Robinson, Jackie with Alfred Duckett. *I Never Had It Made.* New York: G. P. Putnam's Sons, 1972.

Sanders, Ronald. *Reflections on a Teapot.* New York: Harper and Row, 1972.

Schuller, Gunther. *Early Jazz: Its Roots and Musical Development.* New York: Oxford University Press, 1968.

Seldes, Gilbert. *The Seven Lively Arts.* New York: Harper and Bros., 1924.

Seymour, Harold. *Baseball: The Early Years.* New York: Oxford University Press, 1960.

Shapiro, Nat and Nat Hentoff, eds. *Hear Me Talkin' to Ya.* New York: Dover Books, 1955.

Shapiro, Nat (ed.). *Popular Music.* New York: Adrian Press, 1964.

Shaw, Arnold. *The Rock Revolution.* New York: Macmillan: 1971.

Shelton, Robert, and Burt Goldblatt. *The Country Music Story.* Secaucus, N.J.: Castle Books, 1971.

Slater, Philip. *The Pursuit of Loneliness: American Culture at the Breaking Point.* Boston: Beacon Press, 1970.

Spaeth, Sigmund G. *The Facts of Life in Popular Music.* New York: McGraw-Hill, 1934.

Spitzer, Marian. *The Palace.* New York: Atheneum Publishers, 1969.

Stearns, Marshall W. *The Story of Jazz.* New York: Oxford University Press, 1956.

Sudhalter, Richard M., Philip R. Evans, and William Dean Myatt. *Bix: Man and Legend.* New York: Schirmer Books, 1974.

Talamini, John T. and Charles Page, eds. *Sport and Society*. Boston: Little, Brown, 1973.

Toll, Robert C. *Blacking Up: The Minstrel Show in Nineteenth Century America*. New York: Oxford University Press, 1974.

Tucker, Sophie. *Some of These Days*. Garden City, N.Y.: Doubleday and Doran, 1945.

Ulanov, Barry. *A History of Jazz in America*. New York: Viking Press, 1952.

Vallee, Rudy with Gil McKean. *My Time Is Your Time*. New York: Ivan Obolensky, 1962.

White, David M. and Richard Averson. *Sight, Sound and Society: Motion Pictures and Television in America*. Boston: Beacon Press, 1968.

White, Morton and Lucia White. *The Intellectual Versus the City*. New York: New American Library Mentor Books, 1964.

Williams, Martin. *Jazz Masters of New Orleans*. New York: Macmillan, 1967.

Woodward, C. Van. *The Strange Career of Jim Crow*. New York: Oxford University Press, 1966.

Wright, Richard. *Uncle Tom's Children*. New York: Harper and Row, 1965.

Index

247